THE M & E HANDBOOK SERIES

Mercantile Law

P W D Redmond LL.M

*Barrister, Formerly Senior Lecturer in Commercial Law
at the City of London College*

Revised by

R G Lawson PhD

*Senior Lecturer in Law
University of Southampton*

FIFTH EDITION

Pitman Publishing Limited
128 Long Acre, London WC2E 9AN

A Longman Group Company

© Pitman Publishing Ltd 1979

First published 1964
Reprinted 1965
Second edition 1968
Reprinted 1969
Reprinted 1970
Reprinted 1971
Reprinted 1971
Third edition 1972
Reprinted 1973
Fourth edition 1974
Reprinted 1975
Reprinted 1977
Fifth edition 1979
Reprinted with amendments 1982
Reprinted 1986

ISBN 0 7121 1288 X ✓

Typeset, printed and bound in Great Britain

M & E HANDBOOKS

M & E Handbooks are recommended reading for examination syllabuses all over the world. Because each Handbook covers its subject clearly and concisely books in the series form a vital part of many college, university, school and home study courses.

Handbooks contain detailed information stripped of unnecessary padding, making each title a comprehensive self-tuition course. They are amplified with numerous self-testing questions in the form of Progress Tests at the end of each chapter, each text-referenced for easy checking. Every Handbook closes with an appendix which advises on examination technique. For all these reasons, Handbooks are ideal for pre-examination revision.

The handy pocket-book size and competitive price make Handbooks the perfect choice for anyone who wants to grasp the essentials of a subject quickly and easily.

Preface to the Fourth Edition

A further edition of *Mercantile Law* has been necessitated by
the many new pieces of legislation that have found their way
to the statute book, and by the need to incorporate many recent
judicial decisions. In particular the Fair Trading Act 1973, has
made necessary the inclusion of a completely new chapter,
and the Supply of Goods (Implied Terms) Act 1973, has forced
considerable changes to the chapter dealing with sale of goods.
In addition I have taken the opportunity to revise completely the
system of cross-referencing throughout the book, to bring it into
line with other HANDBOOKS now in print, and it is hoped that
this will make it easier to use.

The book is intended as a series of concise and comprehensive
lecture or study notes for students preparing for professional or
other examinations in Mercantile Law. It follows the pattern of
the HANDBOOK on *General Principles of English Law*, so as to
facilitate the studies of those who have already used the more
elementary book.

Before commencing to work through this book the student is
advised to study the syllabus for his particular examination, since
the detailed requirements of different institutions vary considerably. Most examinations in commercial law cover contract,
agency, partnership, sale of goods, and negotiable instruments,
with the addition of one or some of the other topics covered in
this book. The student should therefore compare his syllabus
with the contents pages of this book to see what, if anything, he
can safely leave out.

As to the method of study, the student is advised to go through
this HANDBOOK chapter by chapter. Read first through the
headings and bold-printed paragraph heads to see what the chapter is about. Then do a slower detailed reading (ignoring references to cases and statutes) and concentrating on understanding

the text. Only at the third reading should the student commence memorisation (leaving cases and statutes to the end).

Progress Tests are placed at the end of each Part for self-examination and revision. Try to answer each question and then check your answer with the text (by means of the paragraph references given). The easiest way to memorise the subject is to make constant use of the Progress Tests in this way.

In addition a large number of specimen questions from actual examination papers are printed throughout the book. These questions are printed by permission of the bodies concerned, and I gratefully acknowledge my debt to the following:

Institute of Chartered Accountants (I.C.A.)
Association of Certified Accountants (A.C.A.)
Institute of Cost & Management Accountants (I.C.M.A.)
Institute of Bankers
Institute of Chartered Secretaries and Administrators
 (I.C.S.A.—formerly C.I.S.)

In preparing this edition for the press I have been greatly assisted by suggestions for revision from several people, and particularly Mr B. S. Grewal, of South West London College, and Mr J. P. Meader, of Salisbury College of Technology, to whom my thanks are due. I would also like to take this opportunity to express my gratitude to the late Sir William Arnold, former Bailiff of Guernsey, for his encouragement.

March, 1974   P.W.D.R.

Preface to the Fifth Edition

Since the last edition of this book, much of it has been overtaken by events. Notable legislative happenings have been the Consumer Credit Act 1974, the Insolvency Act 1976 and, especially, the Unfair Contract Terms Act 1977. Case law too has continued to enliven the fabric of our law. And here and there I have ventured to add material which is not new but, I believe, of sound illustrative value. Peter Redmond gave me a superb text. The excellence of his work remains, I hope, undiminished.

April, 1979   R.G.L.

Contents

TABLE OF CASES

PART ONE

THE LAW OF CONTRACTS

CHAPTER I

Nature and Classification of Contracts

NATURE OF CONTRACTS

1. Definition of contract. A contract is a legally binding agreement: that is, an agreement which will be enforced by the courts. Sir William Anson, in his *Principles of the Law of Contract*, defined a contract as "a legally binding agreement made between two or more persons, by which rights are acquired by one or more acts or forbearances on the part of the other or others."

2. Consensus ad idem. An agreement occurs when two minds meet upon a common purpose. This meeting of minds is called *consensus ad idem*, i.e. consent to the matter.

Absence of consensus may make a contract null and void, e.g. where the parties are fundamentally mistaken as to each other's intentions: *Raffles* v. *Wichelhaus* (1864), *see* IV, **5**.

3. Agreements which are not contracts. Mere domestic or social agreements are not usually intended to be binding, and therefore are not contracts

EXAMPLES: (1) Three friends joined to enter a newspaper competition and agreed to share any winnings. HELD: They intended to create legal relations and their agreement was therefore a binding contract: *Simpkins* v. *Pays* (1955). (2) A husband promised to pay a housekeeping allowance to his wife. HELD: A mere domestic arrangement, with no intention to create legally binding relations, therefore no contract: *Balfour* v. *Balfour* (1919). (However where the spouses are legally separated it will be presumed that they did intend to create a legally binding contract: *Merrit* v. *Merrit* (1970).)

4. Intention to create legal relations. A binding contract is usually in the nature of a commercial bargain, involving some exchange of goods or services for a price (called the consideration).

But even such bargains will not be legally binding if the parties intend otherwise, i.e. do not intend to create legal relations.

In considering whether sufficient intention to create a binding contract is present, two situations are possible.

(*a*) Where the parties expressly deny the intention. Here the courts will almost invariably hold that there is no contract:

EXAMPLES: (1) A written commercial agreement described itself merely as an "honourable pledge" and stated expressly that it was not "to be subject to the jurisdiction of any court." HELD: The parties did not intend to create legal relations, and the agreement was not a contract: *Rose & Frank Co.* v. *Crompton Bros.* (1923). (2) A condition imposed by a football pool laid down that the relationship should not be legally binding. HELD: No intention to create legal relations: *Appleson* v. *Littlewoods Ltd.* (1939). (This is a common condition of entrance in football pools, etc.)

(*b*) Where the parties do not expressly deny intention to create legal relations. Here it is in each case a question of construction for the Court to decide as to whether a contract is intended.

Thus: (*i*) in commercial agreements there is a rebuttable presumption that a contract is intended; but (*ii*) in social and domestic or family agreements there is a rebuttable presumption that no contract is intended. (But note that in each case the presumption is rebuttable by evidence to the contrary.)

EXAMPLES: (1) C persuaded her niece, P, to sell her own house and come and live in C's on condition that C would leave her house to P by will. After some time C ejected P from the house, and refused to leave it to her by will. P claimed damages for breach of contract. HELD: Although a family agreement, there was consideration for C's promise and evidence of intention to create legal relations. P was therefore entitled to damages: *Parker* v. *Clarke* (1960). (2) B and O habitually rode in each other's cars. Neither had insurance to cover injury to passengers. While in O's car, B was injured through O's negligence and sued for damages in contract or in tort. B had contributed to petrol costs and claimed this gave rise to a contract. O claimed: (*i*) there was no intention to create a binding contract; and (*ii*) B had consented to the risk of injury, since there was a notice in the car disclaiming liability to passengers. HELD: There was no contract, and B could not get damages (either in contract or in tort): *Buckpitt* v. *Oakes* (1968).

If the car owner had advertised for someone to share petrol costs, as he can do under the Transport Act 1978, it is more likely to be presumed that a contract exists. Note that under the Unfair Contract Terms Act 1977, liability for negligence causing death or personal injury cannot be excluded: *see* II, **18** below.

CLASSIFICATION OF CONTRACTS

5. Contracts of record. These are obligations whose terms are recorded by a court of record, e.g. the Supreme Court or a County Court.

They are not true contracts, since the obligations of the parties arise independently of any agreement and solely by reason of entry upon the court records. Two types are as follows.

(*a*) *Judgments:* by which a court imposes on some person a legal obligation, e.g. to pay damages. This judgment, when enrolled on the court records, constitutes a contract of record between the parties to the action in which the judgment was pronounced.

(*b*) *Recognisances:* written acknowledgment of a debt due to the Crown, made before a judge or authorised officer, and en-rolled on the court records, e.g. a promise to "keep the peace" or to attend court when called (an accused person in a criminal case was sometimes released on bail pending trial, on his own recog-nisance, i.e. a promise to attend when called, or to forfeit a stated sum of money); but *see* the Bail Act 1976, s. 8 (3).

6. Contracts by deed (specialty contracts). A contract by deed is a promise written on paper or parchment, signed, sealed, and delivered (either actually or constructively) by the promisor to the promisee or his agent.

(*a*) *Execution of deed:* when a deed has been "signed, sealed, and delivered" it is said to be executed, and it becomes legally binding immediately (unless it is directed to be held by the recipient in escrow).

(*b*) *Escrows:* an escrow is a deed executed subject to a condition that it is not to become effective until the condition is satisfied, e.g. the occurrence of a certain event, or the expiry of a period of time. Escrows are usually delivered to a neutral intermediary, with instructions not to complete delivery to the promisee until further instructions from the promisor.

(c) *Sealing and delivery:* sealing a deed is usually done by affixing a disc or wafer of red paper to the bottom of the deed (next to the signature of the person signing). Delivery is largely a matter of intention; thus it may be by actually handing over the deed to the promisee, or by giving him the keys to a box in which the deed is kept (constructive delivery). It has been held by the Court of Appeal that, as a matter of law, it is not necessary for the due execution of a deed that there should be any physical seal attached to, or impression on, the paper. A document purporting to be a deed was capable in law of being such, even though it bore nothing more than an indication of where the seal should be. This particular document had a circle in which there were letters showing that this was where the seal should go. The signature had been placed across the circle and a witness had signed a clause saying that the document had been signed, sealed and delivered in his presence. The court said that this was enough evidence that the document had been executed by the party as his deed: *First National Securities Ltd.* v. *Jones* (1978).

(d) *Indentures and deeds poll:* a deed to which there is only one party is called a deed poll, e.g. a deed of gift. A deed to which there are two or more parties is called an indenture, e.g. any contract by deed.

7. Characteristics of contracts by deed

(a) *Consideration:* a deed does not require to be supported by valuable consideration, like simple contracts: *see below*.

(b) *Merger:* a special contract absorbs, or merges into itself, any earlier simple contract made between the same parties and on the same terms.

(c) *Limitation of actions:* an action for breach of a specialty contract can be commenced at any time within twelve years of the breach occurring; but an action for breach of a simple contract must generally be commenced within six years: Limitation Act 1980, and *see* V, **15**.

NOTE: Formerly a person who had signed a deed could not thereafter deny the accuracy of statements made therein, i.e. he was estopped from denying the accuracy of the deed. This was called estoppel by deed. The rule is now obsolete and evidence is admissible to show that the deed is inaccurate, like any other contract.

8. Simple contracts. Simple or "parol" contracts are by far the most common and important variety. They are informal contracts and may be made in any way—orally, in writing, or by implication from conduct. A person who takes a seat in a bus is entering into an implied contract to pay his fare.

A simple contract must possess the following essentials.

(*a*) An offer and unqualified acceptance thereof: *see* II, **1–15**.

(*b*) Intention to create legal relations: *see* **4** above.

(*c*) Valuable consideration: *see* III, **10–12**.

(*d*) Genuineness of consent (*consensus ad idem*), e.g. the agreement must not have been induced by fraud or coercion: *see* IV.

(*e*) Capacity of parties: *see* III, **20–28**.

(*f*) Legality of objects: *see* IV, **25**.

(*g*) Possibility of performance: *see* IV, **4**.

(*h*) Certainty of terms: *see* II, **21–23**.

VOID, VOIDABLE AND UNENFORCEABLE CONTRACTS

9. Void contracts. A void contract is one which is destitute of legal effect, i.e. of which the court will take no notice, for example, contracts void on the grounds of fundamental mistake: *see* IV, **1–7**.

Property transferred under a void contract can usually be recovered as the transferee can have no legal right to it: *Chappell* v. *Poles* (1837). But if the contract is void on the grounds that its object is illegal or contrary to public policy property transferred is generally irrecoverable; *see* IV.

10. Voidable contracts. A voidable contract is one which can be made void by one party, at his option. Thus a contract induced by fraud can be avoided by the party misled whenever he chooses: *see* IV.

11. Unenforceable contracts. An unenforceable contract is one which, though perfectly valid in all other respects, lacks some technical requirement needed to make it enforceable, e.g. some necessary written evidence. Such a contract will not be enforced by the courts unless and until the defect is rectified.

Thus contracts for the sale of land or any interest therein must be evidenced in writing, signed by the defendant, before they can be the subject of a successful action at law: Law of Property Act 1925, s. 40.

But such unenforceable contracts are not void, and therefore if they have been performed and property has been transferred the court will not intervene to set the agreement aside. Thus if A orally agrees to buy B's house and pays a deposit to B, then later changes his mind and refuses to sign a written contract to purchase the house, B will be unable to sue A for damages or performance of the contract but will be able to keep A's deposit, and the court will not assist A to recover it: *Monickendam* v. *Leanse* (1923).

QUASI-CONTRACTS

Sometimes the law imposes obligations of a contractual nature even where no true agreement exists between the parties. The object of such imposition is to prevent a person obtaining "unjust enrichment" merely because there is no contract between himself and the person seeking the court's aid. The chief examples of such artificial or *quasi-contracts* are given below.

12. Money paid to the use of another. If A, at the express or implied request of B, pays to X a sum of money legally owed by B to X, the law implies a quasi-contract between A and B under which B must compensate A for the sum paid, e.g. where A pays rent owed by B to prevent the landlord seizing A's goods, which are stored at B's premises: *Edmunds* v. *Wallingford* (1885).

13. Accounts stated. Where there has been a series of transactions between A and B and they agree a balance, showing a sum payable by A to B, the agreed balance constitutes an "account stated." If B now has occasion to sue A for the amount so stated, he does not need to prove the details of the transactions between them but can rely entirely on the account stated as an admission of indebtedness.

14. Total failure of consideration. Where a valid contract has been made between A and B (supported by consideration) but subsequently B fails to provide any of the promised consideration, there is said to be a total failure of consideration and A can sue for the recovery of any money he has paid.

(Contrast the situation where the consideration has only partially failed, e.g. where A pays money for goods to B, who later delivers some but not all of the goods ordered. If A decides to accept this partial delivery, which he is not obliged to do, A can sue for damages for breach of contract, and the damages will be measured as the amount needed to compensate him for his loss, i.e. he is unlikely to recover all the money he has paid. If A decides that he will not accept partial delivery, which he is entitled to do, he can recover all the money paid).

15. Money had and received. If A wrongfully obtains money to which B is legally entitled, B can sue A for recovery of the money in a quasi-contractual action for money had and received, e.g. where an employee receives money on behalf of his master and refuses to pass it on to the proper recipient.

Thus where B used the authority of his army uniform to assist him in smuggling activities, it was held that the army, as his employer, was entitled to the profits he had made out of the smuggling: *Reading* v. *Attorney-General* (1951).

16. Money paid under mistake of fact. Where money is paid under a mistake of fact it is generally recoverable by the payer, e.g. where an employer overpays wages under a mistake as to the employee's entitlement: *Lener* v. *L.C.C.* (1949). Where a local authority had overpaid an employee it was estopped from recovering amounts where the employee had, in good faith and without notice of the claim and also in reliance on the representation, so changed his position that it would be inequitable to ask him to repay the money: *Avon County Council* v. *Howlett* (1981).

NOTE: Money paid under mistake of law is generally irrecoverable, since ignorance of the law is no excuse (*ignorantia juris neminem excusat*). But to this rule there are the following exceptions: (1) where the payee knew of or induced the payer's mistake: (2) where the money was paid to an officer of the court, e.g. a trustee in bankruptcy: *Ex parte James* (1874); (3) where money was paid under unjustified threat of legal proceedings against the payer; (4) where the payee was under a fiduciary duty to the payer, e.g. where paid by a client to his solicitor; (5) where the mistake of law is treated as one of fact, e.g. (*i*) mistakes of foreign law; (*ii*) mistakes as to private proprietary rights.

17. Quantum meruit. Where there is a breach of an essential condition in a contract, the injured party may either (*a*) seek to enforce the contract and sue for damages by way of compensation or (*b*) treat the contract as discharged, in which case he cannot sue for damages for its breach.

However where he treats the contract as discharged, and has incurred expenses under it, he is entitled to bring a quasi-contractual action for compensation for work done. This is called a *quantum meruit* action (literally "how much is it worth?"): *see* V, **30**.

In addition to providing a remedy in certain cases of breach of contract like those above, *quantum meruit* may also be used by the court to impose quasi-contractual liability where there is no contract between the parties but justice requires that some remuneration should be paid for work done.

> EXAMPLE: L, a builder, did certain work for D on the under-standing that D would give him a contract later for some major building work. D did not give L the expected contract and L sued for (1) damages for breach of contract or (2) *quantum meruit* relief. HELD: There was no contract between L and D and therefore L could not get damages, but he was entitled to reasonable remuneration on a quasi-contract: *William Lacey Ltd.* v. *Davis* (1957).

CHAPTER II

Formation of Contracts

In order to constitute a contract there must be an offer, express or implied, by one person (the "offeror"), and unqualified acceptance, express or implied, by the person to whom the offer is made (the "offeree") The House of Lords has emphasised that save in exceptional circumstances, a binding contract requires an offer and an acceptance: *Gibson* v. *Manchester City Council* (1979).

RULES GOVERNING OFFERS

1. How made. An offer may be oral, written, or implied from conduct. Thus an implied offer is made by a bus company when it sends its buses along the street and stops them at fixed places to let people get on (the people who then get on a bus are thus accepting the offer by implication).

2. To whom. An offer may be specific, i.e. to a particular person or group of persons, or general, i.e. to the world at large.

(*a*) *A specific offer* can usually be accepted only by the person or persons to whom it was made: *Boulton* v. *Jones* (1857).

(*b*) *A general offer* can be accepted by anyone (and usually without prior notification of intention to accept).

Thus a newspaper advertisement offering £100 to anyone who contracted influenza despite using a patent medicine in a specified way was held to be (*i*) a general offer, (*ii*) which could be accepted by conduct, (*iii*) without previously notifying the offeror of the acceptance: *Carlill* v. *Carbolic Smoke Ball Co.* (1893).

3. Communication to offeree. The offer must be communicated to the offeree before it can be accepted.

EXAMPLE: A seaman helped to navigate a ship home, and before sailing wrote to the owners telling them of his intention and asking a particular wage for his services. The owners did not receive the letter of offer until the ship was nearly home.

HELD: The owners had no reasonable opportunity to accept or reject the offer, therefore the seaman could not compel them to pay him wages for navigating the ship: *Taylor* v. *Laird* (1856).

4. Certainty of offer. The offer must be definite, not vague or illusory Thus a promise to pay an increased price for a horse "if it proves lucky to me" is too vague: *Guthing* v. *Lynn* (1831).

5. Intention to create legal relations. The offeror must intend the creation of legal relations i.e. must intend that if his offer is accepted a legally binding agreement shall result: see *Balfour* v. *Balfour*; I. 3. The House of Lords has indicated that there is an intention to create legal relations where "free" medallions are given away with so many gallons of petrol purchased: *Esso* v. *Commissioners of Customs and Excise* (1976).

6. An offer must be distinguished from the following.

(a) *An invitation to treat* (invitation to make offers), e.g. an auctioneer's request for bids (which will themselves be offers): *Payne* v. *Cave* (1789); or the display of goods in a shop window with prices marked upon them: *Fisher* v. *Bell* (1961); or the display of priced goods in a self-service store: *Pharmaceutical Soc.* v. *Boots, etc.* (1953). But indicating that medallions are given away with the purchase of petrol is probably not an invitation to treat, but is an offer: *Esso* v. *Commissioners of Customs and Excise* (1976).

(b) *A mere statement of intention*, e.g. an announcement of a forthcoming auction sale. Thus a person who attends the advertised place of auction could not sue for breach of contract if the sale were cancelled: *Harris* v. *Nickerson* (1873).

(c) *A mere communication of information* in the course of negotiations, e.g. a statement of the price at which one is prepared to consider negotiating the sale of a piece of land: *Harvey* v. *Facey* (1893).

EXAMPLE: In discussing a possible sale of land, A wrote offering £20,000 and B replied: "As you are aware that I paid £25,000 for this property, your offer of £20,000 would appear to be at least a little optimistic. For a quick sale I would accept £26,000 ..." A replied accepting this offer. HELD: B's letter was an offer which A had accepted, so making a contract: *Bigg* v. *Boyd Gibbins Ltd.* (1971) C.A.

7. An offer lapses under the following circumstances.

(*a*) *If either offeror or offeree dies before acceptance: Kennedy* v. *Thomassen* (1929). But the death of the offeror may not invalidate subsequent acceptance provided: (*i*) the offeree did not know of the death when he accepted. and (*ii*) the personality of the offeror is not vital to the contract: *Bradbury* v. *Morgan* (1862).

(*b*) *If it is not accepted within* (*i*) the specified time (if any), or (*ii*) a reasonable time, if none is specified.

What is a reasonable time depends on the circumstances. Five months has been held to be an unreasonable delay in accepting an offer to take shares in a company: *Ramsgate Hotel* v. *Montefiore* (1866).

(*c*) *If the offeree does not make a valid acceptance*, e.g. makes a counter-offer or conditional acceptance; or. if a particular manner of acceptance has been requested, he accepts in some other manner, e.g. by sending a letter by mail when a reply by hand was requested: *Eliason* v. *Henshaw* (1819), U S.A. case.

NOTE: Where a counter-offer is accepted the terms of the counter-offer then form the basis of the resulting contract (and not the terms of the original offer): *Davies & Co.* v. *William Old* (1969).

8. An offer may be revoked any time before acceptance.

(*a*) *Revocation must be communicated.* Until the offeree actually receives the revocation, he is entitled to accept and so create a binding contract.

EXAMPLE: A sent an offer by cable to B on the 1st October requesting acceptance by the same method. B received the offer on 11th October and immediately cabled acceptance. On 8th October A had posted a letter revoking the offer, which did not reach B till after he had cabled his acceptance. HELD: B had accepted before receiving the revocation, therefore a contract was made and the revocation was ineffective: *Byrne* v. *Van Tienhoven* (1880).

(*b*) *Indirect communication.* If the offeree learns of the revocation, he cannot later accept, even though he learns indirectly, e.g. where a prospective purchaser of land learns through a reliable third party that the offeror has sold the land to someone else. he cannot then accept the offer and sue the offeror for damages: *Dickinson* v. *Dodds* (1876).

NOTE: An offer for shares or debentures in a public company made as a result of an advertisement or prospectus cannot be revoked until the 3rd day after the opening of the subscription lists: Companies Act 1948, s. 50 (5).

9. Options. An offer to keep an offer open for a specified time (an *option*) is not binding unless (*a*) made under seal, or (*b*) supported by valuable consideration, like any other simple contract: *Routledge* v. *Grant* (1828).

PROBLEMS: (1) A wrote offering to sell a car to B and to keep the offer open "till Wednesday noon." On Tuesday B learned through overhearing a conversation that A had sold the car to C on Monday. Can B now accept A's offer and sue A for damages for breach of contract? (*See* **8** above.) Would it make any difference to your answer if B had paid A 25p to keep the offer open till Wednesday? (*See* **9** above.) (2) A published an advert saying that he would pay £100 to the first person to swim a particular lake on 1st April. B swims the lake and claims the reward. A now says the advert was a joke. Can B compel payment of the reward? (*See* **2** and **5** above.)

NOTE: In a unilateral contract, which is where A promises to give B something if B first does something for A (see the example in (2) above), it has been said that "although the offeror (A in our example) is entitled to require full performance of the condition which he has imposed and although short of that he is not bound, once the offeree (B in our example) has embarked on performance of the condition (as by starting to swim across the lake) there is an implied obligation on the part of the offeror not to prevent performance and he cannot revoke his offer": *Daulia Ltd* v. *Four Millbank Nominees Ltd.* (1978).

RULES GOVERNING ACCEPTANCE

10. How made. Acceptance may be oral, written or implied from conduct: *Carlill* v. *Carbolic Smoke Ball Co.* (1893).

But if a particular method of acceptance is required the offeree must accept in the prescribed manner: *Eliason* v. *Henshaw* (1819).

11. Unqualified acceptance. Acceptance must be unqualified and must correspond with all the terms of the offer.

A counter-offer or conditional acceptance operates as a rejection of the offer, and causes it to lapse. Thus where a house is offered for sale at £1000 and the offeree counter-offers £950, the offer lapses: *Hyde* v *Wrench* (1840).

Similarly a conditional acceptance "subject to a proper contract being drawn up" causes lapse of offer: *Eccles* v. *Bryant* (1948) (but an agreement "subject to contract" would be binding if the phrase simply meant the agreement was to be subject to the terms of a contract already existing).

12. Positive conduct. There must be active acceptance: mere passive intention to accept is ineffective.

Thus an offer by letter containing the words, "If I hear no more, I shall consider the horse is mine," is incapable on its own of constituting its own acceptance. There must be some positive communication of acceptance by the offeree; it would not be enough to show that the offeree intended to accept but died before writing a letter of acceptance: *Felthouse* v. *Bindley* (1862). Furthermore. where goods are sent unrequested to a private individual, they can become his after six months without him having to do anything: Unsolicited Goods and Services Acts 1971 and 1975.

13. Communication of acceptance. Normally an acceptance is ineffective unless and until it is communicated to the offeror.

EXCEPTIONS: (1) Where the offeror expressly or impliedly waives communication, e.g. where a general offer requires merely conduct as its acceptance: *Carlill* v. *Carbolic Smoke Ball Co.* (1893). Similarly an offer of a reward is accepted by doing what is required, without any previous communication: *Williams* v. *Carwardine* (1833). (2) Where the contract is made by post, or the post is envisaged as the means of communication, e.g. in most commercial contracts today. Here acceptance is complete as soon as it is posted, provided it is properly stamped and addressed: *Household Fire Insurance Co.* v. *Grant* (1879).

In postal cases therefore it does not matter if the letter of acceptance is lost in the post and never reaches the offeror: the contract is complete as soon as the letter of acceptance is posted. As a matter of commercial expediency the Post Office is treated as agent for the offeror, and communication to the agent is treated as communication to the principal.

The same rule applies to telegrams (but where the method of communication is instantaneous, e.g. telex or telephone, acceptance is not complete until it actually reaches its destination: *Entores* v. *Miles Far East Corpn.* (1955)).

Where acceptance is to be "by notice in writing to the offeree," mere posting of acceptance does not constitute notice—actual delivery must be proved: *Holwell Securities* v. *Hughes* (1973).

NOTE: Mere posting is not sufficient in contracts governed by the Uniform Laws on International Sales Act 1967.

14. Motive for acceptance. No one can accept an offer in ignorance of its existence, but provided he knows of the offer his motive for accepting is usually irrelevant.

EXAMPLE: C offered a reward for information leading to the arrest of a criminal. W provided the information (knowing of the offer) but saying that she did so simply "to ease her conscience." Therefore C refused to pay the reward. HELD: Since W knew of the offer and accepted it, her motive for doing so was irrelevant and she was entitled to the money: *Williams* v. *Carwardine* (1833).

15. Tenders. A tender is a form of offer for the supply of goods or services, usually made in response to a request for tenders. Tenders take the following forms.

(a) *Single offer*, e.g. a tender to build a factory. Acceptance of such a tender constitutes a contract.

(b) *Standing offer*, e.g. a tender to supply goods as and when required. Here the tenderer must supply as and when agreed, whenever an order is made. But he cannot insist on any orders being made at all.

EXAMPLE: P tendered to supply goods up to a certain amount to the L.C.C. over a certain period. The L.C.C.'s orders did not come up to the amount expected and P sued for breach of contract. HELD: Each order made a separate contract and P was bound to fulfil the orders made, but there was no obligation to make any orders at all: *Percival Ltd.* v. *L.C.C.* (1918).

(c) *Sole supplier*. The person seeking the tender may agree to take all his requirements for certain goods from the tenderer. This agreement does not oblige him to make any orders at all, but if he does require goods within the category agreed he must take them from the tenderer: *Kier* v. *Whitehead Iron Co.* (1938).

STANDARD FORM CONTRACTS

There is an increasing tendency for an offeror to write out the contract entirely himself, and then demand that the offeree shall accept the detailed terms of the offer without modification.

The offeror may state all his terms in one document or, as in the case of railway tickets, may simply incorporate by reference certain standard conditions contained in another document. These "offers with terms annexed" are subject to special rules. They include most forms of transport ticket, by air, sea, or rail, many printed leases, and most contracts for the supply of gas, electricity, etc.

16. If the contract is signed by the offeree, he is bound by all the conditions contained in the document signed even if he has not read them: *L'Estrange* v. *Graucob* (1934).

EXCEPTIONS: (1) Where he can prove he signed the document under a fundamental mistake as to its nature (not merely as to its contents). This is the Common Law defence of *non est factum.* It covers, for example, cases where a person is induced to sign a cheque on the mistaken assumption that it is merely a guarantee: *Foster* v. *Mackinnon* (1869), and *see* IV, **7**. (2) Where he can prove that he was induced to sign as a result of a misrepresentation by the offeror, or the offeror's agent, whether innocent or fraudulent: *Curtis* v. *Chemical Cleaning & Dyeing Co. Ltd.* (1951); *Mendelsohn* v. *Normand Ltd.* (1970); *Evans & Son* v. *Merzario* (1976). (3) Where, in a hire purchase contract, the hirer signed the contract at a place other than the trader's place of business, the hirer can cancel his signature within four days of signing: *see* X, **68**.

17. If the contract is unsigned, e.g. railway tickets, the offeree is bound by all the terms in the document or annexed to it if:

(*a*) a reasonable man would assume the document to be contractual, e.g. not merely a receipt for money: *Chapelton* v. *Barry U.D.C.* (1940);

(*b*) reasonable care was taken by the offeror to bring the terms of the offer to his attention, e.g. by a notice "for conditions see Company's rules and regulations" clearly displayed on the face of the ticket.

If the notice given is reasonable the contract is binding whether the offeree reads the conditions or not: *Parker* v. *S.E. Railway*

(1877), or even whether the offeree is illiterate and unable to read them: *Thompson* v. *L.M.S. Railway* (1930); but if it is known that the person cannot read the clause because he is not English, he is not bound by it: *Geier* v. *Kujawa* (1970);

(*c*) notice of annexed conditions must be contemporaneous with the making of the contract: *Olley* v. *Marlborough Court Ltd.* (1949) and *Thornton* v. *Shoe Lane Parking* Ltd (1971).

NOTE: An oral contract could also contain exemption clauses, but they would clearly be harder to prove.

EXAMPLES: (1) C took a deck-chair from a p'le under a notice, "Hire of chairs—3d." Later an attendant came round to collect the money and C paid him, receiving in return a ticket which said on it, "The Council will not be liable for any accident or damage arising from hire of chair." C put the ticket in his pocket without reading it, thinking it was merely a receipt. The chair collapsed and he was injured and sued the Council. HELD: The Council could not rely on the exclusionary notice ticket, since none of rules (*a*), (*b*), or (*c*) above was satisfied: *Chapelton* v. *Barry U.D.C.* (1940). (2) O registered at a hotel by signing the visitors' book, and then went to his room where was displayed a notice excluding the hotel's liability for articles lost. HELD: He made his contract when he signed the book, and the hotel could not rely on the exclusionary notice since it was not brought to his attention contemporaneously with the making of the contract: *Olley* v. *Marlborough Court Ltd.* (1949). (3) B booked a passage for P and himself on D's vessel. He later received tickets containing an exclusion clause. It was held that the contract was made before the tickets were received, so the exclusion clause had no effect: *Hollingworth* v. *Southern Ferries* (1977).

18. Exemption clauses. Annexed conditions are usually aimed at exempting the offeror from some legal liability to which he would otherwise be subject, e.g. liability for negligence in carrying out the contract. Exemption clauses are viewed with increasing disfavour by the courts, and both statutory and judicial restrictions have been imposed on their employment.

(*a*) *Statutory restrictions* Examples are as follows.

(*i*) The Unfair Contract Terms Act 1977 limits the effectiveness of exclusion clauses in contracts of sale and hire-purchase. In contracts made by businesses with consumers clauses excluding the implied terms as to description, quality and fitness for purpose are void. The use of such clauses is also unlawful by virtue of the Consumer Transactions (Restrictions on Statements) Orders 1976 No. 1813 and 1978 No. 127. In contracts made between businesses or between private parties, clauses excluding these terms are valid if they can be shown to be reasonable.

(*ii*) The same Act also imposes restrictions on some exclusion clauses in contracts made on written standard terms or between a business and a consumer (i.e. whether or not on written standard terms). Clauses covered by this part of the Act, s. 3 are only valid if proved to be reasonable. The clauses which are covered by the Act are the following: (1) those which seek to exclude or restrict liability for breach of contract; (2) those which claim to allow a contractual performance "substantially different" from that expected; (3) those which claim to allow no performance at all.

(*iii*) The Act states that no exclusion clause can restrict or exclude liability for negligence resulting in death or personal injury. Where negligence results in any other type of loss, such as damage to property, the clause is valid if it can be proved to be reasonable.

(*iv*) The Unfair Contract Terms Act s. 8, makes void any term in a contract seeking to exempt a party from legal liability for any misrepresentation made by him before the contract was entered into (unless it is shown that the clause was reasonable).

(*v*) The Consumer Credit Act 1974, s. 173, makes void a term in a contract which excludes the protection afforded by the Act.

(*vi*) The Supply of Goods (Implied Terms) Act 1973 makes void clauses seeking to avoid the warranties as to title and merchantable quality implied into redemptions of trading stamps for goods.

(*b*) *Judicial restrictions.* The attitude of the courts can be summarised as follows.

(*i*) An exclusion clause will never be enforced unless adequate advance notice of it has been given to the other party: *Parker* v. *S. E. Railway* (1877).

(*ii*) Under the *contra proferentem* rule exclusion clauses are narrowly construed, against the person who inserted them.

(*iii*) Where the parties are on unequal footing, the court will more readily reject an exclusion clause designed to protect the stronger party. In one case, a young songwriter made an agreement with a publishing company for a five-year period. It was a particularly stringent standard form contract, for example, there was no obligation on the publishers to publish any of the songs produced. It was said, in finding that the contract could not be enforced, that the courts intervene to protect those "whose power is weak against being forced by those whose bargaining power is stronger to enter into bargains which are unconscionable": *Schroeder (A) Music Publishing Co. Ltd.* v. *Macaulay* (1974). *See also Clifford Davis Management* v. *W.E.A. Records Ltd.* (1975) and *Lloyds Bank* v. *Bundy* (1975).

(*iv*) Where the exclusion clause seeks to evade liability for breach of a fundamental term of the contract the courts will be particularly reluctant to enforce it: *Suisse Atlantique etc.* v. *N. V. Rotterdamsche Kolen Centrale* (1966), and *Harbutt's Plasticine Ltd.* v. *Wayne Tank and Pump Co. Ltd.* (1970): *Wathes (Western) Ltd.* v. *Austins (Menswear) Ltd.* (1976)

EXAMPLES: Exemption clauses were thus held void where (1) a bailee for safe custody handed the goods deposited to a stranger instead of returning them to the bailor: *Alexander* v. *Railway Executive* (1951); (2) a bailee stored goods in a warehouse other than that agreed with the bailor and the goods were destroyed by fire: *Lilley* v. *Doubleday* (1881). Where a bailee loses goods, the onus is on him to show he was not in fundamental breach: *Levison* v. *Patent Steam Carpet Cleaning Co.* (1977).

19. Indemnity clauses. The Unfair Contract Terms Act, s. 4, controls clauses which require a consumer to indemnify another party for liability which the latter might incur through negligence or breach of contract. Such clauses are now only valid if they are proved to be reasonable.

20. Guarantees. Where a guarantee is provided by a manufacturer that he will make good loss arising from negligence in the distribution or manufacture of the goods, this guarantee cannot exclude liability for the loss or damage: s. 5 of the 1977 Act.

NOTE: The Consumer Transactions (Restrictions on Statements) Order 1976 requires all guarantees (whether given by the manufacturer or the retailer) to be accompanied by a statement to the effect that the consumer's rights against the retailer are unaffected.

CERTAINTY OF TERMS

21. Terms must be certain. It is for the parties to make their intentions clear in their contract. The court will not enforce a contract the terms of which are uncertain.

Thus an agreement to agree in the future ("a contract to make a contract") will not constitute a binding contract, e.g. a promise to pay an actress "a West End salary to be mutually agreed between us" is not a contract, since the salary is not yet agreed: *Loftus* v. *Roberts* (1902). Similarly an agreement providing that the price will be subject to later negotiations is not a contract, since contracts to negotiate are not known to the law: *Courtney* v. *Tolaini* (1975).

Similarly, where the terms of a final agreement are too vague, the contract will fail for uncertainty, e.g. sale of a van "on hire-purchase terms" is too vague, since there are several types of hire-purchase agreement: *Scammell* v *Ouston* (1941).

22. Id certum est quod certum reddi potest (*that is certain which can be reduced to certainty*).

An agreement which at first sight appears to be too vague may be enforced under the following conditions.

(*a*) If the parties themselves have provided machinery in the contract for resolving the uncertainty, e.g. where no price was fixed for the sale of petrol, but the agreement stated that all disputes should be referred to arbitration, it was held that the arbitrator could fix the prices and so resolve the uncertainty: *Foley* v. *Classique Coaches Ltd.* (1934). Also where a five-year contract for the supply of chickens failed to state the number of chickens, but contained an arbitration clause, it was held that the numbers could be fixed by arbitration: *F. & G. Sykes* (*Wessex*) *Ltd.* v. *Fine Fare Ltd.* (1966).

(*b*) The deficiency can be remedied by the court implying a term, either (*i*) from the course of dealing between the parties in the past (if any), or (*ii*) from trade usages in the particular trade (if any), or (*iii*) where certain terms are implied by statute in similar contracts, e.g. the Sale of Goods Act 1979.

The court may always imply a term into a contract to save it from collapse, but will do so only where it is clearly necessary and equitable: *The Moorcock* (1889).

23. Meaningless clauses. An agreement which is definite on the whole will be enforced, notwithstanding the presence of some

meaningless or unnecessary words or phrases. The court in such
a case will ignore the meaningless words and enforce the contract
without them (unless the parties have given such a phrase a
common meaning): *Nicolene Ltd.* v. *Simmonds* (1953).

TERMS OF A CONTRACT

24. Express or implied terms. The parties may expressly state
every term of their contract with varying degrees of precision;
or they may simply agree the basic purpose of the contract and
leave the detailed terms to be deduced from the surrounding
circumstances.

Contractual terms are of two kinds: (*a*) conditions (main
terms); or (*b*) warranties (subordinate terms). Whether a term
is a condition or a warranty is a question of intention to be
deduced by the court in the light of the surrounding circumstances. Mistaken use of the words "condition" or "warranty"
by the parties will not be regarded as conclusive.

25. Conditions. A condition is an essential term, which goes to
the root of the contract, i.e. it may constitute the main purpose of the agreement, or one of several main purposes.

Breach of condition entitles the injured party to treat the
contract as at an end: *Behn* v. *Burness* (1863), and *see* V, **23–29**.
(Alternatively he may treat the breach as a mere breach of warranty, claim damages and insist on the contract being performed.)
The Sale of Goods Act 1979 declares, ss. 13 and 14, that the
implied terms as to description, quality and fitness for purpose
are conditions, as is the seller's duty to have a right to sell: s.
12 (1).

NOTE: Fundamental term. This is a condition so important that
it constitutes the fundamental purpose of the contract, in the
view of the Court. Where there is breach of such a term (fundamental breach) the courts will not allow the contract-breaker
to escape liability by relying on even an express exemption
clause unless the clause clearly covers the particular breach:
Suisse Atlantique etc. v. *N. V. Rotterdamsche Kolen Centrale*
(1960) H.L. (*the Suisse Atlantique* case); *Photo Procuction Ltd.*
v. *Securicor Transport Ltd.* (1980).
There is no fundamental breach where breach is caused by
circumstances beyond the control of the non-performing party

and an exemption covers the situation: *Trade & Transport Incorporated* v. *Iino Kaiun Paisha* (*The Angelia*) (1973).

26. Kinds of condition.

(*a*) *Condition precedent:* a condition that the contract shall not bind one or both of the parties until such condition is fulfilled, e.g. "this contract is not to be binding until the war ends."

(*b*) *Condition subsequent:* a condition under which the contract shall cease to be binding at the option of one party on the happening of a certain event, e.g. "this contract shall cease to be binding if war breaks out." This is called a determinable contract and remains binding until the condition subsequent is fulfilled; contrast a voidable contract, which can be made completely void at the option of one party.

(*c*) *Condition concurrent:* a condition under which performance by one party is made dependent on performance by the others at the same time, e.g. payment of price upon delivery of goods ordered.

27. Warranties.
A warranty is a subordinate term, subsidiary to the main purpose of the contract; S.G.A. 1979, s. 61 (1).

Breach of warranty entitles the injured party to sue for damages, but he cannot regard the contract as at an end and must perform his part of it.

EXAMPLE: B promised to attend rehearsals for six days before a concert, but arrived in London only in time for two days' rehearsals, whereat G claimed the contract was discharged by breach of condition. HELD: Attendance at rehearsals was a warranty only and therefore the contract was not discharged, though G was entitled to damages: *Bettini* v. *Gye* (1876).

The obligations on the seller that the goods are free from any encumbrance and that the buyer will enjoy quiet possession are *warranties:* Sale of Goods Act 1979, s. 12 (2).

28. Ex post facto warranties.
Where a breach of condition occurs the injured party can (*a*) treat the contract as discharged, or (*b*) if he prefers he may treat the breach as breach of a warranty, go on with the contract and sue for damages.

In some cases he must adopt the second alternative, e.g. where in a contract for sale of goods the purchaser has accepted a substantial part of the goods, before discovering a breach of condition, he must treat the breach as a breach of warranty: S.G.A. 1979, s. 11 (1).

This treating a breach of condition after it has occurred as though it were a breach of warranty is called treating it as breach of an *ex post facto* warranty, i.e. a warranty after the event.

29. Implied terms. The general rule is that the parties are presumed to have expressed their intentions fully.

The courts will only imply additional terms where it is strictly necessary to give effect to the clear intentions of the parties, or where custom or statute requires the implication: *The Moorcock* (1889), and *see* **22.**

When express terms are clear and unambiguous, the court will only imply a term if it is clear that the parties must have intended it to form part of the contract: *Trollope & Colls* v. *N.W. Metropolitan Regional Hospital Board* (1973).

> EXAMPLE: C's insurance company employed the X garage to repair C's car, damaged in an accident. The Court found that there was an implied contract between C and X (contrary to X's claim that its only contract was with the insurance company). There was no term in this implied contract fixing the time to be taken for the repairs: X took eight weeks and C claimed damages for unreasonable delay. HELD: In the interests of business efficacy the Court implied that repairs must be completed in a reasonable time (in this case five weeks) and awarded damages to C: *Charnock* v. *Liverpool Corporation* (1968); *see* also *Brown & Davis Ltd.* v. *Galbraith* (1972).

Occasionally, terms are implied by statute: e.g. Sale of Goods Act (contracts of sale): Sale of Goods (Implied Terms) Act (hire-purchase): *see* **25** and **27** above.

30. Terms and representations. Frequently during preliminary negotiations one of the parties (e.g. the seller of goods) may make a series of statements, or representations, to help persuade the other party to enter the contract. Whether such representations become terms in the contract (and so binding the maker) depends on the construction which the court puts upon them.

The test is: Did the plaintiff accept the representations as mere inducements, or did he insist that he would not enter into the contract unless the representations could be regarded as binding conditions or warranties?

The following rules apply.

(*a*) A representation will not be regarded as a term of the contract unless the parties so agree, expressly or by implication.

(*b*) If a representation is treated as a mere inducement, the plaintiff cannot sue for breach of contract if it proves untrue. (Though he may be able to avoid the contract and obtain damages on the grounds of misrepresentation: Misrepresentation Act 1967, *see* IV, **11**).

(*c*) If a representation is agreed by the parties to be a term of the contract, the plaintiff's remedies will depend on whether it is regarded by the court as a condition or as a warranty: *see* **25** and **27** above, and V, **25**.

31. Construction of terms. In construing the terms of a contract the courts apply the following rules.

(*a*) Language used must be construed as far as possible in such a way as to give effect to the intentions of the parties.

(*b*) Words used must be presumed to have their normal literal meaning, unless the contrary is proved.

(*c*) Where there are two possible meanings, one legal and the other illegal, the legal meaning is to be preferred so as to render the contract enforceable. (Illegal contracts are void: *see* IV, **25**.)

(*d*) The contract is to be construed most strongly against the party who drew it up (the *contra proferentem* rule: *see* **18**).

(*e*) Contracts are to be construed according to their proper law, i.e. usually the law of the country in which they were made: *see* **33**.

(*f*) If the contract fails to express the undoubted intentions of the parties, the court will rectify it so as to make it express such intentions: *see* IV, **9** below.

NOTE: In construing the terms of a written contract the court cannot admit evidence of (1) the negotiations preceding contract, or (2) of the parties' intentions during negotiations: *Prenn* v. *Simmonds* (1971) H.L.

32. Collateral contracts. Where A and B enter into a contract the rights and duties arising will normally affect only A and B: *see* Privity of Contract, VI, **1–4**. But sometimes if A was induced to enter into this contract by the representations of X, the court may imply a collateral contract between X and A, the consideration for which is A's agreement to enter into the contract with B.

EXAMPLE: X induced A to buy a car from B on hire-purchase. The hire-purchase contract was between A and B and X was not a party to it. The car was defective and injured A. X's state-

ments as to the condition of the car were found to be false.
HELD: A had no remedy against B, by reason of an exemption
clause. But there was an implied collateral contract between X
and A, under which A promised to buy the car from B; X was
liable in damages for his false statements: *Andrews* v. *Hopkinson* (1956). *See also Evans* v. *Merzario* (1976).

NOTE: Under the Hire Purchase Act 1965 and the Consumer
Credit Act 1974, B would now be liable in contract for misrepresentations by his agent, X: *see* X, **70** below.

CONFLICT OF LAWS

33. Conflict of laws. There is an increasing tendency for mercantile contracts to be made between people in different countries and the question may then arise: which of several possible
systems of law should the English court apply to resolve a dispute
upon the contract?

The general rule is that the "proper law" of a commercial
contract is that which the parties have expressly or impliedly
chosen. This will usually be the *lex loci contractus*—"the law
of the place of contracting," but the court will not be restricted
to the *lex loci* and will make an objective assessment as to which
system of law is most closely and intimately connected: *James
Miller & Partners Ltd.* v. *Whitworth Street Estates Ltd.* (1970).

34. Rules applicable to commercial contracts.

(*a*) Contractual capacity of a party is generally governed by
the law of his domicil (the *lex domicilii*).

A person's domicil is the country in which he resides with
intention to remain there permanently.

(*b*) Whether the contract itself is valid or not depends on the
proper law of the contract, i.e. whether it is void, voidable, or
enforceable.

(*c*) Questions relating to the form of the contract are decided
by reference to the *lex loci contractus.*

(*d*) Procedural matters and questions relating to the evidence
required to prove the contract are governed by English law.

(*e*) Questions relating to construction and discharge of the
contract are governed by its proper law.

(*f*) The legality of the contract is assessed by the following
rules.

(*i*) If the contract is illegal by the *lex loci contractus* it will not be enforced in Britain.

(*ii*) If the contract is legal where made, but would be illegal in the country in which it is to be performed, it will not be enforced in Britain.

(*iii*) A contract valid by its proper law but illegal by English law will not be enforced in Britain.

CHAPTER III

Form, Consideration and Capacity

Generally a contract can be made in any form, but in exceptional cases the law lays down a particular requirement, e.g. that the contract shall be by deed.

All simple contracts must be supported by consideration, that is by some element of exchange which is measurable in money or money's worth, e.g. goods in return for cash, or services in return for wages or goods.

Generally any person can make any sort of contract, i.e. has full capacity to contract. But certain special classes of person suffer from contractual incapacities of various kinds, e.g. minors.

FORMAL REQUIREMENTS

1. Generally no formality. Most contracts can be made in any form, i.e. orally, by writing, by telephone, telegram, or by deed.

But in the following special cases the law requires that a particular form shall be adopted, usually to provide better evidence of the terms and so prevent disputes.

2. Contracts void unless made by deed.

(*a*) Promises of gifts: *Rann* v. *Hughes* (1778).

(*b*) Transfers of British ships or shares therein.

(*c*) Conditional bills of sale: *see* XVI, **13**.

(*d*) Certain documents creating or transferring estates or interests in land, e.g. conveyances of land, legal mortgages, and leases for more than three years: Law of Property Act 1925.

Note that corporations' contracts formerly had to be made by deed if the contract was other than of day-to-day or trivial importance. This rule has been abolished and corporations can now make their contracts in whatever form would be appropriate to private individuals: Corporate Bodies Contracts Act 1960.

3. Contracts void unless fully written. These include the following.

(*a*) Bills of exchange: Bills of Exchange Act 1882, s. 3 (1).

(*b*) Assignments of copyrights: Copyright Act 1956, s. 36.

(*c*) Contracts of marine insurance: Marine Insurance Act 1906.

(*d*) Transfers of shares in registered companies: Companies Act 1948.

(*e*) Acknowledgements of statute-barred debts: Limitation Act 1980.

(*f*) Articles of association of registered companies.

(*g*) Moneylending contracts.

(*h*) Contracts of employment.

NOTE: Hire-purchase contracts, credit sales and conditional sales are unenforceable unless written in proper form and signed by the hirer (or purchaser): Hire Purchase Act 1965, Consumer Credit Act 1974, and *see* X, **67**

4. Contracts unenforceable unless "evidenced" in writing. Note that these contracts are merely unenforceable unless in the required form, while those in **2** and **3** above are void: *see* I, **10** (meaning of void, etc.).

Contracts in this class are as follows.

(*a*) *Contracts of guarantee* (*see* below)*:* Statute of Frauds 1677, s. 4.

(*b*) *Contracts for the sale or other disposition of land* or any interest therein. This includes contracts to grant mortgages, leases, etc.: L.P.A., s. 40. (Notice that the contract to dispose of land must be evidenced in writing, while the conveyance which effects the actual transfer must be by deed: *see* **2** above.)

NOTE: Section 4, Statute of Frauds, originally applied to several types of contract besides guarantees, e.g. contracts for sale of goods worth more than £10, contracts not to be performed within one year of their making, executors' promises to pay a deceased's debts out of their own pocket, etc. But the L.R. (Enforcement of Contracts) Act 1954 reduced this list to guarantees only; the other contracts formerly covered by the Statute of Frauds can now be made in any form.

(*c*) *Contracts for directory entries:* Unsolicited Goods and Services Acts 1971 and 1975.

5. Contracts of guarantee. A guarantee is a contract "to answer for the debt, default or miscarriage of another": s. 4, Statute of

Frauds; that is, a contract to discharge another's obligations if that other fails to do so himself, sometimes called a contract of secondary liability (for guarantees generally, *see* XVII).

Contrast contracts of indemnity: promises to discharge another's obligation or to ensure that it is discharged, i.e. a contract in which the indemnifier accepts primary liability (indemnities do not need to be evidenced in writing).

> NOTE: Guarantees do not need to be evidenced in writing if they are merely part of larger transactions, e.g. where, on his appointment, an agent guarantees to make good losses incurred by his employer if any of the clients introduced by the agent fail to pay their debts. Here the guarantee is merely part of the contract of agency and therefore the whole contract can be oral if so desired: *Eastwood* v. *Kenyon* (1840),

The Unfair Contract Terms Act 1977, s. 5, makes special provision for the guarantee of consumer goods Where loss or damage arises from a defect in the goods, and results from negligence in the manufacture or distribution of the goods, no contract term or notice can exclude or restrict liability by referring to a guarantee. This rule only applies to "third party" guarantees, such as those provided by manufacturers.

The same Act, s. 4, controls indemnity clauses. A consumer cannot be made to indemnify another for that other's negligence or breach of contract, unless the clause is reasonable (*see* X 23).

6. Meaning of "evidenced in writing." The minimum of necessary written evidence suffices, provided it contains all the material terms of the contract, i.e. any signed note or memorandum of material terms on any scrap of paper.

The note or memorandum must contain the following.

(*a*) *The signature of the* "*party to be charged*" or of his agent, i.e. the signature of the defendant in any action brought upon the contract. It need not be signed by the plaintiff in the action.

(*b*) *All material terms* of the contract, i.e. (*i*) names of the parties or sufficient identification; (*ii*) description of the subject-matter, e.g the address of a house being sold; (*iii*) the price or other consideration.

> NOTE: Although, like other simple contracts, guarantees must be supported by consideration, the consideration does not need to be expressly stated in the memorandum of guarantee: Mercantile Law Amendment Act 1856.

7. When and how made. The note or memorandum can be made at any time after the contract is agreed, providing it is made (and signed by the defendant) before the contract is disputed in court.

It may consist of several documents, provided there is sufficient evidence to connect them beyond reasonable doubt, e.g. a letter headed "Dear Sir" might be linked to the envelope which contained it, so identifying the recipient: *Long* v. *Millar* (1879).

PROBLEM: A contracted to buy a house from B, vacant possession to be given on completion. A paid a 10 per cent deposit and B gave him a signed receipt which identified the parties, stated the purpose of the deposit, but contained no mention of vacant possession. Would this receipt be a sufficient memorandum? Would it be sufficient if it mentioned the requirement as to vacant possession?

8. Effect of non-compliance. If a contract required to be evidenced in writing is not so evidenced it is unenforceable. Therefore, although it may be perfectly lawful, if one party breaks the contract the other cannot sue him for damages for breach of contract in the normal way (but he would be entitled to keep any deposit he had obtained: *see* I, **11**).

NOTE: (1) The parties retain all other rights, except action in the courts. Thus, in an oral contract for the sale of land which fails through the fault of the purchaser, the vendor would be entitled to retain a deposit the purchaser had put down (normally 10 per cent) and the court would not assist the purchaser to recover it: *Monickendam* v. *Leanse* (1923) and *see* I, **11**. (2) If one party has fully performed his part of the contract the court may give him an order for specific performance, commanding the defendant to perform his side of the bargain despite the absence of written evidence (this is the Equitable Doctrine of Part Performance, and it applies only to contracts for the transfer of some interest in land).

9. The Doctrine of Part Performance. An oral contract for the transfer of any estate or interest in land is unenforceable by action: L.P.A., s. 40 (Breach of such contract does not give rise to any action for damages.)

But if A has performed his part of the contract and B then refuses to perform his part, the court will intervene to save A from hardship by ordering B to perform his side of the bargain.

Such an order for specific performance is discretionary and will only be granted under the following conditions.

(*a*) Where the contract is one of which specific performance can be ordered, i.e. where damages would be inadequate to compensate the plaintiff, and performance can be compelled without requiring constant supervision by the court: *see* Specific Performance, V. **31**.

(*b*) The act of part performance relied on is referable to the contract alleged: *Wakeham* v *McKenzie* (1968)

(*c*) The act of part performance relied on is such that it would amount to fraud on the part of the defendant to take advantage of the absence of writing

(*d*) There is sufficient oral evidence of the material terms of the contract.

EXAMPLES: (1) X orally promised a woman to leave her his house in his will if she gave up her own house and came to keep house and care for him until his death. She did so, but paid for her own board. When he died his will made no mention of the bargain. She sued the executors. HELD: Her actions were sufficiently clear part performance of the oral contract: *Wakeham* v. *McKenzie* (1968). (2) P wrote asking C to come and live with him, and promised to leave his house to C. C sold his own home and went to live with P. Later P ejected C, who sued for specific performance. HELD: C's sale of his own home taken in conjunction with P's request and promise constituted a binding contract, under which C was entitled to live in O's house and to inherit it on O's death: *Parker* v. *Clarke* (1960).

VALUABLE CONSIDERATION

10. Importance of consideration. The courts will not enforce a simple contract unless it is supported by valuable consideration, which is therefore an essential element in most contracts.

(Consideration is not necessary in specialty contracts or contracts of record: *see* I, **5–8**.)

11. Meaning of "valuable consideration." It has been defined as the price for which a promise is bought (Sir Frederick Pollock).

Consideration itself means "some right, interest, profit, or benefit accruing to one party or some forbearance, detriment, loss or responsibility given, suffered or undertaken by the other": *per* Lush J., *Currie* v. *Misa* (1875).

Consideration therefore means the element of exchange in a bargain, and in order to satisfy the requirements of English law it must be valuable consideration, i.e. something which is capable of being valued in terms of money or money's worth, however slight. It may take the form of money, goods, services, a promise to marry, a promise to forbear from suing the promisee, etc.

12. Kinds of consideration.

(a) *Executory consideration*, i.e. where the consideration consists of a promise to do something in the future (such as to render a service at a future date).

(b) *Executed consideration*, i.e. where the act constituting the consideration is wholly performed.

Thus if X pays a shopkeeper now for goods which are promised to be delivered later, X has executed his consideration, but the shopkeeper is giving executory consideration, i.e. a promise to be executed in the future.

RULES RELATING TO CONSIDERATION

These require to be fully learned and understood, and are set out in detail below

13. Necessity for consideration. Every simple contract must be supported by valuable consideration, otherwise it is normally void.

EXCEPTIONS: (1) *Gratuitous bailments*. A bailment is the delivery of a chattel to a hirer or borrower for some limited purpose or period. Most bailments are for reward, i.e are supported by some payment, but even where the bailment is gratuitous it is still recognised as an enforceable contract: *Bainbridge* v. *Firmstone* (1838) (In such cases the courts tend to regard the owner's parting with possession of his chattel as sufficient notional consideration, so that this is not a real exception to the doctrine of consideration.) (2) *Gratuitous services when performance commenced* If A gratuitously promises to dig B's garden, and fails to do so, B cannot sue A for breach of contract since there is no consideration for A's promise. But it has been suggested that if A once commenced the digging, he would be under an obligation to exercise reasonable care in the work and could be sued for damages if he were negligent.

14. Legality of consideration. The consideration must be legal, e.g. not some illegal act, such as paying someone to commit a crime.

If the consideration is illegal, the contract is void: *see* IV, 25–29.

15. Consideration must move from the promise. That is, a person seeking to enforce a simple contract in court must prove that he himself has given consideration in return for the promise he is seeking to enforce.

EXAMPLE: D had supplied goods to a wholesaler, X, on condition that any retailer to whom X resupplied the goods should promise X not to sell them to the public without fulfilling stated conditions. X supplied goods to S upon this condition, but nevertheless S sold them in breach of stated conditions. HELD: There was a contract between D and X, and a contract between X and S, but none between D and S. Therefore D could not obtain damages from S. The main reason for this decision was the fact that D could not show that he himself had given any consideration for S's promise to X: *Dunlop Pneumatic Tyre Co. v. Selfridges Ltd.* (1915) (affirmed in *Scruttons Ltd. v. Midland Silicones Ltd.* (1962), *H.L.*).

NOTE: Compare this rule with the Doctrine of Privity of Contract, *see* VI, **1**. In effect, in any contractual action, the court asks two implied questions which must be satisfied before the plaintiff can succeed in his action: (1) Is the plaintiff a party to the contract he seeks to enforce? (privity of contract) and (2) if so, has he given consideration for the promise he seeks to enforce? In *Dunlop Pneumatic Tyre Co. v. Selfridges Ltd* (1915) the plaintiff failed to supply satisfactory answers to both questions.

16. It must be something more than the promisee is already bound to do for the promisor. That is, the person seeking to enforce the promise must show that he himself has undertaken some obligation to the promisor beyond what he was already bound to do either (*a*) as part of his legal duty as a citizen, or (*b*) as part of a private contractual duty owed to the promisor.

EXAMPLE: If a seaman deserts his ship—so breaking his contract —and is induced to return to his duty by the promise of extra wages, he cannot later sue for the extra wages since he has only done what he was already contracted for: *Stilk* v. *Myrick*

(1809). BUT NOTE: Performance by A of an existing duty owed
to B will suffice to support a promise by C to A.

Thus where A was engaged to marry B, and C promised A a
sum of money to carry out this promise to B, it was HELD that
A could sue C for the money as soon as he had performed his
promise and married B: *Shadwell* v. *Shadwell* (1860).

17. Consideration must be real. That is, it must not be vague,
indefinite, or illusory, e.g. a son's vague promise to "stop being
a nuisance" to his father: *White* v. *Bluett* (1853).

Although the consideration must be real, it need not be
adequate, i.e. it is up to the parties to fix their own prices, and
providing there is some definite valuable consideration the
court will not set a contract aside merely because the price is
inadequate: *Haigh* v. *Brooks* (1839).

But a ridiculously inadequate consideration may be prima
facie evidence of misrepresentation or coercion: *see* IV.

EXAMPLE: A bought a guarantee contract from B which later
turned out to be unenforceable. HELD: A had got what he
wanted and could not later rescind the contract merely because
it turned out to be worth less than he thought: *Haigh* v. *Brooks*
(1839).

18. Consideration must not be past. That is, a promise made in
return for some past service is unenforceable, e.g. where, having
bought a horse, the purchaser promised to give the seller an extra
sum because of his satisfaction with the purchase, it was HELD
that the promise was unenforceable since it related to a past sale,
and the purchaser was therefore receiving no new benefit as
consideration for his new promise: *Roscorla* v. *Thomas* (1842).

EXCEPTIONS: Past consideration is sufficient in the following
cases: (1) *To revive a statute-barred claim*, a mere written
acknowledgement is enough without any fresh consideration:
Limitation Act 1980 (for limitation of actions, *see* V, **15**). (2)
A bill of exchange can be supported by any antecedent debt
or liability: B.E.A. 1882, s. 27. (3) Where the past consideration was rendered in response to an earlier request by the person who subsequently promises to pay for the service rendered:
the rule in *Lampleigh* v. *Braithwait* (1615). Here the promisor's
request is held to imply a promise to pay a reasonable sum later
and the subsequent promise to pay merely fixes the sum:
Stewart v. *Casey* (1892).

EXAMPLE: A asked B to use his influence to obtain a royal pardon for A, who had committed a crime. B did as he was asked, and later (in consideration of this past service) A promised to pay B £100. HELD: B could enforce payment: *Lampleigh* v. *Braithwait* (1615).

19. Payment of a smaller sum will not discharge a liability to pay a larger: the Rule in *Foakes* v. *Beer* (1884) Thus if A owes B £100 and B agrees to accept £50 in complete discharge of the debt there is nothing to stop B later changing his mind and suing for the remaining £50

EXCEPTIONS: (1) *Where the smaller sum is paid in a form or manner different* from that originally intended, e.g. where the smaller sum is paid earlier than the debt was due, or where a money debt is settled in goods, or is paid by handing over "a horse, hawk, or robe": *Pinnel's Case* (1602). But it is important to note that the creditor's acceptance of the smaller sum must be voluntary. Thus where a debtor put pressure on his creditor to accept a smaller sum, it was held that the acceptance was not binding: *D. & C. Builders Ltd.* v. *Rees* (1966). (2) Where (*i*) the creditor promises to accept a smaller sum (*ii*) intending his position to be relied upon and (*iii*) the debtor alters his financial position in reliance on the promise, the creditor may be estopped from going back on his promise, even though it was unsupported by consideration.

EXAMPLE: A leased property to B at a rent of £2,500 p.a but promised to accept half this sum during the war years, and B relied on this promise, making no attempt to earn the money necessary to pay the full rent. If later A went back on his promise and sued for the full rental the court would exercise its equitable discretion and estop A from retracting his promise: The High Trees Case (*Central London Property Trust* v. *High Trees House* (1947)).
This is an application of the principle of equitable estoppel, whereby a man may be prevented from denying any promise unconscionably even though it was unsupported by consideration. But the High Trees rule can only be raised as a defence, and not as a cause of action by the debtor, e.g. where a creditor has retracted his promise to accept a smaller sum and has forced the debtor to pay him the full amount, the debtor could not use the High Trees rule as the basis of an action to recover the extra money paid: *Combe* v *Combe* (1951).

CONTRACTUAL CAPACITY

The general rule is that all persons have full capacity to make binding contracts, but the following exceptional cases exist: *see also* Minors, **25** below.

20. Aliens. They have full capacity, save that they cannot own or hold shares in British ships: Merchant Shipping Act 1894, s. 1.

Aliens residing in countries at war with Britain are classed as enemy aliens (whatever their nationality). They cannot sue in British courts during war-time, but can be sued; and if sued they can defend the action, appeal, and lodge counter-claims in the normal way, either personally or through agents: *Porter* v. *Freudenberg* (1915).

21. Foreign sovereigns and diplomats. They have diplomatic immunity and cannot be sued in British courts, unless they voluntarily submit to the jurisdiction: Diplomatic Privileges Act 1964. *See also* the State Immunity Act, 1978 (no immunity in respect of commercial contracts; or contracts to be performed wholly or partly in the United Kingdom).

NOTE: Diplomatic immunity does not arise until the diplomat's appointment is accepted by the British Government: *R.* v. *Pentonville Prison Governor, ex parte Teja* (1971).

22. Married women. They now have full contractual capacity, can sue or be sued in their own names, can be bankrupted for their debts, etc.: L.R. (Married Women & Tortfeasors) Act 1935.

The common law doctrine of a wife's agency of necessity was abolished under s. 41 of the Matrimonial Proceedings and Property Act 1970.

23. Mental patients and drunkards. Their contracts are voidable, if (*a*) they were so drunk or mentally unbalanced as not to understand what the contract was about, and (*b*) the other party was aware of this: *Imperial Loan Co.* v. *Stone* (1892). Such voidable contracts can be ratified during lucid or sober intervals.

The Sale of Goods Act 1979, s. 2, lays down that lunatics, drunkards, and minors are bound to pay a reasonable price for necessaries (*see* Minors, below).

24. Corporations. A corporation is an artificial personality recognised by the law. Consequently it can only contract through human agents.

Under the *Ultra Vires Doctrine* a statutory or registered corporation can only contract validly within the powers conferred upon it. Any contract which is *ultra vires* ("beyond the powers") is void. (Corporations created by royal charter are not subject to the doctrine, though if they exceed their authority their charter may be revoked.)

NOTE: (1) *Statutory companies*, i.e. those created by special Act of Parliament: the statute will define the company's powers, and any contract beyond those powers is void absolutely. (2) *Registered companies*, i.e. those incorporated by registration under the Companies Acts: their powers are not usually expressly stated, but such companies must register a memorandum of association in which the objects of the company must be stated. The powers of the company will then be such powers as are necessary to the achievement of its objects. Any contract which exceeds such powers is void and cannot be ratified even by the unanimous vote of all the members: *Ashbury Carriage Co.* v. *Riche* (1875).

Registered companies must also have articles of association which govern the internal regulations of the company, e.g the rights of members and the powers of directors If the directors exceed the powers delegated to them by the articles, the contract is voidable by the company and is said to be "*ultra vires* the directors" (but if the contract in question is within the powers of the company itself, it can ratify such contract if it wishes). But by the European Communities Act 1972, s. 9, in favour of any person dealing in good faith with a company, any contract made by directors on behalf of the company is deemed to be *intra vires* and valid.

CAPACITY OF MINORS

25. Minors' contracts. A minor attains his majority at the first instant of his eighteenth birthday: Family Law Reform Act 1969. (Formerly the age of majority was twenty-one.)

Minors' contracts are roughly divisible into three classes: binding. voidable, and void.

26. Contracts binding on minors.

(a) *Contracts for "necessaries,"* i.e. goods and services necessary to maintain the minor, having regard to his social position.

Goods: A minor must pay (*i*) a reasonable price for goods (*ii*) suitable for his condition in life and (*iii*) to his actual requirements, at the time of (*iv*) sale and (*v*) delivery: S.G A. 1979, s. 2 (before he can be made to pay for goods, the supplier must prove all five points).

Goods may be classed as necessaries even if they are luxuries, provided they have some actual utility and fit the actual requirements of the minor, e.g. an engagement ring: *Elkington* v. *Amery* (1936).

EXAMPLE: A minor ordered eleven fancy waistcoats, which could have been considered necessaries having regard to his financial position. HELD: He could not be made to pay for them, as he was already sufficiently supplied with articles of this kind: *Nash* v *Inman* (1908).

NOTE: Goods necessary when ordered might have ceased to be necessary by the time they were delivered, e.g where a minor orders a suit from a tailor but buys other suits before that ordered is actually delivered. Here the minor could not be made to pay the tailor.

(*b*) *Beneficial contracts relating to education or training*, e.g. contracts intended to assist the minor in training for adult life or for a career (non-educational contracts would not be binding even if beneficial).

These contracts are binding even if they contain one or two burdensome terms, providing they are on the whole beneficial to the minor.

EXAMPLES: (1) A contract signed by a young boxer, which was intended to protect him from exploitation during his minority, contained a clause by which he was to forfeit his pay for a fight if disqualified for fouling. HELD: This clause was burdensome but was binding since the contract as a whole was beneficial: *Doyle* v. *White City Stadium* (1935). (2) C contracted with a publisher to publish his autobiography, since his wife and child needed money. Later C tried to avoid the contract. HELD: It was binding, as beneficial in earning C a livelihood: *Chaplin* v. *Leslie Frewin (Publishers) Ltd.* (1966).

27. Contracts void against minors. The following are absolutely void against a minor.

(a) Contracts to repay money lent or to be lent.

(b) Contracts for goods supplied or to be supplied, other than necessaries.

(c) All accounts stated, e.g. IOUs: Infants Relief Act 1874, s. 1.

NOTE ALSO: (1) A minor incurs no liability by signing a bill of exchange (such as a cheque) whether as drawer, indorser, or acceptor: B.E.A. 1882, s. 22. (2) If a minor fraudulently mis-represents his age in order to obtain a loan of money, he cannot be made to repay the loan; nor can he be sued for damages for fraudulent misrepresentation, since this would amount to indirect enforcement of the void contract of loan: *Leslie* v. *Sheill* (1914). (3) If a minor obtains unnecessary goods under a void contract, he must return them if possible. If it is impossible (perhaps because the goods have been consumed), he cannot be made to pay any compensation for them: *Stocks* v. *Wilson* (1913). But if he has sold such goods to another person, he is liable for damages for the tort of con-version since he had no right to the goods and has dealt with them in a manner inconsistent with the rights of the true owner: *Ballett* v. *Mingay* (1943) (4) A minor can only recover money he has transferred under a void contract if he has received no benefit under the contract: *Steinberg* v. *Scala Ltd.* (1923). (5) If an adult guarantees a loan made to a minor, the guarantee is void as well as the contract of loan: *Coutts & Co.* v. *Browne-Lecky* (1947). (6) If a minor borrows money to buy necessaries he must repay the loan, as the lender is placed in the position of the seller of the necessaries, i.e. is subrogated into the position of the seller.

28. Contracts voidable by a minor.

(a) *Contracts requiring express repudiation* before or within a reasonable time after reaching eighteen, e.g. contracts involving a continuing interest in property of a permanent nature, such as leases of land or contracts to take shares in a company.

Such contracts will become binding unless repudiated by the minor within a reasonable time after his eighteenth birthday. Thus if a minor leases a flat, he must pay rent while he is in occupation but can repudiate the lease and escape liability for future rent any time until a few weeks after his eighteenth birth-day; if he fails to so repudiate he will become liable for all the rent up to his majority and for the whole of the lease thereafter: *Davies* v. *Beynon-Harris* (1931).

(*b*) *Contracts not requiring express repudiation*, e.g. trading contracts and promises to marry. These remain voidable, even after the eighteenth birthday and even if confirmed by a fresh promise after eighteen, unless such promise was supported by fresh and additional consideration (otherwise any purported ratification by the minor after eighteen is ineffective: Infants Relief Act 1874, s. 2).

Thus a trading contract is not binding on a minor even if beneficial to him. And if a minor in business receives payment for goods sold by him, but refuses to deliver them, he cannot usually be sued for their value: *Cowern* v. *Nield* (1912).

CHAPTER IV

Void, Voidable and Illegal Contracts

These include contracts invalidated because they rest upon some fundamental mistake of fact (void), contracts induced by misrepresentation or coercion (voidable), and contracts which are contrary to some statute or to Common Law (void and illegal).

MISTAKE

1. Effect of mistake. The general Common Law rule is that mistake made by one or both parties in making a contract has no effect on the validity of the contract, e.g. where a person pays an excessive price for goods under a mistake as to their true value: *Leaf* v. *International Galleries* (1950).

However where the parties contracted under a fundamental mistake of fact, the contract may be void if:

(*a*) the mistake is one of fact, and not of law or opinion; and

(*b*) the mistake is so fundamental as to negative the agreement.

For a mistake to be "operative", it must exist at or before the time when the contract was made. Thus, there is no mistake where parties to a contract for the sale of a building believe it is not listed, if the listing occurs after they have made their contract: *Amalgamated Investment and Property Co. Ltd.* v. *John Walker & Sons Ltd.* (1976).

Mistake which thus renders a contract void is called "operative mistake."

2. Mistakes of law and of fact. Mistakes of law generally have no effect, since "ignorance of the law is no excuse" (*ignorantia juris neminem excusat*).

In two exceptional cases, however, mistakes of law are treated as though they were mistakes of fact.

(*a*) *Mistake of foreign law*, since the laws of a foreign country require to be proved in British courts as ordinary facts.

(*b*) *Mistake as to private rights*, e.g. a right of property, as where a purchaser buys property which already belongs to him: *Cooper* v. *Phibbs* (1867) (*see* NOTE, "Money paid under mistake of law," I, **16**).

3. Operative mistakes of fact. It is difficult to deduce consistent principles from the numerous cases on this subject, but it is fairly well established that in the following cases a fundamental mistake of fact will avoid a contract.

(*a*) Common mistake as to the existence of the subject-matter of the contract.

(*b*) Mutual mistake as to the terms of an offer, or the identity of the subject-matter.

(*c*) Unilateral mistake as to the identity of the person contracted with.

(*d*) Unilateral mistake as to the nature of a contract signed.

NOTE: *Common mistake* is where both parties make the same mistake. *Mutual mistake* is where each makes a different mistake, i.e. they misunderstand one another. *Unilateral mistake* is where only one party is mistaken. Unilateral mistake is generally of no effect, unless (1) it concerns some fundamental fact, and (2) the other party is aware of the mistake. Thus unilateral mistake has no effect where it relates merely to an error of judgment by one of the parties.

4. Common mistake as to existence of subject-matter, i.e. where, unknown to both parties, the subject-matter has been destroyed before the contract was made.

EXAMPLES: (1) The sale of a life insurance policy on the life of a person who, unknown to purchaser or seller, is already dead: *Scott* v. *Coulson* (1903) (2) The sale of goods which unknown to the contractors, have already been destroyed: *Couturier* v. *Hastie* (1856), and Sale of Goods Act 1979, s. 6 (*see* X. **28**).

NOTE: Mistakes as to the quality of the subject-matter generally have no effect. The general maxim of English law is *caveat emptor* ("let the buyer beware") and if a man mistakenly pays an unduly high price for something he has only himself to blame for the bad bargain.

EXAMPLES: (1) L paid a senior employee £50,000 compensation for loss of office when dismissing him before his contract had expired. Later L discovered that the employee had committed breaches of duty which would have entitled L to dismiss him without compensation. HELD: L could not recover the money on discovering the truth, since the House of Lords considered that the mistake related only to the quality of what was purchased, namely release from the contract of employment: *Bell* v. *Lever Bros.* (1932). (2) L bought from G a painting which both mistakenly believed to be by Constable and of great value. Later L discovered it was by an unknown artist and comparatively worthless. HELD: L could not avoid the contract, as his mistake related only to the quality of the subject-matter: *Leaf* v. *International Galleries* (1950).

5. Mutual mistake.

(*a*) *As to the terms of the offer.* Where the parties misunderstand each other as to the terms of the offer, the contract will be void if the mistake is sufficiently fundamental.

Here there is no real concurrence of offer and acceptance, since the offeree is accepting on a mistaken understanding of what the offeror intended.

EXAMPLE: A and B contracted to ship a cargo on the Peerless from Bombay. Unknown to either party there were two ships of the same name, and both were at Bombay and were due to sail on different dates. A had in mind one of the two ships, and B had in mind the other. HELD: The contract was void: *Raffles* v. *Wichelhaus* (1864).

(*b*) *As to the identity of the subject-matter*, i.e. the parties misunderstand each other as to what is to constitute the subject-matter of the contract.

EXAMPLE: At an auction X, misled by the catalogue, bid an absurdly high price for some tow (thinking it was hemp) and the auctioneer accepted the bid thinking that X was merely mistaken as to the value of tow. HELD: Contract void: *Scriven* v. *Hindley* (1913).

6. Unilateral mistake as to the identity of the person contracted with. Such mistake will only operate to avoid the contract where:

(*a*) the identity of the person contracted with is of fundamental importance; and

(*b*) this is made clear by the party mistaken before or at the time of contracting (so that the other party knows of the mistake).

NOTE: Where the parties contracted "face to face" the presumption is that there can be no mistake as to identity: *Lewis* v.

Averay (1971). (But this presumption may be rebutted by clear evidence to the contrary: *Ingram* v. *Little* (1960).)

EXAMPLES: (1) A rogue, X, entered a jeweller's and offered to buy goods. His offer was accepted, and he then offered to pay by cheque. The jeweller accepted the cheque, but said delivery would be delayed until the cheque was cleared. The rogue then said he was a well-known person and asked to take some of the jewels immediately. Deceived as to his identity, the jeweller let him take some of the jewels. X took the goods and sold them to a pawnbroker, and the cheque proved worthless. HELD: The contract was made before the identity became important, therefore it was not void on the grounds of mistake: *Phillips* v. *Brooks* (1919) (the contract was probably voidable on the grounds of misrepresentation). (2) L advertised his car for sale and B, a rogue, answered, describing himself as a well-known film-star. L was impressed and accepted B's cheque after B had produced a film-studio admission card as proof of identity. B then took the car and sold it to A, a *bona fide* purchaser. When L discovered the fraud he sued A to recover the car. HELD: L intended to contract with the man he met "face to face" and the contract was therefore not void for mistake, but merely voidable for misrepresentation: *Lewis* v. *Averay* (1971) C.A.

7. Unilateral mistake as to nature of a contract signed. Generally a person who signs a contract is bound by it, even if he has not read it: *L'Estrange* v. *Graucob*, *see* II. **16.**

But a person who signs a document under a fundamental mistake as to its nature may have it avoided, e.g where A is induced to sign a negotiable instrument believing it is merely a guarantee: *Foster* v. *Mackinnon* (1869). Notice that the mistake must be as to the fundamental legal nature of the document—not merely as to its contents.

EXAMPLES: (1) A, who was senile, was persuaded to sign a bill of exchange under the misapprehension that it was a guarantee. HELD: The bill was void for mistake: *Foster* v *Mackinnon* (1869). (2) A executed a transfer of land under a misapprehension as to its contents and effect. HELD: Contract not void. The mistake was not sufficiently fundamental: *Howatson* v. *Webb* (1907). (3) G, an elderly lady, signed without reading a document which L informed her was a gift transferring her house to her nephew P. In fact it was a transfer on sale (for

£3000) to L. G sought to have the sale annulled. HELD: She failed on the facts of the case because: (*a*) the document was not radically different in type from what she thought she was signing; (*b*) she was careless and (*c*) she had failed in her evidence to show that she would not have signed had she known the true facts: *Saunders* v. *Anglia Building Society* (1971) H.L.

(4) In another case, a person signed a form in blank addressed to a finance house, believing it to be a hire-purchase agreement. It was, in fact, a loan agreement. It was held that a binding contract existed between the signatory and the finance house. The signatory was under a duty of care to ensure that the completed document represented his true intention. He had not shown he had acted carefully, so he was bound by his signature: *U.D.T.* v. *Western* (1975).

8. Mistake in equity. The Common Law rules relating to mistake stated above render the contract either completely void or completely valid, even though neither conclusion may be completely just.

But since the Judicature Acts (1873–75) allow Equity to be administered in all courts to modify the Common Law in the interests of justice, the courts have used equitable principles to achieve a compromise result where it would be unjust to one or both of the parties to apply the Common Law doctrine rigidly in cases of mistake.

Equity will thus intervene for the following purposes.

(*a*) *To rectify* (amend) a written instrument containing patent errors of expression.

(*b*) *To refuse to order specific performance* of a contract against a defendant who is labouring under a mistake such that it would be grossly unjust to compel him to perform his contract, e.g. where A, by a slip of the pen, writes offering to sell land to B for '£1,250" when he meant to write "2,250." Here if B tries to enforce a contract at the lower price equity will refuse to help him and will protect A against the consequence of his mistake: *Webster* v. *Cecil* (1861).

(*c*) *To set aside an agreement on terms* fair to all parties, where Common Law will not declare it void: *Solle* v. *Butcher* (1950). See also *Grist* v. *Bailey* (1966) where a sale of a house was held voidable on grounds of common mistake as to value, which was not sufficient to render the contract void at law. This discretionary power to rescind the contract operates only if:

(*i*) the contract is not void at common law (but merely voidable in Equity): see *Lewis* v. *Averay* (1971);

(*ii*) there is a fundamental mistake common to both parties; and

(*iii*) the party seeking rescission is not at fault. (The maxim is: "He who comes to Equity must come with clean hands.")

9. Rectification. Where a written contract does not accurately express the intentions of the parties, the court will amend (rectify) the contract to make it express the true intentions. The party seeking rectification must prove the following.

(*a*) The mistake to be rectified lies only in the words used.

(*b*) There is a complete and final contract between the parties.

(*c*) There is clear oral or written evidence of the true intention of the parties.

(*d*) The mistake is common to both parties: *Craddock Bros.* v. *Hunt* (1923).

MISREPRESENTATION AND FRAUD

10. Caveat emptor. In English law a person is generally under no duty to disclose all facts in his possession to the other contracting party. Each must protect his own interests unaided. The rule is "buyer beware" (*caveat emptor*). Keeping silent therefore is generally not actionable, even though it causes damage to the other party.

EXAMPLE: H sold pigs "with all faults" to W, knowing that they had swine fever, and that W was unaware of this. HELD: W could not have the contract set aside: *Ward* v. *Hobbs* (1878).

11. Misrepresentation. But where one party makes a positive false statement which deceives the other, this may amount to misrepresentation rendering the contract voidable at the option of the party misled.

The deceived party may also be entitled to damages: (*a*) for deceit, if he can prove fraud, or (*b*) for negligent misrepresentation, unless the defendant can show that he had reasonable grounds for believing that what he said was true: Misrepresentation Act 1967, s. 2(1).

12. What is misrepresentation? A misrepresentation is (*a*) a false statement (*b*) of material fact, (*c*) made by a party to the contract or his agent, (*d*) which induces the other party to enter into the contract.

Misleading conduct may also amount to misrepresentation, if it presents a misleading picture about material facts and satisfies (c) and (d) above.

NOTE: (1) *The statement must be of fact*, not of law or opinion (but an opinion expressed by a person who might be expected to know the facts, e.g. by a technical expert on his own subject, may amount to a statement of fact: *Brown* v. *Raphael* (1958)). (2) *It must be of material importance* in the transaction, e.g. in the sale of a car a statement that the car is in good working order But representations relating to trivial matters, such as the condition of the windscreen wipers, would not amount to actionable misrepresentation. (3) *It must be made by a party to the contract* or his agent, i.e. not by a mere bystander. Thus where A invests money in a company in reliance on a false statement by the company's auditor in the company's balance sheet, A cannot sue the company for misrepresentation because the contract is between him and the company and the auditor is not an agent for the company for the purpose of making statements to lure investors: *Candler* v. *Crane Christmas* (1951) (but an action might be possible against the auditor for the tort of negligence: *Hedley Byrne & Co* v. *Hellers, etc.* (1964), H.L). (4) *It must be relied upon*, i.e. it must succeed in inducing the offeree to enter into the contract. Thus, A sold a broken gun to B and patched the barrel with clay to conceal the crack. B did not examine the gun and therefore was not deceived by the patch. HELD: The misrepresentation was not actionable, since it had no effect on B: *Horsfall* v. *Thomas* (1862) (5) *It must be by positive words or conduct*, not by mere silence unless the silence amounts to active concealment of facts, or silence about some facts puts those revealed into a false and deceptive light. Thus where a company's prospectus showed that it had paid dividends for several years, without disclosing that these had been paid out of reserves as the company was trading at a loss, it was HELD that the omission was deceptive and amounted to misrepresentation: *R.* v. *Kylsant* (1923). (6) *Statements true when made but becoming false before the contract is made must be corrected*. Thus R arranged to sell a business to Y and estimated profits at £2000 p.a. By the time the sale was completed the profits had fallen considerably. HELD: A's failure to disclose the change amounted to misrepresentation: *With* v. *O'Flanagan* (1936).

Thus an exceptional duty of disclosure is imposed in (5) above where silence is actually deceptive, and in (6) where facts true when stated subsequently become untrue before negotiations are completed. A further duty of disclosure is imposed in *uberrimae fidei* contracts: *see* **19** below.

13. Innocent misrepresentation. If a person makes a misrepresentation believing what he says is true he commits innocent misrepresentation, providing he had reasonable grounds for his belief.

The party misled may:

(*a*) affirm the contract and treat it as binding or may rescind the contract by notifying the other party and—where necessary—obtaining the court's assistance to secure restitution;

(*b*) sue for damages under the Misrepresentation Act 1967, s. 2. If he obtains damages, he cannot also rescind the agreement. *See also* **14**(*b*).

14. Damages for innocent misrepresentation. Formerly a plaintiff could not secure damages for innocent misrepresentation, but the Misrepresentation Act 1967 gives a right to damages in certain cases.

(*a*) Where the misrepresentation was made negligently. Note that negligence is presumed; the defendant can only escape liability for damages if he can show that he had reasonable grounds for believing what he said was true at the time the contract was made: s. 2(1).

(*b*) Where the plaintiff has sought rescission, the court has power to award damages in lieu of rescission: s. 2(2).

NOTE: Any exemption clause seeking to exclude liability for misrepresentation is void unless it satisfies the requirement of reasonableness: s 3, as substituted by the Unfair Contract Terms Act 1977: *Howard Marine* v. *Ogden* (1978).

Damages are also obtainable against the makers of innocent misrepresentation made in a company prospectus: Companies Act 1948, s 43.

15. Fraudulent misrepresentation. "An untrue statement made knowingly, or without belief in its truth, or recklessly, careless whether it be true or false": *per* Lord Herschel, *Derry* v. *Peek* (1889).

Thus if the maker believes that his representation is true, he cannot be guilty of fraud, even if he was negligent or unreasonable in saying what he did: *Akerhielm* v. *De Mare* (1959). (But in such cases he may be liable for damages for the tort of negligence: *Hedley Byrne & Co.* v. *Hellers, etc.* (1964).)

16. Remedies for fraudulent misrepresentation.

(*a*) The plaintiff may sue for damages for the tort of deceit (fraud)

(*b*) The plaintiff may repudiate the contract or have it rescinded by the court (with or without claiming damages for deceit).

(*c*) The plaintiff may affirm the contract and still claim damages for deceit.

17. Limits to the right of rescission. Although the misled party can generally get the contract rescinded (set aside by the court) this right is lost in the following cases:

(*a*) *Affirmation:* where the injured party has expressly or impliedly affirmed the contract after learning of the misrepresentation.

(*b*) *Restitution impossible:* where the parties cannot be restored to their original position, i.e. *restitutio in integrum* (total restitution) is impossible.

(*c*) *Prejudice of third parties:* where an innocent third party has obtained an interest in the subject-matter of the contract in good faith and for value: *see Phillips* v. *Brooks*, **6**. (In that case the innocent purchaser of the jewels from the rogue was held entitled to them since he had bought them from a person with a voidable title to them before that title was avoided and without notice of the fraud: *see* X, **35**).

(*d*) *Undue delay:* where in a case of innocent misrepresentation the plaintiff delays unreasonably in seeking rescission, the court may refuse to grant him the discretionary remedy of rescission: *Leaf* v. *International Galleries* (1950).

NOTE: Formerly rescission was unobtainable where a contract had been performed under the Rule in *Seddon* v. *N.E. Salt Co.* (1905). This rule was abrogated by the 1967 Act, s 1.

18. Representation as terms of a contract. If a misrepresentation is made during negotiations and is later incorporated as a term of the contract, the remedies of the injured party will be basically those for breach of contract. The remedies available will then depend on whether the term concerned is a condition or a warranty: *see* II, **24**.

NOTE: Formerly rescission was unobtainable in such circumstances. But the injured party may now rescind for misrepresentation: 1967 Act, s. 1.

19. Contracts uberrimae fidei ("of the utmost good faith"). Although there is no general duty of disclosure, in some exceptional contracts the law imposes a special duty to act w'th the utmost good faith, i.e. to disclose all material information.

Failure so to disclose renders the contract voidable at the option of the other party (and note the duty of disclosure imposed in ordinary contracts in certain circumstances: *see* **12** (5) and (6) above).

EXAMPLES: (1) *Contracts of insurance.* The insured must disclose all facts which might influence the judgment of a prudent insurer, whether to decline the risk or to increase the premium. (2) *Contracts of family arrangement,* for the settlement of family property, etc. Each member of the family must disclose any portions he or she has already received without the knowledge of other members of the family. (3) *Company prospectuses.* Directors, promoters, etc., must make full disclosure of material facts in any prospectus inviting the public to subscribe for shares in the company: Companies Act 1948, s. 43. Failure to do so renders the contract voidable and makes the directors, etc., liable for damages. (4) *Contracts for sale of land.* The vendor must disclose any defects in his title to the land, of which he knows. The duty does not extend to other matters, e.g. there is no obligation to disclose physical defects in the property sold. (5) *Suretyship and partnership contracts.* These contracts are not *uberrimae fidei* at their formation, but since made they impose a duty of utmost good faith on the parties to disclose to each other all material facts coming to light after the making of the contract (*see* Partnership, IX, **13**, and Guarantees, XVII, **4**).

DURESS AND UNDUE INFLUENCE

20. Duress. This means actual or threatened violence to the person (not the property) of the party coerced or to his wife, children, or parents, and its effect is to render the contract voidable at the option of the party coerced.

Threats of imprisonment are included under this head, e.g. where A was induced to part with valuable documents by threats of continued confinement: *Cummings* v. *Ince* (1847).

Contracts made under economic duress may also be void: *North Ocean Shipping Co.* v. *Hyundai Construction Co.* (1978).

21. Undue influence. This means any pressure or coercion, not amounting to duress, which prevents the party coerced from exercising free judgment, and it makes the contract voidable by him at the discretion of the court (thus a plaintiff who proves duress is entitled to rescission, while one who can only prove undue influence is dependent on the discretion of the court).

Undue influence covers all types of pressure not amounting to duress, e.g. moral pressure, threats of violence to property, playing on victim's superstitions. etc.

To be actionable the undue influence need not have been exercised by a party to the contract (cf. misrepresentation).

EXAMPLE: A mother coerced her daughter into making a money lending contract with X, a moneylender, who knew of the mother's actions. HELD: The contract was voidable by the daughter: *Lancashire Loans Ltd.* v. *Black* (1934).

22. Undue influence may be presumed. The court presumes that undue influence has been available to one party (and exerted) in contracts between persons in a fiduciary relationship, i.e. where one party is in a position to influence the other unfairly. Wherever undue influence is thus presumed, the burden of proof will lie on the defendant to disprove its exercise if he wishes to preserve the contract.

Undue influence is presumed in contracts between parent and child, trustee and beneficiary, solicitor and client, doctor and patient, priest and communicant, teacher and pupil, etc.

The defendant can disprove undue influence by showing that:
  (a) full disclosure of all material facts was made;
  (b) the consideration was adequate; and
  (c) the weaker party was in receipt of independent legal advice.

EXAMPLE: The age and health of the person influenced may be relevant. Thus undue influence was presumed between a woman secretary of strong personality and an aged and infirm employer who had been persuaded to make valuable gifts to her: *Re Craig* (1970). Where an elderly farmer mortgages his property to help a company run by his son, the bank must ensure that he has independent advice: *Lloyds Bank* v. *Bundy* (1975).

23. Other cases of undue influence. Even where it is not presumed, undue influence may still be alleged. In such cases the burden of proof lies on the plaintiff to show that such influence existed and was exerted.

EXAMPLE: A nephew managing the affairs of an elderly aunt persuaded her to give him some shares, for the purpose of getting control of the company. HELD: The contract was voidable, despite the fact that she had received independent legal advice, since the lawyer who advised her to make the contract was not informed that the shares were virtually all the property the woman possessed: *Inche Noriah* v. *Shaik Allie Bin Omar* (1929), *see also Hodgson* v. *Marks* (1971).

24. Right to relief lost. Since remedies for undue influence are discretionary, they will only be awarded where the plaintiff's own conduct is equitable. A claim for relief may be disallowed where:

(a) the plaintiff's conduct has been tricky or unfair; or

(b) the plaintiff has delayed unreasonably in seeking rescission of the contract: *Allcard* v. *Skinner* (1887).

ILLEGALITY

25. Meaning of "illegality." An illegal contract is one which is void because (a) it is for an illegal purpose, or (b) it is contrary to some rule of public policy.

The courts will generally give the parties to such contracts no protection at all, even to prevent hardship (except as stated in **29** below). Contrast contracts which are void for some other reason than illegality, e.g mistake, or by s 1 Infants Relief Act, *see* III, **27**; in these cases the court will assist the parties to the extent of ordering the return of property transferred under the contract: *Chappell* v. *Poles* (1837).

26. The Doctrine of Severance. Where a contract is for several independent purposes, some of which are legal and others illegal, the court may sever the illegal terms from the contract and enforce the remaining legal terms: *Pickering* v. *Ilfracombe Rail Co.* (1868), and *see* **48**.

But this is only possible where the legal and illegal terms are clearly independent. The court will not re-write the main terms of the contract so as to make it legal: *Napier* v. *National Business Agency* (1951).

27. Presumption in favour of validity. The courts are reluctant to
declare any contract void on the grounds of illegality and will
do so only where:

    (*a*) a statute clearly prohibits the contract; or

    (*b*) a well-established rule of Common Law makes such con-
tract illegal on grounds of public policy.

Otherwise the general attitude of the courts has been stated
thus: "You have this paramount policy to consider—that you
are not lightly to interfere with the freedom of contract": *per*
Sir George Jessel, in *Printing & Numerical Co.* v. *Sampson* (1875).

28. Consequences of illegality.

    (*a*) The contract is entirely void, unless the Doctrine of
Severance can be applied to save part of it.

    (*b*) Money paid or property transferred under an illegal con-
tract cannot be recovered (subject to the exceptions in **29** below).

The maxim is *in pari delicto potior est conditio defendentis*
("in cases of equal guilt, more powerful is the condition of the
defendant"). Thus where the parties are equally guilty, if the
plaintiff is suing for the return of money paid under the illegal
contract, the court will usually allow the defendant to keep it.
(For the rules applicable where the parties are not equally guilty
see **29** below.)

    (*c*) Negotiable securities, such as cheques and other bills of ex-
change, transferred between the parties to the contract are void
as between them. But an innocent third party who acquires such
securities in good faith and for value can usually enforce them:
see Bills of Exchange, XV, **2**. Thus where A pays a gambling debt
to B by cheque B cannot enforce payment against A; but if B
sells the cheque to C, who buys in good faith and without notice
of any irregularity, C will be able to enforce the cheque. *See also*
Consumer Credit Act 1974, ss. 123–125.

    (*d*) *Ex turpi causa non oritur actio* ("from an evil cause, no
action arises"). Where a plaintiff seeking the court's assistance
has to base his claim on his own illegal or immoral act, his claim
will fail.

    EXAMPLE: A rented a flat to R at £1,200 p.a. To avoid tax they
agreed to describe the money as £450 for rent and £750 for
"services." Later R attempted to bilk A by refusing to pay the
£750 on the grounds that he had received no services, and A
sued for the money. HELD: The contract was illegal as an

attempt to defraud the revenue, and A could not recover the money since he could only get it by admitting that it was really rent and this involved admitting his own guilt. But to prevent R benefiting from this situation the court terminated his tenancy on the grounds that it was illegal, and offered him a new one at the full rent: *Alexander* v. *Rayson* (1936).

29. Recovery of property transferred. Money paid or property transferred under an illegal contract is normally irrecoverable.

EXCEPTIONS: (1) Where the transferor repents of making the contract before any part of the illegal purpose is carried out, or (2) Where: (*i*) He is not *in pari delicto* (equally guilty) with the defendant, e.g. where he was induced to make the contract by the fraud of the defendant (*Shelley* v. *Paddock* (1978)); or (*ii*) The transferee was under a fiduciary duty to protect the plaintiff's interests, and has abused this duty by making the illegal contract, e.g. where he is the plaintiff's solicitor or trustee; or (*iii*) The contract is made illegal by a statute intended to protect a class of which the plaintiff is a member, e.g. a borrower suing to recover excessive interest from a moneylender under a contract illegal under the Consumer Credit Act (which is intended to protect borrowers).

CONTRACTS FORBIDDEN BY STATUTE

30. Contracts for trading or selling on a Sunday. Such contracts are generally prohibited under the Sunday Observance Act 1677. But many of these are in fact made lawful under the Shops Act 1950, under which shops may be licensed to remain open on Sundays.

31. Registration of Business Names Act 1916. Any person trading under a name other than his real name must register such trade name. If he, or his firm, fails to do so any contracts made under the trade name are void: *see* Partnership, IX, **3**.

32. Moneylenders Acts 1900–1927: Consumer Credit Act 1974. These lay down restrictions upon professional moneylenders. A contract made in contravention of the Acts is void.

NOTE: (1) A moneylending contract is not enforceable unless in writing signed by the borrower, and the borrower must receive a copy of the contract within seven days of making it: Moneylenders Act 1927, s. 6. (2) Moneylenders (now properly referred to as creditors) are those whose business includes lending sums up to £5,000. They must be licensed under the Consumer Credit Act 1974. "Creditors" includes every business lending sums up to £5,000, and so includes banks. If such creditors are not licensed by the Office of Fair Trading, they cannot enforce their contracts unless allowed to do so by the Director General of Fair Trading. (3) The Limitation Act 1980 provides a special time limit for actions in respect of certain issues. (4) Under the Moneylenders Act 1927 an annual rate of interest in excess of forty-eight per cent was presumed to be excessive. This has now been repealed by the Consumer Credit Act 1974, ss. 137–140. The position now is that no percentage figure is mentioned. The court instead may re-open any credit agreement which it holds to be extortionate and do justice between the parties. An agreement will be extortionate if: (*i*) it requires payments which are "grossly exorbitant", or (*ii*) it otherwise "grossly contravenes" ordinary principles of fair dealing.

33. Gaming and wagering contracts. A wager is a promise to give or pay something on the ascertainment of an uncertain future event, e.g. a horse race. A bet is a wager on the result of a game.

Such contracts are void under the Gaming and Wagering Acts 1835–1960. The position is complex, but the following basic rules apply.

(*a*) Money earned as commission on bets and wagers is irrecoverable: Gaming Act 1892. An agent cannot therefore recover his commission from his principal. But the principal can recover any winnings received on his behalf by the agent: *De Mattos* v. *Benjamin* (1894).

(*b*) Negotiable instruments given for a bet are given for an illegal consideration and are void as between the parties: Gaming Act 1835. But an innocent third party who becomes a holder in due course of such an instrument may be able to enforce it fully: *see* Bills of exchange, XV, **38**.

(*c*) Money lent to a loser to pay his bets is recoverable: *Re O'Shea* (1911); but not if the lender himself pays the winner, since he is then participating in the forbidden transaction: *Macdonald* v. *Green* (1951).

(*d*) The winner of a wager cannot sue the loser for his winnings, even though the loser later makes a fresh promise to pay supported by fresh consideration: *Hill* v. *William Hill Ltd.* (1949).

This rule still applies, even though the Betting, Gaming and Lotteries Act 1963 legalised gambling in certain circumstances, i.e. the contracts resulting from such legalised gambling were void. *See now* the Gaming Act 1968.

(*e*) Money paid to a stakeholder to retain pending the result of a wager can be recovered from the stakeholder by the payer at any time before he has handed it over to the other party to the wager: *Burge* v. *Ashley & Smith Ltd.* (1900).

(*f*) The essence of a wager is that neither party has any legitimate interest in the uncertain event wagered upon, except the money staked. Where a party has something to gain or lose apart from the money staked, the agreement is not a wager, e.g. insurance contracts. Thus if A insures his life, his ship, or his house against death, loss, or damage, he stands to lose the value of his ship or house (or his life) quite apart from the wager. Although an insurance contract is similar in its other characteristics to a wager, it is valid and enforceable: *see* XII.

CONTRACTS ILLEGAL AT COMMON LAW

34. Contracts tainted with sexual immorality. A contract superficially lawful will be void if, to the knowledge of the parties, its ultimate purpose was immoral, e.g. an ordinary lease of a house would be void if the house was to be used as a brothel.

EXAMPLE: A hired a carriage to a woman knowing that she was a prostitute and would use the carriage for the purpose of soliciting. HELD: The contract was void and he could not recover unpaid hiring charges: *Pearce* v. *Brooks* (1866). This is an example of the working of the maxim *In pari delicto potior est conditio defendentis: see* **28** above.

35. Contracts tending to interfere with the sanctity of marriage, e.g. a promise by a married man to marry another woman as soon as his wife is dead: *Wilson* v. *Carnley* (1908).

Were a married man to promise to marry another woman, the other woman could not sue him for breach of promise if she knew he was married when he made the promise. The right to sue for breach of promise to marry has, however, been abolished by the Law Reform (Miscellaneous Provisions) Act 1970, s. 1.

36. Contracts for the sale of public offices or titles of honour, e.g. a promise to use influence to obtain a title or commission for the promisee in return for money: *Parkinson* v. *College of Ambulance Ltd.* (1925).

37. Contracts to commit crimes or torts, whether in Britain or in any foreign friendly nation, e.g. a contract to smuggle goods into the United States of America: *Foster* v. *Driscoll* (1929).

38. Contracts to obtain an unfair benefit from the government, e.g. a promise to use influence to obtain exemption from a legal duty, such as military service: *Montefiore* v. *Menday Motor Components Ltd.* (1918).

39. Contracts involving trade with an enemy nation are illegal at Common Law and also under the Trading with the Enemy Act 1939.

40. Contracts to defraud the Revenue, see *Alexander* v. *Rayson*, **28** above.

41. Contracts tending to impede the administration of justice, e.g. a promise by an accused person to indemnify someone who has stood bail for him: *Herman* v. *Jeuchner* (1885).

42. Contracts prejudicial to the freedom of marriage, e.g. imposing a general restraint upon a person to prevent marriage, though a particular restraint might be valid if not unreasonable, e.g. a contract forbidding a girl from marrying a particular man.

Marriage brokage contracts are also in this category and are void, i.e. contracts to arrange marriages for a reward: *Hermann* v. *Charlesworth* (1905).

43. Contracts involving champerty or maintenance. Maintenance means giving financial or other assistance to a party to a law suit, where the maintainer has no sufficient legal or moral interest in the case. Champerty means maintenance with a view of sharing the profits of the action. But the Criminal Law Act 1967 states that maintenance and champerty can no longer be punished as a crime or tort.

NOTE: A shared commercial interest is sufficient to negative maintenance: *Martell* v. *Consett Iron Co. Ltd.* (1955).

CONTRACTS IN RESTRAINT OF TRADE

These are contracts which seek to restrict a person from freely exercising his trade or profession. For students of Mercantile Law this is the most important category of illegal contracts.

44. Restraints prima facie void. All restraints on trade are prima facie void, though they may be enforceable if they seek merely to protect some legitimate commercial interest. By contrast, a restraint which seeks merely to prevent competition is always void: *Morris* v. *Saxelby* (1916).

A restraint may be (*a*) general, i.e. forbidding trading through-out a large area, such as throughout the United Kingdom, or Europe, or (*b*) particular, i.e. forbidding trade in some localised area, such as a particular town and its environs. General restraints are more disfavoured than particular restraints.

45. When restraints are valid. A restraint will be held void unless the party seeking to enforce it can prove:

(*a*) that is is reasonable in the public interest;

(*b*) that it is reasonable as between the parties, i.e. seeks to provide reasonable protection for some legitimate interest of the plaintiff, such as trade secrets or business goodwill;

(*c*) that the plaintiff has given valuable consideration for the promise he seeks to enforce. In this type of contract considera-tion is necessary even if the contract is under seal.

Whether a restraint is reasonable or not is a question of law to be decided by the judge; whether the individual restraint under dispute is in fact reasonable is a question of fact in each case.

A restraint which is reasonable between the parties is pre-sumed to be reasonable in the public interest, unless there is some rule of law to the contrary: *Attorney-General of Australia* v. *Adelaide S.S. Co.* (1913).

46. Kinds of restraint. Restraints can be grouped roughly into three categories.

(*a*) Between employer and employee, to prevent the employee competing with his employer after leaving his job: *see* **47** below.

(*b*) Between the vendor and the purchaser of a business, to prevent the seller harming the goodwill of the business sold, *see* **49** below.

(*c*) Between traders, to regulate conditions of trade. These are

now largely governed by statute, e.g. the Restrictive Trade
Practices Act 1976 and the Resale Prices Act 1976.

47. Restraints upon employees. An employer may compel an
employee to sign a covenant promising not to injure the employer's interests either (a) during the continuance of the employment (e.g. by passing confidential information to outsiders), or
(b) after leaving the employment (e.g. by luring away his former
employer's customers).

Such agreements are viewed with disfavour by the courts
because of the element of coercion: *see* Undue Influence, **21**
above. They will only be enforced if they satisfy the tests set out
in **48** below.

NOTE: Apart from any express covenant, an employer is
entitled to prevent an employee from disclosing trade secrets
during the employment or after leaving: *Amber Size & Chemical Co.* v. *Menzel* (1913); or from making a list of the employer's clients with a view to competition after leaving:
Robb v. *Green* (1895). *See also Thomas Marshall (Exports) Ltd.*
v. *Guinle* (1978). But even if an express covenant exists and is
enforceable, the employer loses the right to enforce it if he
himself breaks the contract of employment, e.g. by wrongfully
dismissing the employee: *General Billposting Co.* v *Atkinson*
(1909).

48. Restraints upon employees: when enforceable. Restraints
upon employees will only be enforced if they satisfy the following tests.

(a) The restraint is void unless supported by valuable consideration. The payment of wages is the usual consideration
given by the employer. If therefore the covenant is only imposed
when the employee is leaving, there may be no consideration for
it (unless some special payment is made to bind the contract).

(b) The restraint is void unless the employee has some real
capacity to damage the employer and the covenant seeks to guard
against such damage.

Thus a master is entitled to protection of trade secrets, or to a
covenant that an employee in an influential position will not use
his influence to seduce the master's clients.

Therefore the employee must generally be in some confidential
capacity, e.g. a solicitor's managing clerk: *Fitch* v. *Dewes* (1921);
but not a mere door-to-door salesman: *Mason* v. *Provident*

Clothing Co. (1913); nor a newspaper correspondent: *Leng* v. *Andrews* (1909) (though a newspaper editor might be in a sufficiently confidential capacity).

(*c*) The restraint is void if it seeks merely to restrict or prevent competition.

(*d*) The restraint must be reasonable, having regard to:

(*i*) the type of employment: *Mason* v. *Provident Clothing Co.* (1913).

(*ii*) the period of restraint: *Kores Ltd.* v. *Kolok Ltd.* (1959).

(*iii*) the area of restraint, e.g. a solicitor's managing clerk covenanted not to open a competing practice within seven miles of his former employers. HELD: Reasonable and enforceable: *Fitch* v. *Dewes* (1921).

EXAMPLES: (1) A tailor's assistant covenanted not to open a competing business within ten miles of his former employer's. HELD: Void, because in this particular case the assistant had no confidential relationship with customers and the covenant was therefore aimed merely at preventing ordinary competition: *Attwood* v. *Lamont* (1920), *see also*: *Home Counties Dairies Ltd.* v. *Skilton* (1970)—milk roundsman. (2) S was an estate agent with offices at Dartmouth and Kingsbridge. J was employed at the Kingsbridge office and covenanted not to open a competing business within five miles of Dartmouth or Kingsbridge within three years of leaving the employ. HELD: The restraint was too wide, since J had never worked at Dartmouth, but was valid insofar as it related to Kingsbridge. (This was an application of the Doctrine of Severance: *see* **26** above.) *Seymour* v. *Seymour-Jones* (1966).

49. Restraints on sale of a business. Restraints imposed by the purchaser of a business on the seller, preventing the latter from opening another business in such a way as to damage the goodwill of the business sold, are enforced if reasonable in the circumstances.

Restraints of this kind are more readily enforced than those between employer and employee, because they lack the element of coercion which may be present between the parties in contracts of employment.

A restraint of this kind will be reasonable if (*a*) it satisfies the tests set out in **45** above, and (*b*) it is intended merely to protect the purchaser's investment in the goodwill of the business bought, i.e. not intended to protect other businesses the purchaser already owned, or merely to prevent ordinary competition.

EXAMPLES: (1) N, an inventor of guns, sold his world-wide business to M and promised not to manufacture guns anywhere in the world for twenty-five years. HELD: Reasonable and binding: *Nordenfeldt* v. *Maxim-Nordenfeldt Co.* (1894) H.L. (2) S sold his localised business to C (who already had branches all over Britain) and promised not to open a competing business anywhere within ten miles of any of C's branches. HELD: Void. The restraint was more than was necessary to protect the goodwill of the small local business purchased from S: *British Concrete Co.* v. *Schelff* (1921).

CHAPTER V

Discharge of Contracts

DISCHARGE BY PERFORMANCE

1. Complete performance. In order to effect discharge, performance must be complete and exactly in accord with the terms of the contract.

Partial performance, even if substantial, will not discharge the contract (except in the special cases stated below).

EXAMPLE: A sailor, having signed on to receive a lump sum payment for a complete voyage, died before he completed the journey. HELD: His widow could not claim any part of his wages since he was entitled to payment only if he completed his contracted obligations: *Cutter* v. *Powell* (1795). (NOTE: On the facts this case would now be decided differently, but the general rule it lays down is still valid.)

2. Exceptional cases.

(*a*) *Performance prevented by the promisee.* Here the promisor can obtain compensation for work actually done in pursuance of the contract by suing on a *quantum meruit* claim: *see* **30**.

(*b*) *Partial performance accepted.* If the promisee voluntarily accepts less than complete performance where he had genuine freedom of choice, the promisor is entitled to claim payment on *quantum meruit*, e.g. A contracted to erect a building for B, and when the work was half done A abandoned the job. B had to complete the building himself, but A sued him for work done. HELD: B need pay nothing under the contract, as he had not freely chosen to complete the building himself, but had been compelled to do so by A's breach: *Sumpter* v. *Hedges* (1898).

(*c*) *Divisible contracts.* If performance is to be by instalments payment can be recovered for instalments actually completed (unless the intention of the parties appears to be to the contrary).

(*d*) *Substantial performance*, i.e. where performance is as complete as a reasonable man could expect, even though not strictly in accord with every detail of the contract. This is a question of fact.

EXAMPLES: (1) A decorated B's flat for £750, but because of faulty workmanship B had to pay an extra £290 to complete the job. B refused to pay any money at all to A. HELD: A was entitled to recover the £750, less the £290 paid to make good his defective workmanship: *Hoenig* v. *Isaacs* (1952). (2) A installed a defective central heating system for B at a charge of £560. B had to spend £174 to get C to put the system into working order. HELD: There had not been substantial performance of the contract and B need not pay A anything—not even the £385 that A claimed: *Bolton* v. *Mahadeva* (1972).

3. Tender of performance and payment.

(*a*) *Tender of performance.* It is sometimes sufficient if the promisor attempts to perform his side of the contract. Then, if performance is rejected, the promisor is discharged from further liability and may sue for breach of contract if he so wishes.

(*b*) *Tender of payment.* This relieves the promisor from future liability to make further tenders, but does not discharge him from liability to pay.

Under the Coinage Act 1971, Bank of England notes (and gold coins issued by the Mint) are legal tender for any amount, silver (or cupro-nickel) coins of more than 10p denomination are legal tender up to £10, silver (or cupro-nickel) coins of 10p or less are legal tender up to £5, and bronze coins for any amount up to 20p. (But the debtor should produce the correct amount: the creditor is not obliged to give change: *Robinson* v. *Cook* (1815).)

4. Time for performance or payment. Failure to perform or pay on time may be a breach of warranty but is rarely a breach of condition, i.e. is rarely "of the essence" of the contract.

(*a*) *Time of payment* is not of the essence unless otherwise agreed expressly or impliedly. (This rule is statutorily applied to contracts for the sale of goods: S.G.A. 1979, s. 10.)

(*b*) *Time of performance* is not usually of the essence but may be made so by agreement, and this is usually done in mercantile contracts.

EXAMPLE: O waived the original delivery date but stipulated a later date as final. HELD: This made the later date of the essence, i.e. a condition, of the contract and failure to deliver on the new date entitled O to rescind the contract: *Rickards* v. *Oppenheim* (1950.)

5. Rules re payment of money.

(a) Payment of a smaller sum will not usually discharge liability to pay a larger: *Foakes* v *Beer* (1884), except where the rules in *Pinnel's Case* or the *High Trees Case* apply; *see* III, 19.

(b) Payment to an agent is usually a good discharge, if the agent is held out by the creditor as having authority to receive money.

(c) Payment by a third party is not a good discharge, unless he pays as agent for the debtor: *Smith* v. *Cox* (1940).

(d) Payment to one joint creditor discharges liability to the others: *Kendall* v. *Hamilton* (1879).

(e) Payment by negotiable instrument is conditional payment only, until the negotiable instrument is cashed (or as otherwise agreed).

The creditor can always refuse to take a negotiable instrument such as a cheque and can insist on cash

(f) Payment by post is ineffective if the letter is lost in the post, unless the creditor requested this method of payment: *Pennington* v. *Crossley & Son* (1897).

But if the creditor did request payment by post, payment is effective once posted, even if the letter is lost in the post: *Newman* v. *Ricketts* (1886).

(g) Payment by cheque is prima facie evidence of receipt (once the cheque has been cashed) but a formal receipt can also be demanded: Cheques Act 1957, s. 3.

6. Appropriation of payments.
Where there are several debts outstanding between the parties, it is sometimes important to ascertain what payment has discharged what debt.

The following legal rules apply.

(a) The debtor can appropriate any payment to any debt, no matter which is the longest outstanding.

(b) If the debtor makes no appropriation, the creditor can appropriate in any way he chooses, e.g. applying the money to pay off a statute-barred debt: *Seymour* v. *Pickett* (1905).

(c) The Rule in *Clayton's Case* (1816). If there is a current account between the parties, subject to constant incomings and outgoings, then if neither party makes any express appropriation the law presumes that the first payment in discharges the earliest outstanding debt.

(*d*) Certain rules, not yet in force, are prescribed for credit agreements by the Consumer Credit Act 1974, s. 81.

DISCHARGE BY AGREEMENT

7. Executory contracts, i.e. those wholly unperformed by either side, can be discharged by simple waiver. Consideration for the waiver lies in the exchange of promises not to sue to enforce the contract.

8. Executed contracts, i.e. those wholly or partly performed by one party. Discharge of such contracts must be supported by consideration, or must be under seal.

(*a*) *Deed of release*, for which no consideration is necessary.

(*b*) *Accord and satisfaction*, i.e. a simple contract agreement (the accord) + valuable consideration (the satisfaction) other than performance of the actual obligations under the original contract. The consideration may take the form of some alternative method of performance, or mere executory promises. But some consideration is necessary to prevent the rule in *Foakes* v. *Beer* coming into operation: *see* III, **19**.

9. Substituted agreement. A contract can also be discharged by the parties making a fresh contract in substitution for the old. But this method is available only where the contract is not yet wholly performed on either side, i.e. is still partly executory on both sides.

A new contract substituted for an earlier in this way is called a novation.

10. Variation of contracts. Discharge by agreement may be total or partial.

Variation (which may amount to partial discharge) can generally take any form, except that contracts unenforceable unless evidenced in writing can only be varied in writing: *Morris* v. *Baron* (1918). In the case of credit agreements, certain variations are ineffective unless in a prescribed form: Consumer Credit Act 1974, s. 82.

(Total rescission can always be made in any form, e.g. a specialty contract can be rescinded orally: *Berry* v. *Berry* (1929).)

11. Unauthorised alteration. If one party makes a material alteration to a contract without the consent of the other, the contract is automatically discharged.

A material alteration is one which alters the effect of the contract, e.g. altering the crossing or the amount payable on a cheque.

DISCHARGE BY OPERATION OF LAW

12. By merger. A contract is discharged if it is merged in a higher obligation, e.g. a deed swallows or merges into itself a simple contract on the same terms and between the same parties.

13. Contracts for personal services. These are automatically discharged by death in most cases. Contracts of a non-personal nature may survive for the benefit of the deceased's estate.

14. Discharge in bankruptcy. Where a bankrupt obtains his discharge the order automatically cancels liability on all provable debts existing at that date: *see* XVIII, **15.**

15. Lapses of time: Limitation Act 1980. The Act lays down that actions for breach of contract must be commenced within a certain time after the breach occurs, otherwise the right of action lapses, i.e. is statute-barred. (The right of action is not destroyed by lapse of time, it simply cannot be enforced: *see* **17** below.)

The more important periods of time laid down by the Act are as follows.

(*a*) Six years for actions for breach of simple contracts.

(*b*) Twelve years for actions for breach of speciality contracts.

(*c*) Thirty years in actions of land where the Crown is the plaintiff; twelve years in other cases.

(*d*) Three years where the claim is for damages for personal injury: Limitation Act 1980. But this period can be extended by the court where the plaintiff did not realise he had suffered until more than three years after the breach of contract.

16. When time runs. The limitation period under the Act is generally calculated from the moment the breach occurs, except where:

(*a*) the plaintiff was under a legal disability at the date of the breach, e.g. minority or mental incapacity. Here time runs from the date when the disability ceases, or the plaintiff dies while still disabled: s. 28;

(*b*) the action is based on fraud, mistake, etc. Here time begins to run from the date when the fraud or mistake is discovered by the plaintiff, and not from the date when the cause of action arose: L.A., s. 32.

EXAMPLES: (1) Eight years after his house was built A discovered that in breach of contract the builder had laid defective foundations. HELD: He could not have discovered the truth as the builder had concealed the facts, and consequently his right of action was not barred: *Applegate* v. *Moss* (1971). (2) In order to prevent the L.A. operating, the plaintiff's mistake must be as to facts, e.g. not merely ignorance or mistake as to his rights in law: *Central Asbestos Co. Ltd.* v. *Dodds* (1972).

17. Acknowledgments and part payments. When a right of action has lapsed it may be revived by the following.

(*a*) A written acknowledgment constituting an express or implied admission of liability. Thus a letter admitting liability but refusing to pay and relying on the Limitation Act has been held to be a sufficient acknowledgment for this purpose: *Re Coliseum (Barrow) Ltd.* (1930). (If the written acknowledgment is lost, its contents can be proved by oral evidence: *Read* v. *Price* (1909).);

(*b*) A part payment of a statute-barred debt.

Where there is an acknowledgment or part payment, it starts time running again, i.e. the plaintiff has a further six years (or twelve if a speciality contract is involved) in which to commence action: L.A., ss. 29–31.

NOTE: a part payment into a bank current account which is overdrawn operates to revive the right of action for the whole account, including debts incurred more than six years previously: *Re Footman Bower & Co. Ltd.* (1961).

FRUSTRATION OF CONTRACTS

18. Supervening impossibility of performance. Where at the outset is is clearly impossible to perform a contract, such contract lacks an essential element and is void, e.g. contracts to walk across the Atlantic.

But sometimes a contract possible when made subsequently becomes impossible to perform, e.g. a lawful contract involving trade between Britain and Russia became impossible to perform when the Crimean War broke out between the two countries: *Avery* v. *Bowden* (1856).

The general rule is that supervening impossibility of performance does not discharge the contract, except where the doctrine of frustration applies.

19. Doctrine of frustration. This has been developed to mitigate hardship which might be caused by the supervening impossibility rule stated above.

Under the doctrine of frustration the courts will imply a term into a contract providing for the discharge of the contract if certain types of impossibility arise after the contract is made: *Cricklewood Property Co.* v. *Leighton's Investment Trust* (1945).

20. Frustration occurs in the following cases.

(*a*) Where basis is destroyed. If the contract depends on the continued existence of some thing, and that thing is destroyed, e.g. hire of a theatre frustrated by the theatre being burned down: *Taylor* v. *Caldwell* (1863).

(*b*) Where there is non-occurrence of an essential event. If the contract depends on the occurrence of an event which does not in fact happen, e.g. hire of rooms to watch the coronation procession of Edward VII, frustrated by cancellation of the procession: *Krell* v. *Henry* (1903); contrast *Herne Bay S.S. Co.* v. *Hutton* (1903).

(*c*) Where there is death or illness. A contract for personal services may be frustrated by death or unduly prolonged illness of the employee. What amounts to unduly prolonged illness is a question of fact in each case, e.g. if a concert pianist hired for three performances is ill when due to play at the first, this might amount to frustration: *Robinson* v. *Davison* (1871).

(*d*) Where there is government interference. Where the government prohibits performance for such a period that it would be unreasonable to expect performance after the prohibition ceases: *Metropolitan Water Board* v. *Dick, Kerr & Co. Ltd.* (1918).

(*e*) Where there is a change in law. Where a contract legal when made subsequently becomes unlawful through a change in the legal situation: *Avery* v. *Bowden* (1856).

(*f*) Where the method of performance is impossible. If a particular manner of performance is essential, and when the time comes for performance this particular method has become impossible.

EXAMPLES: (1) A contracted to build for B seventy-eight houses in eight months for £92,000. It was impossible to meet the contract date, and rises in costs added £17,000 to A's bill.

There was no clause in the contract to cover this eventuality. The time ultimately taken by A was twenty-two months. A claimed that the original contract was frustrated by impossibility, and sued for £109,000 on *quantum meruit*. HELD: Contract was not frustrated, and therefore A had no *quantum meruit* claim. He should have foreseen his troubles and written a clause into the contract to cover them: *Davis Contractors Ltd.* v. *Fareham U.D.C.* (1956). (2) Headmaster of school was suspended by his employers after a criminal charge had been made against him, of which he was acquitted six months later. HELD: His enforced absence from his work did not frustrate his contract of employment, since his presence as headmaster was not vital to the continued running of the school: *Mount* v. *Oldham Corporation* (1973). (3) Property was advertised as being suitable for redevelopment. On the date when the parties entered the contract, they did not know that the Department of the Environment proposed to list the building as being of architectural or historical significance. This happened the following day. This brought the development value of the property down to £200,000 from £1.7m. The court said listing was an inherent risk which the purchaser of property had to bear. Listing did not make the contract radically different and so it was not frustrated: *Amalgamated Investment and Property Co. Ltd.* v. *John Walker & Sons Ltd.* (1976).

21. Limits of the doctrine. Frustration does not occur in the following cases.

(*a*) Express terms may cover the contingency complained of. The court will refuse to treat the contract as frustrated where to do so would be contrary to the express terms of the contract: *British Movietonews Ltd.* v. *London, etc., Cinemas Ltd.* (1952), H.L.

(*b*) *Self-induced frustration* cannot be pleaded as grounds for discharge, as it may amount to breach of contract.

Although it used to be thought that the doctrine did not apply to leases, the House of Lords ruled to the contrary in *National Carriers Ltd.* v. *Panalpina (Northern) Ltd.* (1981).

22. Effect of frustration. The contract is discharged for the future (from the date of the frustrating event), but it is not void *ab initio*. Therefore it may be important to ascertain who should bear the loss and who should pay for any services rendered up to the time of frustration.

(a) **Before 1943.** At Common Law the loss lay where it fell, i.e. money which had become payable before frustration remained payable, and money paid before frustration was irrecoverable, but money not due until after frustration ceased to be payable: *Chandler* v. *Webster* (1904).

This harsh rule was later modified to allow apportionment of loss where there had been total failure of consideration: *Fibrosa Case* (1943).

(b) **L.R. (Frustrated Contracts) Act 1943** reformed the above position by providing the following.

(i) Money paid before frustration is prima facie recoverable (unless its retention can be justified by expenses incurred by the recipient before frustration).

(ii) Money due before frustration ceases to be payable (unless needed to cover expenses as in (i) above).

(iii) Benefits received before frustration must be paid for, and a party who has incurred expense before frustration is entitled to compensation therefore.

NOTE: The Act can be excluded by express agreement, and in any case it does not apply to (1) charter parties, (2) carriage of goods by sea, (3) sales of specific goods, (4) insurance contracts.

BREACH OF CONTRACT AND REMEDIES

23. Breach of contract occurs where one party:

(a) repudiates his obligations;
(b) disables himself from performing his part of the contract; or
(c) fails to perform his part of the contract as and when agreed.

24. Anticipatory breach. In (a) and (b) above the breach may occur before the date fixed for performance, e.g. where A hired B to act as a courier commencing employment 1st June but wrote to B in May repudiating the agreement, it was held that B was immediately entitled to sue, and need not wait till the 1st June for his right of action to accrue: *Hochster* v. *De La Tour* (1853). But a party can ignore such a breach, perform his own side, and later claim damages for breach: *White & Carter Ltd.* v. *McGregor* (1962).

25. Effect of breach. The effect depends largely on whether the breach is of a condition or of a warranty: *see* II, 25–27.

(*a*) *Breach of warranty:* the injured party can only sue for damages and must go on with the contract, i.e. the breach does not operate to discharge the contract.

(*b*) *Breach of condition:* the injured party can chose whether:

(*i*) to treat the breach as a breach of ex post facto warranty (and sue for damages while going on with the contract); or

(*ii*) to treat the breach of condition as automatically discharging the contract.

NOTE: If he chooses alternative (*ii*) he cannot also sue for damages for breach. since he has indicated a willingness to regard the contract as dead and has therefore waived his right of action for damages (but if he has incurred expense under the contract he can bring a quasi-contractual *quantum meruit* action for compensation). If he chooses alternative (*i*) he keeps the contract alive, and should immediately commence action to enforce it, i.e. should sue for damages or specific performance. If he delays suing he takes the risk that some unforeseen event may occur to discharge the contract by frustration, thus depriving him of his right of action.

EXAMPLE: A hired B's ship to carry a cargo from Russia. Later B repudiated the contract, thus entitling A either to treat the contract as discharged or to sue for damages. A delayed a decision hoping B would change his mind before the performance date. War broke out between Russia and Britain before the performance date, frustrating the contract. HELD: A had lost his right to sue for damages by his delay: *Avery* v. *Bowden* (1856).

NOTE: In recent times, a somewhat different approach has been adopted. It has been said that many contractual undertakings cannot readily be called "conditions" or "warranties". Instead, the proper approach, it is said, is to examine the consequences of the breach. If the breach is disastrous, the contract may be taken as terminated: if not disastrous, only damages may be claimed: *Hong Kong Fir Shipping Co. Ltd.* v. *Kawasaki Kishen Kaisha Ltd.* (1962); *Cehave N.V.* v. *Bremer* (1975).

26. Remedies for breach. The Common Law remedy is damages by way of compensation. In addition there are the discretionary equitable remedies of specific performance and injunction, which are usually available where damages are inadequate to compensate the plaintiff for the breach.

27. Damages for breach of contract. The plantiff can recover financial compensation for his actual loss, provided it is not too remote.

Under the Rule in *Hadley* v. *Baxendale* (1854) damage is not too remote if:

(*a*) It is the natural consequence of the breach, e.g. B unduly delayed delivery of a mill-shaft to A's mill, whereby the mill was out of action for a considerable time. A had not informed B that the lack of the shaft would necessitate closure of the mill. HELD: A could recover damages for the delay in delivery, but not for loss of profits occasioned by closure of the mill, since there was no way B could have foreseen that his delay would cause the closure: *Hadley* v. *Baxendale*;

(*b*) although not arising naturally from the breach, the damage caused was something which was within the contemplation of the parties when making the contract. (Thus in *Hadley* v. *Baxendale* the mill-owner could have recovered damages for loss of profits if he had informed the carrier of the likely result of delayed delivery.)

EXAMPLE: A contracted to supply a boiler to B's laundry and was five months late in delivery. HELD: B could recover damages for loss of ordinary profits occasioned by the delay since A knew the laundry would be closed pending delivery of the boiler (but B could not recover damages for loss of exceptional profits expected to arise under a valuable contract of which A was not informed): *Victoria Laundry* v. *Newman Industries* (1949): *Parsons* v. *Uttley Ingham* (1978).

28. The measure of damages. Damages for breach of contract are intended to compensate the plaintiff, not to punish the defendant.

NOTE: (1) The plaintiff must mitigate or minimise his loss as far as he reasonably can; he cannot recover additional damages for loss occasioned by his failure to do so: *British Westinghouse Electric & Manufacturing Co. Ltd.* v. *Underground Electric Rail Co. Ltd.* (1912). Thus if an employee is wrongfully dismissed he can recover damages for loss of wages, but must reduce his loss as much as he can by seeking new employment. He will not recover extra heavy damages if he is out of work for a long time, by reason of his own failure to seek work: *Brace* v.

Calder (1895). (2) Interest on any sum claimed is not allowed unless: (*i*) the parties have previously so agreed, or (*ii*) the claim is on a bill of exchange or promissory note, or (*iii*) the court exercises its statutory discretion to award interest under the L.R. (Miscellaneous Provisions) Act 1934. (3) The plaintiff must quantify his loss of profit in financial terms. If he cannot do so, he may recover wasted expenditure, even though the expenditure was incurred before the contract was made (provided it was within the contemplation of the parties at the time of contracting): *Anglia Television* v. *Reed* (1971). *See also Cullinane* v. *British "Rema" Mfg. Co.* (1954). (4) The plaintiff can claim his loss even where his acts of mitigation have made matters worse. It is only necessary that he does what seems reasonable at the time: *Daily Office Cleaning Contractors Ltd.* v. *Shefford* (1977).

29. Penalties and liquidated damages. Where the amount of compensation claimed is left to be assessed by the court, damages claimed are called unliquidated damages.

But sometimes the parties agree in advance the amounts payable in the event of breach. Such an amount is called liquidated damages, and in any action for breach of such contract the court will award the pre-assessed sum unless it has been fixed in such a way as to break the rules against penalties.

Liquidated damages are a genuine pre-estimate of the measure of loss which a breach of the contract is likely to cause. A penalty on the other hand is a sum fixed at random to frighten a party into performing his contract: *Dunlop Pneumatic Tyre Co.* v. *New Garage Co.* (1915).

A sum is a penalty if:

(*a*) it is extravagant having regard to the maximum possible loss which could result from the breach;

(*b*) failure to pay a sum of money results in liability to pay a larger sum;

(*c*) a single sum is payable on the occurrence of any of several events of differing degrees of importance: *Kemble* v. *Farren* (1829).

If a sum is held to be a penalty the court will not award it, but will make its own assessment of damages. The fact that the parties describe a sum as a penalty or a clause as a "penalty clause" is not decisive. The court will apply the above tests in each case, and if satisfied that the sum is a genuine pre-estimate of loss the court will award it to the plaintiff as liquidated damages.

30. Quantum meruit. Where there has been a breach of condition and the injured party has elected to treat the contract as at an end, he cannot later sue for damages for breach of the contract since he has already accepted breach as terminating the contract's existence. However, in such cases, if he has incurred loss, he can bring a quasi-contractual *quantum meruit* action for compensation for work done, expense incurred, etc.: *see* **I, 17.**

A quantum meruit (literally "how much is it worth?") claim can thus arise where:

(*a*) the defendant has abandoned or repudiated the contract, e.g. where after commissioning a writer to do a series of articles, a magazine closes down before the series is completely written: *Planché* v. *Colburn* (1831). The writer could not sue for breach of contract here because he had not completed his own side of the bargain;

(*b*) under a void contract one party has done work and the defendant has received the benefit of it: *Craven-Ellis* v. *Canons Ltd.* (1936). Here again the plaintiff could not have sued on the contract since it was void;

(*c*) the parties have agreed to terminate the contract but the plaintiff has performed a substantial part of his own side of the bargain. Here he can sue on a *quantum meruit* claim, but not on the contract since he has accepted termination: *Dakin* v. *Lee* (1916);

(*d*) one party has obtained a benefit which he could not reasonably expect to get without paying for it, e.g. where a builder leaves building materials on X's land and X uses the materials, the builder can sue for the value of the materials: *Sumpter* v. *Hedges* (1898) and *see* **2** above.

Similarly if a grocer by mistake leaves goods at the wrong house and the occupant uses the goods, the grocer could sue for their value.

31. Specific performance. This is a discretionary remedy for breach of contract and consists in a court order compelling the defendant to perform his side of the bargain. It may be awarded in addition to or instead of damages.

Specific performance will only be awarded where:

(*a*) damages would be inadequate to compensate the plaintiff, e.g. in contracts to sell or lease land, or for the sale of valuable

and unique chattels such as rare paintings. It will not be awarded
in ordinary contracts for sale of goods where the plaintiff could
easily obtain replacement articles with the money received as
damages, e.g. in sales of ordinary cars, books, furniture.

Under a contract made in March 1970, the plaintiff agreed to
buy all its petrol and diesel fuel from the defendant for at least
ten years. The defendant company attempted to terminate the
agreement when the market for oil was in an unusual state. The
court granted an interlocutory injunction restraining the threatened breach because the court could order specific performance
of a contract to sell and purchase chattels which were not specific,
or ascertained where, as the evidence showed here, damages
would not be an effective remedy: *Sky Petroleum Ltd.* v. *V.I.P.
Petroleum Ltd.* (1974);

(*b*) the enforcement of the order would not require constant
supervision by the court, e.g. not in building contracts or
contracts of employment;

(*c*) the contract is equally enforceable by both parties. Thus
a minor plaintiff cannot obtain specific performance of a
contract which would not be enforceable against him, since it
would be impossible for the adult defendant party to claim
specific performance against the minor (in such cases the minor
can of course obtain damages): *Johnson* v. *Agnew* (1978);

(*d*) the plaintiff himself has acted fairly and equitably. He
cannot obtain specific performance if his own conduct has been
tricky or unfair: *Webster* v. *Cecil* (1861), *see* **IV, 8.**

32. Injunctions. An injunction is a discretionary court order and
is either:

(*a*) *prohibitory:* forbidding a person to do something; or

(*b*) *mandatory:* commanding a person to do something.
Mandatory injunctions are rarely granted since they might call
for supervision by the court, which may not have the resources to
enforce the injunction adequately.

Injunctions may take the following forms.

(*a*) *Quia timet injunctions:* issued to prevent an apprehended
injury before it has occurred, but where there is reasonable
ground for fearing a breach of contract may occur.

(*b*) *Interim or interlocutory injunctions:* usually granted pending
the decision of a case, e.g. prohibiting the defendant from taking
disputed property overseas until the dispute as to its ownership
has been settled in court.

(c) *Perpetual:* issued when a dispute has been finally settled, e.g. where an interim injunction is made perpetual when the dispute has been finally settled in court.

33. Injunctions to restrain breaches of contract. An injunction is a suitable additional or alternative remedy to damages where the plaintiff wants to prevent the defendant breaking the contract, or continuing to break it.

Injunctions may be available where specific performance is not. Thus a contract of personal services cannot be enforced by an order for specific performance, since this would necessitate constant supervision by the court. But the court might in such a case grant a prohibitory injunction, forbidding the defendant from breaking the contract (and threatening him with imprisonment if he disobeys).

An injunction will only be granted to restrain a breach of contract if the clause the plaintiff seeks to enforce is negative in substance, though it may be positive in form. Thus a contract under which a film star is to work exclusively for a plaintiff company appears positive in form, but has a negative meaning, i.e. that the film star must not work for anyone else. An injunction could be granted therefore to prevent the film star working for anyone else: *Warner Bros.* v. *Nelson* (1937).

CHAPTER VI

Privity, Assignment, and Negotiability

PRIVITY OF CONTRACT

1. Doctrine of Privity. A contract is a private relationship between the parties who make it, and no other person can acquire rights or incur liabilities under it.

Compare this rule with the separate rule that "consideration must move from the promisee." The two rules together mean that a person seeking to sue upon a contract must satisfy the court: (*a*) that he is a party to the contract he seeks to enforce, and (*b*) that he has given consideration for the promise he seeks to enforce (or that the contract is under seal): *see* III, **10–12**.

Contrast a legal duty with a contractual duty. A legal duty is one which, if not performed, can be sued upon by any person injured by the breach of duty; actions for tort are actions for breach of this sort of duty. A contractual duty is one which is owed only to the other party to the contract, and only that party can sue to enforce it (also contractual duties arise by agreement, while legal duties are imposed by the law independently of any agreement between the parties).

2. Scope of Doctrine. The Doctrine of Privity has two aspects.

(*a*) No one can acquire rights under a contract to which he is not a party.

(*b*) No one can incur liabilities under a contract to which he is not a party.

EXAMPLE: B sold his business to C on condition that C should pay (1) £6.50 per week to B for life, and (2) £5 per week for life to Mrs B after B's death. B died and C refused to pay Mrs B, since she was not a party to the contract. HELD: (1) Mrs B was not a party to the contract and therefore could not personally enforce it, but (2) as administratrix of her late husband's estate (which was a party to the contract) she could enforce the contract: *Beswick* v. *Beswick* (1968): *Scruttons Ltd.* v. *Midland Silicones Ltd.* (1962): *N.Z. Shipping Co.* v. *Satterthwaite* (1975).

3. Acquisition of rights. If A and B make a contract whereby B is to pay A to do something for X, X cannot sue A if he fails to do what he promised. It makes no difference if X has given consideration for the promise—he cannot sue unless he is a party to the contract: *Price* v. *Easton* (1820), nor that B and X are closely related: *Tweddle* v. *Atkinson* (1861).

EXCEPTIONS: (1) *Constructive trust* Where B is regarded as a trustee for X, X may sue A (and join B as co-defendant) if the contract between B and A is broken. (A constructive trust is one imposed by the courts to prevent injustice, and arises independently of any agreement between the parties.) (2) *Resale Prices Act 1976, s. 26.* A retailer who obtains goods from a wholesaler with notice of restrictive conditions imposed on resale of the goods by the original supplier may be bound by such conditions, even though they arose from the contract between the wholesaler and the supplier (to which the retailer was not a party): *Goodyear Tyre & Rubber Co. Ltd.* v. *Lancashire Batteries Ltd.* (1958). (3) *Negotiable instruments.* If X is the holder for value of a bill of exchange he may sue the drawer (A) upon the bill: *see* XV, **37, 38.** (4) *Agency.* Where B is secretly acting as agent for X, X can intervene to enforce the contract between A and B, in which case B drops out and the contract subsists directly between A and X. This is called the Doctrine of the Undisclosed Principal: *see* VIII, **17.** But it has also been held that where a person makes a contract for a holiday for himself and his family, he can recover damages for everyone for the disappointment suffered when the holiday is a disaster: *Jackson* v. *Horizon Holidays* (1975). (5) *Road Traffic Act* 1972, s. 149. Persons specified in a third party car insurance policy can sue the insurance company to enforce the policy for their own benefit. (6) *Law of Property Act* 1925, s. 56, states that a person may take "an immediate or other interest" under a contract, providing it is in writing. But the House of Lords has refused to regard this provision as creating a general exception to the doctrine of privity: *Beswick* v. *Beswick* (1968). (7) *Road Traffic Act* 1972, s. 148(4). This provides that insurance covers any person driving a motor vehicle with the consent of the owner.

4. Acquisition of liabilities. A contract between A and B cannot impose liabilities on X, save in the following exceptional cases.

(*a*) Resale Prices Act 1976, s. 26: *see* **3** above.

(*b*) Commercial usage or trade customs may so provide.

(*c*) Sale of ships. If X buys a ship from B which has previously been chartered by A, he may be bound by the terms of the charterparty if he has notice of its terms: *Strathcona S.S. Case* (1926).

(*d*) Restrictive covenants affecting land. These may run with the land, i.e. if X buys land he may be bound by a covenant between A and B, the seller of the land, provided (*i*) X accepts the covenant when buying the land, or (*ii*) the covenant is registered at the Land Charges Registry under the Land Charges Act 1972.

TRANSFER AND ASSIGNMENT OF CONTRACTS

5. Transfer of contracts. Rights and liabilities under a contract can be transferred in some cases. In this situation, in accordance with the Doctrine of Privity, if in a contract between A and B, B transfers the contract to X, B drops out of the contract which now subsists between A and X. B thereafter generally has no further rights or obligations under the contract.

6. Transfer of liabilities. This is only possible where:

(*a*) the contract so provides; or

(*b*) the parties later so agree. If the parties to a contract agree that it cannot be assigned, any purported assignment is therefore invalid and the intended assignee has no rights under the original contract: *Helstan Securities Ltd.* v. *Hertfordshire County Council* (1978).

Transfer is effected by cancellation of the existing contract between A and B and substitution of a new agreement between B and X, i.e. a novation.

NOTE: In a contract between A and B, if performance is not a personal matter, B can always delegate performance to some other person, e.g. his employee. This does not involve transfer of the contract, and privity still exists between A and B who remain fully liable on the contract.

7. Assignment of rights: choses in action. A right or benefit arising under a contract is called a *chose* (or "thing") *in action*, i.e. a personal right of property which can usually be enforced only by suing (by action) and not by taking physical possession: *Torkington* v. *Magee* (1902). Contrast a *chose in possession*, which is a piece of property capable of actual physical possession, e.g. goods, ships.

Whether the benefit of a contract can be assigned depends on the intention of the parties. Thus a contract of employment cannot usually be assigned, unless otherwise agreed.

Choses in action can be assigned in two ways: (*a*) in accordance with s. 136, Law of Property Act 1925, and (*b*) in accordance with the rules of equity (i.e. any assignment not complying with s. 136, L.P.A.).

8. Statutory assignments: L.P.A. 1925, s. 136. Such an assignment operates to transfer (*a*) the full legal obligation, (*b*) the right to enforce the obligation, and (*c*) power to give a valid discharge.

REQUIREMENTS: (1) The assignment must be absolute, i.e. of the whole debt or other obligation. (2) The assignment must not be by way of charge only. (3) It must be in writing, signed by the assignor. (4) It need not be supported by valuable consideration. (5) Express notice in writing must be given to the obligee by the assignee, to avoid the obligee performing the contract for the benefit of the assignor.

Thus if A owes B £100, B can sell his right to collect payment to X (in the form set out above), and this will entitle X to enforce the debt against A. But X should notify A of the assignment to avoid A paying B.

9. Effect of statutory assignments.

(*a*) The assignee (X) can sue in his own name to enforce the chose in action, e.g. by suing A for debt.

(*b*) The assignee (X) takes subject to equities having priority over his assignment, e.g. if A has paid part of his debt to B before receiving notice of the assignment X cannot compel A to pay the full amount (but must try to recover the money from B).

10. Equitable assignments. This means any assignment which though valid fails to comply with the requirements of s. 136 L.P.A., e.g. an oral assignment.

In an equitable assignment the assignee (X) cannot sue in his own name, but must join the assignor (B) as co-plaintiff in any action against the debtor or other obligee (A), or as co-defendant if he refuses. Thus the action will be either X and B. v. A, or X v. B and A.

ESSENTIALS: (1) Intention to assign (no particular form is necessary). (2) Notice is necessary to the obligee to prevent him paying the assignor: the Rule in *Dearle* v. *Hall* (1828).

(3) Value is necessary only in assignments of future rights, e.g. the assignor's expectations under a will.

11. Negotiable instruments. Some choses in action possess the quality of negotiability, e.g. cheques and other bills of exchange. These negotiable instruments are freely transferable by mere delivery (with or without indorsement by the transferor), and the transferee usually obtains an indefeasible title free of equities, etc.

Negotiability must therefore be distinguished from assignability. If a chose is merely assignable, the assignee obtains no better rights to the chose than were possessed by the assignor; but if the chose is negotiable, the transferee may obtain a better right than that possessed by the transferor: *see* Negotiable Instruments, XV, **2**.

CHAPTER VII

Fair Trading

FREEDOM TO CONTRACT

1. Freedom to contract. It is traditionally a basic principle of English law that a man should be free to make whatever contract he chooses, provided it is not illegal. However this presupposes that both parties to a contract have equal freedom. In practice however, over the last fifty years, the courts have increasingly recognised that too often "the freedom is all on one side" (Lord Denning).

Thus where a person buys a railway or bus ticket he has little real choice as to whether he agrees or does not agree to the terms imposed on the contract by the carrier: *see* II, **16–18** above. If the carrier imposes exemption clauses restricting his common law liability, the passenger either accepts them or is debarred from travelling.

As explained in II, the courts have attacked this situation by applying the *contra proferentem* rule, i.e. construing the contract stringently against the person who lays down the terms in it. Also in recent years the courts have shown themselves hostile to any exemption clause which would, if enforced, eliminate the true or fundamental purpose of the contract: *see* the *Suisse Atlantique Case*, II, **25** above.

In the same way the legislature has increasingly shown hostility to the imposition of one-sided terms in contracts, or to situations which in a more general sense involve unfair trading. This hostility has culminated in the Fair Trading Act 1973, and the Unfair Contract Terms Act 1977 (II, **18**) which set out to establish machinery for the protection of the consumer of goods or services and also co-ordinate and reform earlier statutory regulations relating to monopolies and restrictive trade practices.

2. Earlier restrictions on freedom to contract. These can roughly be summarised as follows.

    (*a*) *Judicial restrictions.*
        (*i*) The *contra proferentem* rule; *see* II, **18**.
        (*ii*) The fundamental term doctrine: *see* II, **18**.

(b) *Statutory restrictions.*

(i) The Restrictive Trade Practices Act 1976: *see* **11–12** below.

(ii) The Monopolies and Mergers Act 1965: *see* **7–10** below.

(iii) The Resale Prices Act 1976: *see* **13** below.

(iv) The Trade Descriptions Act 1968: *see* **14** below.

The judicial controls still apply to contracts generally, but the statutory controls have now largely been amalgamated by the Fair Trading Act 1973, which reforms and—in parts—replaces the earlier statutes within the specialised fields to which they relate. This chapter deals with the more important statutory controls; judicial controls are dealt with in IV.

FAIR TRADING ACT 1973

3. Objects. The main objects of the Act are as follows.

(a) The appointment of a Director-General of Fair Trading and of a Consumer Protection Advisory Committee (to advise the Director and the Secretary of State for Trade on the protection of consumers).

(b) To confer on the Director and the Committee and on the Restrictive Practices Court and on certain other courts new functions for the protection of consumers.

(c) To reform the law relating to monopolies and restrictive practices, and extend the law relating thereto.

(d) To regulate pyramid selling and similar trading schemes.

(e) To amend the provisions regarding trade descriptions, and certain other matters.

4. The Director-General. He is appointed (for a period not exceeding five years) by the Secretary of State for Trade: s. 1.

(a) *Chief functions.* These are:

(i) to review the supply of goods and services to consumers in the U.K. for their better protection;

(ii) to review commercial activities in the U.K. with regard to monopoly situations;

(iii) to advise the Secretary of State of matters appearing to him to be detrimental to the interests of consumers in the U.K.: s. 2.

(b) *Reference to Restrictive Practices Court.* The Director has power to refer cases of unfair trading to the R.P. Court, where the persons at fault refuse or fail to amend their conduct: ss. 34, 35.

(c) *Monopolies.* The Director is empowered to ascertain whether a monopoly situation exists in the supply of goods or services to the public; he may refer the case to the Monopolies and Mergers Commission for investigation and possible prosecution of the offenders: ss. 44, 50.

5. Consumer Protection Advisory Committee. This consists of not fewer than ten and not more than fifteen members appointed by the Secretary of State for Trade, either full- or part-time: s. 3. The Committee acts as watch-dog for the public in all matters relating to "consumer trade practices."

(a) Consumer trade practices mean practices relating to the supply of goods or services to consumers, and affecting (i) terms and conditions of supply and the method of communication of such terms etc., (ii) promotion, advertising and methods of selling, (iii) packaging and delivery, (iv) methods of securing payment from the customer: s. 13. Any Minister or the Director may refer a case to the Committee if the interests of consumers in the U.K. are affected: s. 14. The Committee may require the Director to use his powers to carry out any necessary investigation: s. 14.

(b) Action by Secretary of State may follow a recommendation of the Committee (s. 22), and on prosecution an offender may be fined up to £1,000 (as increased by the Criminal Law Act 1977) or sentenced to imprisonment: s. 23.

(c) Defences include honest and reasonable mistake, and that the defendant took all reasonable precautions to avoid commission of an offence: s. 25.

6. Other provisions of the Act. These relate mainly to monopolies and restrictive practices, and are dealt with separately in the following notes.

MONOPOLIES AND MERGERS COMMISSION

7. Monopolies and Mergers Commission. This was originally set up by the Monopolies Act 1948, and its powers and functions have been gradually extended. Under its new name the Commission consists of not fewer than ten and not more than twenty-five members appointed by the Secretary of State: s. 4.

(a) *Functions.* The Commission investigates any question referred to it:

(*i*) with respect to the existence of a monopoly situation;

(*ii*) with respect to a transfer of a newspaper;

(*iii*) with respect to certain commercial mergers: s. 5.

(*b*) *Monopoly references.* These may be made by the Director where they relate to supply of goods or services: s. 50. In addition any Minister or the Secretary of State may make such references to the Commission, over a wider field. The Commission has wide powers to investigate and report to the appropriate Minister, and recommend appropriate action: s. 54. In its report the Commission specifies the ways in which a monopoly appears to be detrimental to the public interest; s. 56.

8. Monopoly situations. The Fair Trading Act 1973 sets out specific types of situation to be dealt with by the Commission.

(*a*) A monopoly situation in relation to the supply of goods shall be deemed to exist if:

(*i*) at least one quarter of such goods as are supplied in the U.K. are supplied by or to one person or inter-connected group of persons or bodies corporate, or

(*ii*) agreements are in operation as a result of which such goods are not supplied in the U.K. at all: s. 6.

(*b*) A monopoly situation in relation to the supply of services shall be deemed to exist if one person (or inter-connected group) controls one quarter of the supply in the U.K. or is in a position to prevent any supply at all: s. 7.

(*c*) A monopoly situation in relation to exports shall be deemed to exist if at least one quarter of the goods in question (produced in the U.K.) are produced by one person or inter-connected group, or if any agreements exist which prevent or distort competition in relation to the export of such goods: s. 8.

9. Mergers. The Commission has jurisdiction to supervise, investigate and—where necessary—stop commercial mergers of such a nature that they affect the public interest, in particular mergers of newspapers.

(*a*) *Newspaper merger references.* Where newspapers owned by a newspaper proprietor, when taken with the circulation of the paper to be acquired, have a circulation of 500,000 copies or more per issue, any merger is void unless made with express permission of the Secretary of State: s. 58. Where application for permission is made to the Secretary, he will refer the case to the Commission for investigation, and the Commission will report within three months giving reasons for its decisions: ss. 59, 60.

(b) *Other merger references.* Where it appears to the Secretary of State that two or more enterprises (of which one at least is carried on in the U.K.) have lost their distinct independence (i.e. have "merged"), and (i) supply at least one quarter of the goods or services in their field in the U.K., or (ii) the value of the assets taken over exceeds £15 million, he may refer the case to the Commission for investigation: s. 64. Businesses cease to be distinct enterprises if they (i) come under common ownership or control, or (ii) or cease to trade as a result of an agreement between them to prevent competition: s. 65. The Commission must report within six months, stating reasons for its conclusions: ss. 70, 72.

10. References other than monopoly and merger references. The Secretary of State or any other Minister may require the Commission to report on the general effect on the public interest of (a) practices of a specified class of persons adopted for the purpose of achieving a monopoly situation, or (b) any practices appearing to be uncompetitive practices: s. 78. In this way restrictive labour practices may be referred to the Commission to ascertain whether they operate adversely to the public interest: s. 79. (Restrictive labour practices mean those designed to restrict competition unnecessarily, and which do not relate merely to rates of remuneration: s. 79.)

Under the Competition Act 1980 the Director General of Fair Trading may ask the Commission to decide if an anti-competitive practice is contrary to the public interest. The Commission can also under this Act be asked to carry out efficiency audits into public and quasi-public bodies, and the Act gives the government the power to ask the Director General to enquire into prices of "major public concern".

RESTRICTIVE TRADE PRACTICES

11. Restrictive trade practices. The Restrictive Trade Practices Act 1976 lays down regulations under which the Restrictive Practices Court may invalidate agreements between groups of persons which interfere with freedom of competition, e.g. by fixing prices throughout a particular industry. The Fair Trading Act 1973 repeals parts of these Acts and introduces many amendments, e.g. in particular the former office of Registrar of R.T.

Practices is abolished and his functions are handed over to the Director-General of Fair Trading.

The Restrictive Practices Court is staffed by High Court judges and specially appointed industrial experts and has itself High Court status, and wide powers. Appeal on questions of law lies to the Court of Appeal, but on questions of fact the R.P. Court's decision is final.

12. Registration of agreements. Agreements are registrable if:

(*a*) they are between two or more persons or bodies in the U.K. carrying on business in the production or supply of goods or services, or

(*b*) they involve the acceptance by two or more parties of restrictions on pricing of goods or services, conditions of supply, etc.

The Director has power to demand registration (or cause to be shown why an agreement should not be registered) wherever he thinks an agreement of the kind noted is in existence.

It is presumed that any registrable agreement is contarary to the public interest, and the onus of proving that it is not is on the persons seeking to uphold it.

The Restrictive Practices Court will only uphold an agreement if it is satisfied that:

(*a*) it is reasonably necessary to protect the public;

(*b*) removal of the restrictions would not be beneficial to the public;

(*c*) it is reasonably necessary to protect the legitimate interests of the parties to it;

(*d*) removal of the restrictions would adversely affect employment in the industry in question;

(*e*) it does not unduly restrict or discourage competition: R.T.P. Act 1976.

13. Resale Prices Act 1976. This renders void any agreement purporting to fix resale prices of goods (only net books and medicaments are exempt), unless approved by the R.P. Court. Agreements must be registered with the Director, and the Court will only declare such agreements valid if they appear in the public interest, e.g.:

(*a*) by preserving quality or variety of goods;

(*b*) by preserving the number of retail outlets;

(*c*) by preserving the level of prices against undue increase;

(*d*) by preventing sale in such a way as to damage health;

(*e*) by preserving standards of sales service or after-sales service.

TRADE DESCRIPTIONS ACT 1968

14. Trade Descriptions Act 1968. This makes it a criminal offence for anyone in course of trade to apply a false description to goods, or to supply goods to which one has been applied: s. 1.

The description complained of must be false to a material degree: s. 3. It may relate to quantity, quality, size, composition, fitness for any particular purpose, testing of goods, place or type of manufacture, name of manufacturer, identity of previous owner (of used goods) etc.: s. 2. It is also an offence falsely to indicate that goods are being sold below the price recommended by the manufacturer or main distributor: s. 11. False indications of price reductions are also punishable where goods have not been offered for sale at the higher price for at least twenty-eight days within the preceding six months: s. 11. It is also unlawful to claim that goods are "worth £X" or that they cost "£X" elsewhere: price Marking (Bargain offers) Order 1979. And recommended prices may not be used with regard to beds, electrically powered and similar domestic appliances and apparatus, consumer electronic goods, carpets and furniture: Bargain offers order.

With regard to provision of services (as distinct from goods) it is an offence in the course of trade to make a statement which the maker "knows to be false," or "recklessly": s. 14.

EXAMPLES: (1) Omission of words "ex Channel Islands" from log-book of car when sold has been held to be an offence: *R.* v. *Haesler* (1973) C.A. (2) To describe an unroadworthy car as "beautiful" or as in "showroom condition" is a false trade description: *Robertson* v. *Dicicco* (1973): *Hawkins* v. *Smith* (1978). (3) D was repairing a car for X, a dealer, to whom D had sold the car. X brought a prospective purchaser to look at the car, and D falsely described it as having a "good little engine." HELD: D committed an offence, even though he was not a party to the sale: *Fletcher* v. *Sledmore* (1973). (4) Tour agency's brochure praised a hotel which did not yet exist. HELD: An offence: *R.* v. *Clarksons Holidays* (1972). (5) The Act does not cover mere predictions for the future as distinct from statements as to existing fact. Tour agent who predicted high quality for a future hotel was held not liable under the Act: *R.* v. *Sunair Holidays* (1973): *British Airways Board* v. *Taylor* (1976). (6) Falsification distance shown on car's odometer is capable of being a false trade description, if used to assist in persuading the purchaser to buy: *Tarleton Engineering Co.* v. *Nattrass* (1973). (7) Disclaimers are often used to avoid offences under the Trade Descriptions Act, particularly with regard to odometer readings. But these disclaimers will only be effective if they are as "bold, precise and compelling" as the trade description they are seeking to disclaim: *Norman* v. *Bennett* (1974): *R.* v. *Hammerton Cars Ltd.* (1976).

MISCELLANEOUS MATTERS

15. Pyramid selling. This is a trading tactic whereby a supplier or manufacturer of goods engages participants (who may likewise be encouraged to engage others) to help him sell his wares to the public in return for a commission (and sometimes requiring the participants to invest money in the project). Thus A manufactures goods and supplies them to B as agent for sale on commission, and B in turn involves C and D, who in turn involve E, F, G, etc.

The Fair Trading Act brings such trading schemes under the surveillance and control of the Secretary of State for Trade: s. 118. The Secretary of State is empowered to make regulations generally for schemes of this kind, and also to prohibit individual suppliers from operating particular schemes: s. 119. The regulations are the Pyramid Selling Schemes Regulations 1973 No. 1740. Persons who operate such a scheme contrary to the regulations commit a criminal offence and on conviction can be fined up to £1,000 (as increased by the Criminal Law Act 1977) or imprisoned for up to two years: ss. 120, 122.

16. Creation of new offences. The Fair Trading Act effectively grants the Secretary of State power to create new offences relating to unfair trading. Procedure is for the Director to refer a practice he considers reprehensible to the Consumer Protection Advisory Committee on the grounds that:

(*a*) it may mislead or confuse consumers as to quality or quantity of goods or services; or

(*b*) it may mislead consumers as to their rights or obligations, or subject them to undue pressure; or

(*c*) it may impose inequitable terms on consumers.

If the Committee then (within three months of the reference to it) advises such action, the Secretary of State may then prohibit the particular practice, or nullify exemption clauses in contracts complained of, or demand that contracts complained of shall embody certain clauses for the protection of the consumers, etc. Breach of the Secretary of State's prohibition will constitute an offence under the Act. To date, three statutory instruments have followed upon recommendations by the Committee.

(*a*) The Mail Order Transactions (Information) Order 1976 No. 1812.

(*b*) The Consumer Transactions (Restrictions on Statements) Order 1976 No. 1813, as amended by the Consumer Transactions (Restrictions on Statements) (Amendment) Order 1978 No. 127.

(*c*) The Business Advertisements (Disclosure) Order 1977 No. 1918.

PROGRESS TEST 1

LAW OF CONTRACTS

1. How does a binding contract differ from other agreements? What kinds of contract are there, and what are their characteristics? (I, 1–4, 5–8)

2. What is a quasi-contract? When if ever can money be recovered on the grounds of mistake in payment? (I, 12–17)

3. Distinguish an offer from: (*a*) an invitation to treat, and (*b*) a statement of intention. (II, 1–6)

Apply the rules of offer and acceptance to the following situations.

(*i*) Bidding at an auction.

(*ii*) Putting a coin in a slot machine.

(*iii*) Display of goods in a shop or self-service store.

(*iv*) Boarding a bus.

4. Comment on the statement that there cannot be a contract to make a contract. (II, 21)

A agreed orally to sell his house to B for £10,000 "subject to contract." The next day C offered A £10,500 for the house, and A accepted this offer and sold the house to C. Can B sue A for breach of contract?

Would it make any difference to your answer if the agreement between A and B was in writing? (II, 11, 13; III, 4)

5. In what circumstance may an offer: (*a*) lapse, and (*b*) be revoked? (II, **7, 8**)

6. A wrote to B offering to sell his house for £10,000, the offer to remain open "until Wednesday noon." On Tuesday A sells his house to C. What remedies, if any, has B against A? Would it make any difference to your answer if B had paid A 5p to keep the offer open till Wednesday? (II, **9**)

7. When if ever may communication of acceptance be dispensed with? (II, **13**)

8. What is a tender, and what forms may a tender take? (II, **15**)

9. In what circumstances may an offeree be bound by the terms of a written offer which he has not read? Where such terms are designed to limit the liability of the offeror, what is meant by saying that they are interpreted *contra proferentem*? (II, **17, 18**)

10. In what circumstances may the court imply a term in a contract? (II, **22**)

11. Distinguish between conditions and warranties in a contract, and explain what is meant by *ex post facto* warranties. (II, **24–28**) Why is it important to distinguish between a term of a contract and a mere representation made during negotiations? (II, **30**)

12. What is meant by the proper law of a contract, and why is it important? (II, **33, 34**)

13. What contracts are void unless made (*a*) by deed, or (*b*) in writing? What contracts are merely unenforceable unless supported by written evidence? What is the distinction between void and unenforceable contracts? (III, **1–4**)

14. Define "consideration." When if ever is a simple contract enforceable when unsupported by valuable consideration? (III, **10–12**)

15. What is a guarantee, and how does it differ from an indemnity? Is it true to say that a guarantee does not need to be supported by consideration? (III, **4, 5**)

16. What is meant by evidence in writing, in contracts covered by s. 40, Law of Property Act? How does the doctrine of part performance modify the application of this section? (III, **6–9**)

17. Explain the difference between executory, executed, and past consideration. Why is the distinction between executed and past consideration important?

A fell into a river and shouted for help. B hearing the cry rescued him, and in gratitude A promised B £1,000. A now refuses to pay the money. Can B recover it by an action for breach of contract? (III, **12, 18**)

18. Explain briefly the rule in *Foakes* v. *Beer* (1884) and any exceptions of which you know. (III, **19**)

19. What contracts are (*a*) binding on a minor, (*b*) voidable at the minor's option? What must be proved by a shopkeeper suing a minor for the price of goods supplied? (III, **26–28**)

20. When, if ever, may a contract be avoided at Common Law on the grounds of mistake (*a*) of law, or (*b*) of fact? What relief is available in Equity in cases of mistake? (IV, **1–3, 8**)

21. When if ever may a person who has signed a written acceptance of an offer evade the consequences of his signature? (II, **16**; IV, **7**)

22. "Mistakes in the formation of contracts may be common, mutual or unilateral." Discuss this statement, and explain the cases where such mistakes may avoid a contract. (IV, **1–8**)

23. What is "misrepresentation"? When, if ever, is there a positive duty of disclosure imposed on a party to a contract (IV, **12, 19**)

24. Distinguish between innocent, negligent and fraudulent misrepresentation and explain the remedies available for each. (IV, **13, 17**)

25. Explain the importance of the distinction between a mere misrepresentation, and a misrepresentation which has become a term of a contract. (IV, **18**; II, **22–28**)

26. "Adequacy of consideration is of itself no grounds for avoiding a contract, but it may be evidence of undue influence." Explain this statement. (III, **13**; IV, **20–22**)

27. What is meant by an "illegal" contract, and what are the consequences of illegality? (IV, **25–29**)

28. Explain briefly the main provisions of the Moneylenders Acts and the Consumer Credit Act 1974 in regard to loans by professional moneylenders. (IV, **32**)

29. Summarise briefly the rules relating to gaming and wagering contracts and their effects. (IV, **33**)

30. "Restraints of trade are prima facie void." How far is this true? (IV, **44–46**)

31. Explain briefly the cases in which the courts will enforce covenants by an employee not to compete with his former employer. (IV, **47–48**)

32. State briefly the five ways in which a contract may be discharged. (V)

33. "To effect discharge, performance must be complete." What exceptions are there to this rule? (V, **1, 2**)

34. Explain briefly the rules relating to the appropriation of payments by a debtor, or creditor. How does the rule in *Clayton's Case* affect the position? (V, **6**)

35. Explain what is meant by: (*a*) Deed of Release; (*b*) Accord and satisfaction; (*c*) Novation; (*d*) The rule in *Morris* v. *Baron*. (V, **8–10**)

36. When are rights of action arising under a contract liable to lapse? How may such lapsed rights be revived? (V, **15–17**)

37. "Supervening impossibility of performance has no effect on contracts." Discuss this statement. (V, **18–22**)

38. A, in Whiteland, and B, in Redland, made a contract for the supply of machines by A, for which B paid in advance. The contract contained a clause stating: "this contract shall be avoided and the loss shall lie where it falls if war breaks out between Whiteland and Redland." War does break out, when A has supplied only half the machines. The contract was made in England, and B wants to know whether he can recover any of his money under the L.R. (Frustrated Contracts) Act 1943. Advise him. (V, **25, 26**)

39. What is meant by "anticipatory breach of contract"? A was due to perform a contract on the 1st May, but in April repudiated his obligations. On 29th April the contract became illegal through a change in the law. B, the other party to the contract, commenced an action for breach of contract on 30th April. Discuss. (V, **20, 24**)

40. Explain briefly the rule in *Hadley* v. *Baxendale* (1854). What is meant by saying that the plaintiff must mitigate his loss? (V, **27, 28**)

41. Distinguish between penalties and liquidated damages in the law of contracts, and explain when interest may be allowed on sums claimed by way of unliquidated damages. (V, **28, 29**)

42. "You cannot both treat a breach of condition as discharging a contract and also sue for damages for the breach." Discuss this statement. Explain how the plaintiff might have a right of action on a *quantum meruit* claim in these circumstances. (V, **25, 30**)

43. Explain when the court may award the discretionary remedies of specific performance or injunctions in actions upon contracts. (V, **31, 32**)

44. The rule that an outsider cannot claim benefits or incur

liabilities under a contract is not invariably applicable. Discuss.
(VI, 1–4)

45. Why is it easier to transfer the benefit than the burden of a contract? Distinguish between legal and equitable assignments of choses in action, and explain how the effects differ. (VI, 5–10)

46. What is meant by the *contra proferentem* rule? How is it applied by the courts in the construction of exemption clauses in contracts? (VII, 1; II, 18)

47. Summarise the main purposes of the Fair Trading Act 1973, and outline the functions of the Director-General of Fair Trading. (VII, 3, 4)

48. Explain the functions and powers of the Monopolies and Mergers Commission and state what is meant by a "monopoly situation." (VII, 7–9)

49. What agreements must be registered under the Restrictive Trade Practices Act, and in what circumstances will they be enforced? (VIII, 12)

50. What constitutes a "false description" under the Trade Descriptions Act 1968. Give examples from recent cases. (VII, 14)

SPECIMEN QUESTIONS

1. (*a*) "In the formation of a contract consideration must be real but need not be adequate." Explain the meaning of this statement.

Does a promise made without consideration ever affect the promisor's position?

(*b*) Oris, a greengrocer, wished to go to Italy for his annual holiday. He requested Robert, a friend and a neighbour, to look after his children for two weeks. Robert looked after the children while Oris was away. On his return Oris told Robert "I am grateful for your help and promise to pay you £50 as a reward at the end of this month."

Oris has now changed his mind and refuses to pay £50 to Robert. Advise Robert. *A.C.A.*, *December* 1970.

2. (*a*) What is a penalty and how does it differ from liquidated damages?

(*b*) Distinguish between a *quantum meruit* claim and a claim for damages. In what circumstances is a *quantum meruit* claim appropriate? *A.C.A.*, *June* 1970.

3. (*a*) What is generally the purpose of exemption clauses in

contracts? In what circumstances are such clauses enforced by the courts?

(b) A bought an electric blanket manufactured by X Ltd. from B, a dealer in electrical goods, and gave it to C as a birthday present. Owing to defective manufacture the blanket caught fire the first time it was used and C was badly burned. C wishes to recover compensation. Advise him. *A.C.A., December 1971.*

4. C went to D's circus, and bought a ticket at the entrance. On the back of this ticket there was printed notice: "The management accept no responsibility for the safety of their audiences." Just before the circus was due to start an announcement was made to a similar effect. During the performance the stand upon which C was seated collapsed due to the fact that D's workmen had erected it carelessly, and C was injured.

Advise C. *C.I.S., December 1972.*

5. On 1st January D wrote to C offering to sell him his motor car for £500. On 1st June C replied saying, "I accept your offer, but I consider that £450 is enough." D had in fact sold the car to X on 1st May.

C consults you as to his rights: advise him. *C.I.S., June 1972.*

6. What are the requirements for establishing a defence of *non est factum* to a contractual claim? *C.I.S., June 1972.*

7. J bought a ticket for a world cruise from the agents of K. & Co., a shipping line. J was allergic to a certain type of deodorant; so, after he had paid the agent for the ticket and put it way in his wallet, he asked the agents' clerk whether this deodorant was in use on the ship. The clerk said that it was not. There was a statement on the ticket that "The company accept no responsibility for any illness or other physical loss occasioned to passengers as a result of the state of the ship or of the use of any preparations or appliances thereon."

The deodorant in question was in fact in use on the ship. J went on the cruise and became ill as a direct consequence of inhaling it.

Advise J. *C.I.S., June 1971.*

8. (a) "An offer and an invitation to treat must be carefully distinguished, but a tender may be either." Discuss.

(b) In the course of a conversation, A offered to sell his caravan to B for £100. B replied that he would like time to think it over, and A said "I will give you three days." That same day B posted a letter to A enclosing a cheque for £100 and agreeing to buy the caravan. On the same evening A and B chanced to meet and A informed B that he had just sold the caravan to C for £120. Advise B. *A.C.A.*, *December* 1971.

9. "No one can claim the benefit of a contract unless he is a party to it."

Consider this statement. *C.I.S.*, *June* 1971.

10. (*a*) Explain the rules the Courts will apply in the assessment of unliquidated damages in an action for breach of contract.

(*b*) Golden Films Ltd. decided to make a film and engaged Sir Austin, a famous actor, as the leading man. Before engaging Sir Austin Golden Films Ltd. had already incurred expenses in employing a script editor and a director. Sir Austin's engagements abroad were such that he could not perform the contract. So he repudiated the contract. Golden Films Ltd. accepted the repudiation but were unsuccessful in finding a suitable replacement.

Advise Golden Films Ltd. whether they can:

(*i*) sue Sir Austin for specific performance,

(*ii*) recover the expenses incurred before the contract in the form of salaries. *A.C.A.*, *June* 1973.

11. (*a*) Explain the equitable remedies for a miskake which is not recognised as an operative mistake at common law.

(*b*) Justine, an accountancy student, advertised his Mini for sale for £400. A rogue, posing as "Sir Richard" the famous film producer, offered to buy the car. Justine accepted "Sir Richard's" offer and received a cheque signed "Sir Richard." He was worried that the cheque might be worthless and was reluctant to let the rogue remove the car. Noticing Justine's hesitation the rogue produced a special identity card authorising "Sir Richard" to enter the famous Brightwood Studios. Justine, being satisfied about Sir Richard's identity, handed over the log book and allowed him to remove the car. The rogue, now posing as Justine, has sold the car to David. David bought the car in good faith. Justine has received a letter from his bank that the cheque signed "Sir Richard" has been dishonoured.

Advise Justine as to whether he can sue David and recover the car. *A.C.A.*, *June* 1973.

12. (*a*) "The mere fact that one of the parties to a contract acted under a mistake does not, as a general rule, affect the validity of the contract." When will a mistake by one of the parties affect the validity of the contract?

(*b*) B, a builder, submits an estimate to H, a householder, for the erection of a garage. H, who is satisfied with the price quoted, asks B to do the work. While building is still in progress B discovers that he made a mistake in his calculations on which the estimate was based and he asks your advice as to whether he is bound by his estimate which formed the basis of the contract with H. *C.I.S., June* 1970.

13. (*a*) Distinguish carefully between conditions and warranties as terms of a contract. How will the court decide whether a contractual term is a condition or a warranty?

(*b*) A, who wishes to take his family on a holiday, rents from B a villa for the month of August at an agreed rent. The agreement signed by A and B states *inter alia* that the villa is two hundred yards from the beach and that it has been recently redecorated. What action may A take if he discovers in July that the villa is a good mile from the beach? Would your answer differ if the bungalow was in fact only two hundred yards from the beach but had not been decorated for five years? Give reasons for your answer. *C.I.S., June* 1970.

14. (*a*) What rules do the courts apply in determining whether or not a covenant in restraint of trade is valid?

(*b*) D sold his newspaper shop to a large company which operated newspaper shops all over Britain. In the contract of sale D convenanted not to open a competing business within five miles of any of the purchaser's branches within five years. Three years later D, who had become bored with retirement, opened a small newspaper shop three miles from one of the branches of the company that had purchased his business, but over a hundred miles from the shop he had sold. The company now seek an injunction to stop D from trading. Will their application be successful? *A.C.A., December* 1971.

PART TWO

AGENCY AND PARTNERSHIP

CHAPTER VIII

Agency

FORMATION OF AGENCY

1. Definition of agency. An agent is a person who is employed to bring his principal into contractual relations with third parties.

Since the agent does not contract on his own behalf, he does not need to possess full contractual capacity, e g. he may be a minor. But the principal must have full capacity to make the contract in question.

NOTE: Under the doctrine of privity of contract, the agent is an outsider to the contract between principal and third party. Therefore he can only enforce the contract on his own behalf against the third party if he has a personal interest in it, e.g. a lien on proceeds of sale, such as is possessed by an auctioneer: *Chelmsford Auctions Ltd.* v. *Poole* (1972).

2. Kinds of agency.

(*a*) *Universal:* an agent appointed to handle all the affairs of his principal. This kind of agency is very rare: it has to be created by deed, and is a form of general power of attorney.

(*b*) *General:* an agent who has authority to represent his principal in all business of a certain kind, e.g. to manage a branch bank.

Such an agent has implied authority to represent his principal in all matters incidental to the business in question. And a third party dealing with the agent is not affected by any secret restrictions on the agent's authority: *Watteau* v. *Fenwick* (1893), *see* **13** below.

(*c*) *Special:* an agent appointed for a particular purpose, not part of his normal business activities, and who is therefore given only limited powers, e.g. where a bank manager is asked by a friend to act as agent in the sale of the friend's house.

(*d*) *Del credere:* an agent employed to sell goods, who promises to make sure that clients introduced by him to his principal will pay for the goods sold. (Note: this is not a contract of guarantee and does not need to be evidenced in writing.)

3. Express appointment. Where the agent is employed to execute a deed on behalf of his principal his appointment must be by deed, and the agency is called a Power of Attorney, e.g. where A is appointed to execute a conveyance of land: *see* the Powers of Attorney Act 1971.

In most other cases the agent's appointment can be in any form.

4. Implied agency. An agency may be implied from certain relationships, e.g. partnership. Thus where a dealer acts as middleman between a hire-purchase finance company and the hirer of goods, there is now an implied agency between the company and the dealer to the extent that the company must accept liability for representations made by the dealer: H.P. Act 1965, and Consumer Credit Act 1974 *see* X, **70** below.

This can be extremely important, particularly in relation to buying an item, such as a motor car, with money made available by a hire-purchase company. Suppose that money is loaned to a customer of a car dealer because the finance house has an agreement with that dealer by which it provides finance to customers of that dealer. Under the Hire Purchase Act, and now under the Consumer Credit Act, the dealer is the agent of the finance house. This means that the latter has to take the responsibility for anything said by the dealer, his agent, in negotiating the supply of the car. The effect is that if, for instance, the dealer (the agent) has made a misrepresentation, the customer will be able to take action against the finance house (as principal). The customer will be entitled therefore to rescind the credit agreement and the agreement for the supply of the car.

5. Agency by estoppel. Where P allows third parties to believe that A is acting as his authorised agent, he will be estopped from denying the agency (even if in fact he had no authority at all) if such third parties rely on it to their detriment.

This rule applies even where no agency was ever intended by the principal.

Similarly a husband, partner or master, who allows his wife, co-partner or servant to act as his agent cannot evade liability on the agent's contracts even after revocation of the agency unless he has expressly notified third parties with whom the agent has habitually been dealing: *Scarf* v. *Jardine* (1882).

EXAMPLE: L owned a house and allowed his wife to induce S to buy it, though he did not give her authority to sell it. S commenced doing repairs to the house and L then decided he did not wish to sell it. S claimed specific performance and L denied that his wife had authority to sell. HELD: L had allowed S to believe Mrs L was a properly authorised agent and was therefore estopped from denying her authority to contract on his behalf: *Spiro* v. *Lintern* (1973).

6. Agency by ratification. Where (*a*) a duly appointed agent exceeds his authority, or (*b*) a person having no authority purports to act as agent, the principal incurs no liability on the contract supposedly made on his behalf. *See* **14** below.

But in such cases the principal may expressly or impliedly ratify the agent's transaction and so accept liability.

Ratification is only possible where:

(*a*) the agent claimed expressly to be contracting as agent, and named his principal: *Keighley Maxsted* v. *Durant* (1901);

(*b*) the principal had full contractual capacity both (*i*) at the time of ratification, and (*ii*) at the time the agent made the contract. Thus a company after its incorporation cannot ratify a contract supposedly made on its behalf before incorporation, since it did not exist and therefore had no contractual capacity when the contract was made: *Kelner* v. *Baxter* (1866). But where a person purports to contract as agent for a nonexisting company, he will be liable personally on the contract: European Communities Act 1972, s. 9;

(*c*) at the time of ratification the principal had full knowledge of all material facts, or had agreed to dispense with it: *Marsh* v. *Joseph* (1897).

NOTE: Where ratification takes place it is retrospective, i.e. it dates back to the time when the contract was made by the agent. Thus ratification might defeat an attempted repudiation by the third party, made after the date of contracting and on the discovery by the third party of the agent's lack of authority: *Bolton Partners* v. *Lambert* (1889).

7. Agency of necessity. Commercial agency of necessity may arise in favour of a carrier, shipmaster, etc., providing the person claiming it can prove the following.

(a) That it was impossible to get instructions from the principal, e.g. because communication was impossible: *Springer* v. *G. W. Railway* (1921).

(b) That there was a real and definite commercial necessity, e.g. where the master of a ship sells a cargo to prevent it rotting.

(c) That he acted honestly in the interests of his principal while lacking any instructions.

(These rules probably mean that a commercial agency of necessity will only be implied in favour of a person who is already a duly appointed agent for the principal. and who must exceed his instructions in an emergency. It is doubtful whether a person not already an agent could claim an agency of necessity.)

TERMINATION OF AGENCY

8. By act of parties. An agency may be terminated by mutual agreement like any other contract, but in addition the principal may at any time revoke the agent's authority and so prevent him making binding contracts with third parties (though revocation, if unjustified, may leave the agent with a right of action for breach of contract against the principal).

Revocation is not possible in these circumstances.

(a) Where the authority is "coupled with interest," i.e. where the agent was appointed to enable him to secure some benefit already owed to him by the principal: *Smart* v. *Saunders* (1848).

(b) A Power of Attorney (agency granted under a seal) cannot be revoked where it is granted to secure (i) a proprietory interest of the grantee, or (ii) performance of an obligation owed to the grantee.

The power remains irrevocable so long as (i) the grantee continues to possess the proprietary interest, or (ii) the obligation remains undischarged, unless the grantor discharges the obligation, dies, becomes bankrupt or incapacitated, or (if a body corporate) is dissolved: Powers of Attorney Act 1971, s. 4.

(c) Where revocation would involve personal loss to the agent, the principal may be estopped from revoking without the consent of the agent: *Seymour* v. *Bridge* (1885).

(d) The principal cannot revoke in such a way as to damage the interests of innocent third parties. e.g. by breaking contracts the agent has already made with them.

9. By operation of law. Agency is automatically terminated in the following cases.

(*a*) By death of principal or agent, save in some exceptional cases.

(*b*) By bankruptcy or insanity of principal or agent, save in exceptional cases:

> EXAMPLE: X employed T as solicitor to sue Y. T commenced the action and brought the case to court. Unknown to T, X had gone insane in the meanwhile. HELD: T's agency was automatically terminated, and he was therefore liable to Y for damages for breach of warranty of authority: *Yonge* v. *Toynbee* (1910).

(*c*) By frustration: see V, **18**.

(*d*) By intervening illegality.

(*e*) By the agent accomplishing his mission.

(*f*) By effluxion of time, where the agency was created for a limited time.

(*g*) By the principal becoming an alien enemy.

DUTIES OF PRINCIPAL AND AGENT

10. Duties of agent. Apart from the obvious duty to obey the principal's instructions, these are as follows.

(*a*) To exercise due care and diligence on the principal's behalf, plus any special skill he professes to have: *Keppel* v. *Wheeler* (1927).

(*b*) To disclose promptly to the principal any material information he may receive in execution of his task.

(*c*) Not to disclose confidential information entrusted to him by his principal.

(*d*) Not to delegate performance of his duties (*delegatus non potest delegare:* "a delegate cannot delegate"). But this prohibition is not strictly applied, and the agent may usually delegate performance where required by (*i*) commercial usage or (*ii*) necessity, or (*iii*) where expressly or impliedly authorised by the principal: *De Bussche* v. *Alt* (1878).

(*e*) Not to let his interest conflict with his duty, e.g. not to compete with his principal. An agent must maintain a high standard of good faith. Thus is is wrong for a broker employed to buy goods to sell his own goods to his principal without full disclosure: *Armstrong* v. *Jackson* (1917) Similarly an agent should not accept a commission from both parties without his principal's knowledge and consent: *North & South Trust Co.* v. *Berkeley* (1971).

(*f*) Not to make any secret profit. If, beyond his commission, he receives any extra profit in the course of his duties he must disclose this to the principal.

If he fails to do so: (*i*) the principal can sue him for the amount kept secret; (*ii*) the principal can refuse to pay the agent his commission, and can terminate the agency without notice; (*iii*) the principal can sue the agent and the third party for damages to compensate him for any loss he has sustained; (*iv*) the principal can repudiate the contract (whether or not the bribe was effective); (*v*) the agent and the briber are criminally liable: *Salford Corporation* v. *Lever* (1891): *see* the Prevention of Corruption Act 1916.

EXAMPLE: E owned property which D offered to purchase. Before contracts had been exchanged, the defendants made an application for planning permission in the name of E and signed as "agent" for E. Planning permission was given before completion, but unknown to E. It was held that E was entitled to the profits which had accrued to D from the granting of planning permission. D had acted as self-appointed agents and had placed themselves in a fiduciary relationship to E with the result that they were obliged to disclose the application for planning permission: *English* v. *Dedham Vale Properties Ltd.* (1978).

11. Duties of principal.

(*a*) To pay any agreed commission or remuneration and not to prevent or hinder the agent from earning this: *Rhodes* v. *Forwood* (1876).

The agent has a lien over goods belonging to the principal enabling him to retain such goods until his commission is paid.

When commission becomes payable depends on the contract between principal and agent, e.g. when the agent is employed to sell goods or land, his commission may become payable:

(*i*) when he introduces a client (whether sale results or not); or

(*ii*) on completion of the sale, and payment of the price. (The signing of an agreement "subject to contract" does not amount to completion: *Luxor Ltd.* v. *Cooper* (1941).)

(*b*) To indemnify the agent against liabilities properly incurred in the discharge of his duties: *Christoforides* v. *Terry* (1924).

12. Vicarious liability. A master may be liable for wrongs (torts) committed by his agent. The extent of this indirect or vicarious liability depends on whether the agent is:

(*a*) an independent contractor, i.e. an outsider employed to do certain work and told what to do but left free to decide how he will do it. The principal is only liable for his torts if (*i*) he expressly or impliedly commissioned the tort, or (*ii*) he delegated to the contractor performance of a legal duty and the contractor is negligent;

(*b*) a servant, i.e. a person employed as an integral part of the principal's business, who is told both what to do and how to do it: *Mersey Docks etc.* v. *Coggins* (1947).

The principal is liable for all torts committed by a servant *in the course of his employment*, i.e. where the servant does improperly what he is employed to do properly.

NOTE: (*i*) *Course of employment*. What acts are part of the course of employment, or reasonably incidental thereto, is a question of fact in each case: *Chapman* v. *Oakleigh Animal Products Ltd.* (1970). Thus a solicitor was held liable where one of his staff gave fraudulent advice to a client of the firm, despite the solicitor's claim that giving fraudulent advice could not be regarded as part of the course of employment: *Lloyd* v. *Grace, Smith & Co.* (1912). But a bus company was held not liable for the negligent driving of a bus conductor who had temporarily taken over the wheel, since this was not what he was employed to do: *Ricketts* v. *Tilling* (1915). (*ii*) *Express prohibition*. The master is vicariously liable if the servant is doing improperly what he is employed to do properly, even if the master has expressly forbidden the particular wrongful act. Thus a bus company was held liable for an accident caused by bus drivers racing to bus stops, despite the fact that the company had expressly prohibited such racing: *Limpus* v. *L G.O.C.* (1862).

A dairy company was liable when a passenger in a milk-float was injured through the driver's negligence, even though giving lifts was expressly prohibited: *Rose* v. *Plenty* (1976).

EXAMPLE: Bus conductor (contrary to orders) drove a bus at the depot to enable his own bus to be driven out of the depot, and injured fellow-employees. HELD: He was acting outside the course of his employment and his employers were not vicariously liable for his negligent driving: *Iqbal* v. *L.T.E.* (1973).

THE AUTHORITY OF THE AGENT

13. Real and ostensible authority. Extent of the agent's authority depends (*a*) on his contract with his principal, or (*b*) on the law, where this implies a particular authority for particular kinds of agency.

This implied, or ostensible authority, may exceed the agent's actual authority from his principal, and may therefore render the principal liable on contracts made by the agent beyond the limits of his actual authority.

EXAMPLE: The manager of a public house was forbidden to order tobaccos by his principal but did so: HELD: The principal was liable to pay the seller, since a manager of a public house would usually have authority to make orders of this kind, and the seller could therefore rely on the agent's ostensible authority in the absence of express knowledge of the limitation imposed by the principal: *Watteau* v. *Fenwick* (1893).

14. Breach of warranty of authority. Every person professing to act as agent for another impliedly warrants that he has authority to make binding contracts on behalf of his principal.

If therefore an agent lacks the authority he professes to have he is liable to an action for damages for breach of the implied warranty of authority, brought by the person with whom he has been dealing: *Collen* v. *Wright* (1857).

The agent is still liable for damages, even if he was acting in good faith, genuinely believing he had the authority he claimed, e.g. where his authority has been terminated without his knowledge by the death of his principal: *Yonge* v. *Toynbee* (1910).

But he is not liable if his lack of authority was known to the third party at the time of making the contract, or if the third party agreed to exclude the liability for breach of warranty: *Lilly* v. *Smales* (1892).

(Where a dishonest agent deliberately claims authority he knows he does not possess, he is also liable to an action for fraud by the third party whom he has deceived.)

15. Relations between principal and third parties. Generally, once he has made a contract on behalf of his principal the agent drops out of the transaction and privity of contract exists between the principal and the third party: *see* VI, **1-3**.

But the results of an agent's contract differ slightly depending on whether (*a*) he has disclosed the fact of his agency, or (*b*) he has concealed the fact that he is merely an agent for another person.

Each of these possibilities is dealt with separately below.

16. Agent acting for named principal. Here the agent generally incurs neither rights nor liabilities under the contract, and drops out as soon as it is made: *Gadd* v. *Houghton* (1876).

EXCEPTIONS: (1) Where the agent agrees to accept personal liability. (2) Where the agent signs a deed he is personally liable thereon and the principal incurs no liability unless the agent was himself appointed by deed (a power of attorney)—in which case the agent drops out and the principal is liable in the ordinary way. (3) Where the agent signs a bill of exchange in his own name, he is personally liable thereon. (To avoid this he should make it perfectly clear that he is signing merely as agent, e.g. by signing "for and on behalf of" a named principal. A director signing a cheque on behalf of his company should always take this precaution.) (4) Where trade custom makes the agent personally liable, e.g. formerly where an agent acted for an overseas principal, there was a presumption that he accepted personal responsibility; this presumption no longer exists, and the agent is not personally liable in such a case unless it can be shown that he volunteered to accept personal liability: *Teheran-Europe Ltd.* v. *S.T. Belton Ltd.* (1968). (5) Where the supposed agent is in fact the principal, but purports to contract merely as an agent.

17. Agent acting for undisclosed principal. This covers two possible situations: (*a*) where the agent discloses the fact that he is merely an agent, but conceals the identity of his principal, and (*b*) where he conceals the agency altogether, and appears to be acting on his own behalf.

(*a*) *Agency revealed: principal concealed.* Here the agent drops out in the normal way, providing he makes it clear when contracting that he does so merely as agent. If he fails to do so he is personally liable on the contract. (The exceptions stated under **16** above apply to this situation.)

(*b*) *Agency concealed altogether: the Doctrine of the Undisclosed Principal.* Here the third party can enforce the contract against the agent or, when he discovers his identity and existence, against the principal.

The third party thus has an option whether to compel the agent to accept personal liability, or to shift liability to the principal as soon as his identity is revealed.

BUT NOTE: (1) He cannot enforce the contract against both agent and principal. If he sues one he cannot later sue the other. (2) He may be estopped from suing the principal at all if he allows the principal to think he has settled matters satisfactorily with the agent, e.g. by unreasonable delay in taking action against the principal after his identity is revealed: *Heald* v. *Kenworthy* (1855).

SPECIAL CLASSES OF AGENT

18. Factors. A factor is a mercantile agent employed to sell goods for a commission "in the ordinary course of his business," i.e. a professional buying and selling agent: Factors Act 1889. (A factor differs from a broker in that he has possession of the goods to be sold, while a broker usually does not.)

If a factor has possession of goods with the consent of the owner for some purpose other than sale but contrary to his instructions does sell the goods, the purchaser obtains a good title (providing he did not know of the limitation on the factor's authority). In such cases the principal is legally estopped from denying that the purpose of the factor's possession was sale: Factors Act 1889, s. 2. Such an agent cannot pass good title under the Act, unless he has had continuous physical possession of the goods as factor: *Astley Industrial Trust* v. *Miller* (1968).

A factor has a lien over goods in his possession and power to pledge them for security.

19. Brokers. A broker is a commercial agent employed to make contracts between his principal and others for a commission usually called brokerage. (An agent employed to make non-commercial contracts is therefore not a broker, e.g. a contract to hire a singer for a charity concert.)

Unlike factors brokers do not have possession of goods for

sale, and cannot therefore sell in their own name. They have no lien over goods and no power to lodge them for security.

A broker is primarily agent for the seller of goods, but on making a contract with a purchaser he becomes agent for the purchaser also.

20. Auctioneers: *see* X, **61–65.**

21. Position of banks. The relationship between bank and customer is primarily that of debtor and creditor, with the bank usually the debtor (as long as the customer's account is in credit).

In addition there is a complex implied contract between a bank and its customers, which imposes many duties on the bank similar to those of an ordinary agent: *Joachimsson* v. *Swiss Bank Corporation* (1921).

"The limits of a banker's business cannot be laid down as a matter of law;" *Banbury* v. *Bank of Montreal* (1918), but the following general rules apply.

(*a*) The bank is legally bound to honour its customer's cheques up to the limit of his credit (or agreed loan facilities) but not beyond. Thus if the account is £100 in credit and the customer draws a cheque for £100.50, the bank is theoretically entitled to refuse payment (it cannot legally pay part of a cheque).

(*b*) The bank has an implied right to charge reasonable commission for its services (and interest on loans).

(*c*) The bank must not disclose its customer's affairs, save under compulsion of law, e.g. under a court order.

(*d*) Unlike most agents, the bank has a general lien over any of the customer's securities in its possession, e.g. shares, title deeds, insurance policies.

(*e*) Advice on investment is a service offered expressly by most banks. Where offered, there is an implied duty to exercise care in providing advice, and the bank could be liable in negligence if one of its managers gave negligent advice and so caused damage to the customer: *Woods* v. *Martins Bank* (1958).

(*f*) A bank is entitled to dispose as it pleases of money deposited by a customer provided it pays his cheques on demand (during business hours) or through a clearing house.

(*g*) A bank must abide by any express mandate of the customer, and by any express agreement made with him.

(*h*) The bank is entitled to require that the customer shall exercise reasonable care in drawing cheques. If the bank pays a forged cheque and the forgery was facilitated by the customer's carelessness, the loss falls on the customer and not on the bank: *London Joint Stock Bank* v. *Macmillan & Arthur* (1918).

22. Estate agents. These are agents employed to manage property, and also to buy or sell land or houses for a commission (usually paid by the seller).

The scope of their authority as seller's agent varies, but mere engagement of an estate agent does not confer any authority to receive as agent of the vendor a pre-contract deposit. Where a deposit is paid to the agent in such circumstances, the purchaser is at all times until contract the only person with any claim or right to the deposit and his was a right on demand. The vendor has no such claim or right and no control over the deposit. Accordingly, where a vendor has not authorised an agent to receive a deposit on his behalf, he is not liable to repay it on the agent's default: *Sorrell* v. *Finch* (1976).

CHAPTER IX

Partnerships

NATURE AND FORMATION OF PARTNERSHIPS

1. Definition of partnership. "Partnership is the relation which
subsists between persons carrying on a business in common with
a view of profit": Partnership Act 1890, s. 1

Registered, statutory and chartered companies are specifically
excluded from this definition (note also that a non-profit-
making association cannot be a partnership).

Capacity to form a partnership is governed by the ordinary
rules of contractual capacity: *see* III. A minor who remains a
partner after becoming eighteen becomes liable for the firm's
debts incurred after his eighteenth birthday: *Goode* v. *Harrison*
(1821).

2. Tests for establishing partnerships: P.A., s. 2.

(*a*) *Co-ownership* of property does not of itself create a partnership in the property, even though the co-owners share profits.

(*b*) *Sharing of gross returns* of a business does not of itself
indicate a partnership, even if coupled with co-ownership of
the property or business.

(*c*) *Share of profits* is presumptive evidence of partnership, but
the presumption can be rebutted by showing that the purpose
of sharing was for some other reason, e.g.:

(*i*) payment of a debt by instalments out of profits;

(*ii*) remuneration to a servant or agent of the business;

(*iii*) payment of an annuity or portion to a widow or child of
a deceased partner in the business;

(*iv*) payment of interest (varying with profits) on a loan
advanced for use in the business;

(*v*) payment to the seller of the goodwill of a business (where
the consideration is a share of profits).

However if the business goes bankrupt, the recipient of moneys
under (*iv*) and (*v*) above is a deferred creditor in the bankruptcy:
see XVIII, **31.**

NOTE: Whether a partnership exists therefore depends on the circumstances in each case and the intention of the parties. Sharing losses is stronger evidence of partnership than sharing profits, but is still not conclusive: *Walker ı Hirsch* (1884). If executors of a will carry on the testator's business as instructed in the will, they do not automatically become partners: *Re Fisher & Sons* (1912). Even where a partnership exists, a salaried partner on termination of the partnership cannot ask for a winding-up order. He does not share in the equity of the firm, being only entitled to his salary: *Stekel* v. *Ellice* (1973).

3. The firm name. If the partners trade under a firm's name which does not consist of their own true names without any addition, such firm name must be registered, e.g. where A, B, & C trade under the name of X & Co.: Registration of Business Names Act 1916.

In such cases they must register each partner's (*a*) christian and surnames, and any former names, and present and former nationality, (*b*) usual address, (*c*) any other business occupation.

Registration must be effected within fourteen days of commencement of business, and within fourteen days of any subsequent alteration in the required particulars. Registered firms must also publish the names and nationalities of partners in catalogues, circulars, letters, etc.

Default in registration renders the firm's contracts void (and each partner is liable to a £50 fine). The court has a discretion to validate such contracts retrospectively if satisfied (*a*) that the default was accidental, or (*b*) that ratification would be just and equitable: *Re Shaw* (1927).

4. Illegal associations. An association may be illegal because of the following.

(*a*) Its objects are illegal;

(*b*) Its membership exceeds the statutory limits (i.e. twenty in banking and most other partnerships, or more in some firms of solicitors, accountants and stockbrokers: Companies Act 1967);

(*c*) It is an association forbidden by law, e.g. a professional partnership between a solicitor and an unqualified person.

The effects of illegality are that (*i*) the members cannot enforce any rights or obligations among themselves, (*ii*) the members cannot enforce any contract against any innocent outsider, and (*iii*) the illegality cannot be raised as a defence in any action brought against them by an innocent outsider.

DEALINGS WITH OUTSIDERS

5. Agency of partners. Each general partner is an implied agent for the firm, and can make his co-partners liable on debts incurred by him on behalf of the firm: P.A., s. 5. But he has no implied authority to bind the firm in any matter outside the scope of the firm's business: s. 7.

A person dealing with a partner is not affected by any secret restriction on the partner's agency, unless he knows of it or does not believe him to be a partner: s. 8.

Liability of partners for debts and other contractual obligations is joint: s. 9 (contrast liability in tort). Thus a creditor can sue all the partners jointly, or any one of them for the whole debt. But he has only one right of action, and if he obtains judgment for the whole debt against one (even if the judgment is unsatisfied) he cannot later launch proceedings against the others, since he is taken to have waived his rights against them: Rule in *Kendall* v. *Hamilton* (1879).

6. Extent of implied agency.

(*a*) A partner can bind the firm by the following transactions.
(*i*) By selling the firm's goods: *Dore* v. *Wilkinson* (1817).
(*ii*) By purchasing goods for the firm: *Bond* v. *Gibson* (1808).
(*iii*) By accepting payment of debts due to the firm: *Porter* v. *Taylor* (1817).
(*iv*) By engaging or discharging employees: *Birkham* v. *Drake* (1841).
(*b*) In a trading partnership, he has the following additional powers:
(*i*) To borrow money on the firm's credit: *Lane* v. *Williams* (1692).
(*ii*) To sign bills of exchange on behalf of the firm; Bills of Exchange Act 1882.
(*iii*) To employ a solicitor on behalf of the firm: *Tomlinson* v. *Broadsmith* (1896).

NOTE: There is no implied authority (1) to execute deeds—this requires express authorisation by power of attorney: *see* VIII, 1–7; (2) to submit disputes to arbitration; and (3) to give a guarantee in the firm's name, unless the giving of guarantees is within the usual business of the firm.

7. Liability of incoming and outgoing partners.

(a) *Incoming partners.* A new partner is not liable (unless otherwise agreed) for debts incurred before he joined the firm: P.A., s. 17(1).

(b) *Outgoing partners.* A retiring partner is not liable for debts incurred after he retired, but is liable for debts incurred before his retirement: s. 17(2). (Release from this liability is by means of a novation under which the remaining partners are substituted for the retiring partner in respect of his liability to the creditors, with the latters' consent.)

But an outgoing partner remains liable if he has allowed creditors to believe him to be continuing in the firm: s. 36. To protect himself from this liability, he must (*i*) give express notice of his retirement to persons who were dealing with the firm before his retirement, (*ii*) notify persons who trade with the firm in the future by advertising his retirement in the *London Gazette:* s. 36(2).

(c) *Death or bankruptcy.* The estate of a deceased or bankrupt partner is not liable for partnership debts incurred after death or bankruptcy: s. 36(3).

(d) *Dormant partners.* A general partner not known to be a member of the firm to creditors seeking to enforce a partnership debt is not liable for debts contracted after his retirement from active participation.

(e) *Holding out.* A person not a partner who holds himself out, or allows others to hold him out, as being a partner in a firm is liable to persons who rely on such representations as though he were in fact a partner, i.e. he becomes a partner by estoppel: s. 14.

(f) *A continuing guarantee* given to a firm is terminated as to future transactions by any change in the membership of the firm: s. 18. This section does not apply where (*i*) there is an agreement to the contrary, (*ii*) the guarantee relates to past transactions, or (*iii*) the guarantee is given by the firm: *see* Guarantees, XVII.

8. Nature of firm's liability.

(a) Partners are jointly liable for the firm's contracts, unless otherwise agreed: P.A., s. 9 (the liability may be joint and several if the partners expressly so agree).

(b) Partners are jointly and severally liable for torts committed on behalf of the firm: s. 12.

(c) The estate of a deceased partner is severally liable for the firm's debts incurred during his lifetime, subject to the prior payment of his own separate debts: s. 9.

NOTE: Difference between joint and several liability. (1) In joint liability, the plantiff has only one right of action and he may use this either in suing the firm jointly, or in suing any individual partner separately. But if he sues one alone he waives his right of action against the others, and cannot later sue them even though he obtains judgment against the one sued but is unable to get his money because of that partner's insolvency: *Kendall* v. *Hamilton* (1879). (2) In joint and several liability, the plaintiff has several causes of action. He can sue all partners together, or can sue them separately (in successive actions if necessary). (3) As between the partners themselves, whether the liability is joint or joint and several, they must contribute equally to the damages paid.

9. Notices and admissions.

(*a*) Any admissions or representation by a partner in the course of business and about the firm's affairs are evidence against the firm: P.A., s. 15.

(*b*) Notice given bona fide to any active partner concerning business matters operates as notice to the firm: s. 16.

RIGHTS AND DUTIES OF PARTNERS

10. Partnership articles. A partnership may arise by express agreement, or by implication, i.e. where persons conduct a business in common with a view of profit: P.A., s. 1.

Where a partnership is formed by express agreement (the "partnership articles"), the rights and duties of the partners among themselves are regulated by that agreement. Where a partnership arises by implication, or wherever the articles (if any) are silent, the rights and duties of the partners are governed by the Partnership Act 1890.

NOTE: Once formed, a partnership is a relationship requiring the utmost good faith and each partner must disclose to his colleagues all material information coming to his notice: *see* IV, 19.

11. Rights and duties: P.A., s. 24. Unless otherwise agreed, the following rules apply.

(*a*) *Equal shares.* Partners are entitled to share equally in capital and profits, and must contribute equally towards losses (agreement to the contrary may be inferred from past dealings).

(*b*) *Indemnity*. The firm must indemnify a partner against liabilities properly incurred (*i*) in the ordinary course of business, or (*ii*) in anything necessarily done for the preservation of the business.

(*c*) *Interest on advances*. A partner is entitled to interest at 5 per cent on money (other than capital) advanced to the business (but he is not entitled, before the ascertainment of profits, to interest on capital).

(*d*) *Management*. Every partner is entitled to participate in management of the business.

(*e*) *No remuneration*. A partner is not entitled to any remuneration for his services (unless expressly agreed).

(*f*) *New partners* can only be introduced with the consent of all existing partners (notice that there is no implied power to expel partners: *see* **12** below).

(*g*) *Disputes as to ordinary matters* may be settled by majority (but change of business requires unanimous agreement).

(*h*) *Partnership books* are to be kept at the firm's principal place of business and every partner is entitled to inspect them and copy them whenever he thinks fit.

12. Expulsion of partners. A partner can only be expelled from the firm if a power to do so has been conferred by express agreement between the partners: P.A., s. 25. Such power must be executed in good faith and in the interests of the firm, otherwise the expulsion is void: *Blisset* v. *Daniel* (1853).

13. Duties of partners. Apart from any duties imposed by the partnership articles, the following statutory duties are implied.

(*a*) *Uberrima fides*. Partners must render true accounts and full information on partnership matters to their colleagues: s. 28.

(*b*) *To account* for any benefits derived from the partnership business without the consent of the other partners, i.e. a partner must not make "secret profits" (c.f. agents: see VIII, **10**).

(*c*) *Not to compete* with the firm, without the consent of the other partners. Any profits made by such unauthorised competition can be claimed by the firm: s. 30.

14. Partnership property. All partnership property must be held and applied exclusively for the purposes of the firm and in accordance with the partnership articles (if any): s. 20(1).

Whether property is partnership property or not is a question of fact in each case. "Partnership property" includes the following.

(*a*) Property originally brought into the partnership stock: s. 20(1).

(*b*) Property acquired on account of the firm, for the purpose of and in the course of the partnership business: s. 20(1).

(*c*) Property purchased with the firm's money (unless otherwise agreed): s. 21.

(Thus the mere fact that partners are co-owners of land and share its profits does not make it automatically partnership property, unless it falls into one of the above categories: s. 20(3).)

As between partners, partnership land is treated as personal property: s. 22. Land is conveyed to the partners (or to four of them, if there are more than four) as trustees for sale.

15. Execution against a partner. A creditor who obtains judgment against an individual partner cannot seize partnership property in execution of the judgment: s. 23. His rememdy is to appoint a receiver of the debtor partner's share of profits.

By s. 33(2) if a receiver is so appointed, or a partner's share is otherwise charged with payment of his private debts, this entitles the other partners to dissolve the partnership.

16. Assignment of a partner's share. A partner's share in the business is the proportion of the existing assets to which he would be entitled if all the firm's assets were sold and proceeds distributed after discharge of all the firm's debts.

A partner may assign his share (by way of sale, gift, mortgage, etc.) but the assignee does not thereby become a member of the firm, can take no part in management or inspect books, etc., unless the other partners agree: s. 31.

Thus the assignor remains a partner, though his assignee becomes entitled to his share of profits and of the assets in the event of any distribution. The firm's creditors can therefore sue the assignor for the firm's debts, but he can (unless otherwise agreed) claim indemnity from the assignee: *Dodson* v. *Downey* (1901).

DISSOLUTION OF PARTNERSHIP

The effect of dissolution is to terminate the partnership relation, and to entitle the partners (unless otherwise agreed) to share the assets after payment of the firm's debts. Dissolution may occur in the ways listed below.

17. By agreement.

(a) Under the partnership articles, if they provide a method.

(b) By express and unanimous agreement at any time (over-riding the articles).

18. By operation of law.

(a) *Expiration.* If entered into for a fixed term or for a single venture, the firm is dissolved on expiration of the fixed term or termination of the venture. (If however the partnership is continued beyond the term originally agreed, the rights and duties of the partners remain the same: s. 26.)

(b) *Notice.* If entered into for an undefined term, any partner may determine the partnership at any time by notice to the others: s. 26. (If the partnership was originally constituted by deed, the notice must be in writing: s. 26(2).)

The partnership is then dissolved (*i*) from the date stated in the notice or (*ii*) if not stated, then from the date of communication of the notice to the other partners: s. 32.

19. By death or bankruptcy (unless otherwise agreed): s. 33(1). Also if a partner allows his share to be charged with payment of his debts this entitles the others to dissolve the partnership if they wish: s. 33(2).

20. By supervening illegality, i.e. if some event occurs which makes it unlawful for the business to be carried on: s. 34. The partnership in a firm of solicitors is automatically dissolved when one of the partners forgets to renew his practising certificate: *Hudgell Yeates & Co.* v. *Watson* (1978).

21. By court order: s. 35. The court may order dissolution on the application of any partner in the following cases.

(a) *Mental incapacity* of any partner: Mental Health Act 1959, s. 103.

(b) *Permanent incapacity* of a partner (other than the applicant).

(c) *Conduct prejudicial* to the business (by any partner other than the applicant).

(d) *Breach of the partnership agreement* (by any other than the applicant). This includes conduct which makes it impracticable for the other partners to carry on.

(e) Where the business can only be carried on at a loss.

(f) Where, in the opinion of the court, it is just and equitable, e.g. where there are only two partners and they are at logger-heads: *Re Yenidje Tobacco Co. Ltd.* (1916).

22. Notice of dissolution. To avoid incurring liability after dissolution (e.g. by estoppel) a partner may publish notice of dissolution and can compel his co-partners to join him: s. 37.

23. Effect of dissolution. The authority of partners to bind the firm continues so long as is necessary to wind up the business, provided that the firm is in no case bound by the acts of a partner who has been bankrupted: s. 38.

Also each partner has an equitable lien (*see* XVI, **17**) over the firm's assets entitling him to have them applied in payment of the firm's debts, and in payment of whatever is due to partners; this lien can be enforced by injunction forbidding unfair distribution: s. 39.

24. Return of premium: s. 40. To buy entry into an existing firm, a new member sometimes has to pay a premium (in consideration of existing goodwill) in addition to any investment of capital.

On dissolution, he is entitled to demand the return of a proportion of the premium if the partnership was for a fixed term and was dissolved before the expiry of that term, unless dissolution was caused by (a) agreement, or (b) misconduct by the party seeking return of the premium, or (c) death of a partner: s. 40.

The portion returned will usually be in the same ratio to the whole premium as the unexpired term bears to the whole term: *Attwood* v. *Maude* (1868).

25. Dissolution through misrepresentation: s. 41. Where a partnership agreement is rescinded on the grounds of fraud or misrepresentation by any partner, the partner entitled to rescission can also demand the following.

(a) *A lien* on the firm's assets (after payment of debts) for any money he had invested.

(b) *Subrogation*, i.e. a right to stand in the place of any of the firm's creditors for any payment made by him to discharge the firm's debts.

(c) *To be indemnified* by the person guilty of the fraud or misrepresentation against all the firm's debts and liabilities.

(d) Since here rights are without prejudice to other rights, damages may also be claimed under the Misrepresentation Act 1967, s. 2.

26. Profits made after dissolution: s. 42. If a partner dies or retires and the other partners carry on the business after the dissolution, without any final settlement of accounts, the out-going partner or his estate can (unless otherwise agreed) claim:

(a) such share of profits after dissolution as is attributable to the use of his share of the assets (after due allowance for the labour and skill of the continuing partners); or

(b) interest at 5 per cent on the share of the assets. This claim is not exercisable where the articles give continuing partners an option to purchase a deceased or retiring partner's share, and they duly exercise that option.

27. Settling accounts: s. 44. Unless otherwise agreed, the following rules apply.

(a) *Losses* (including deficiencies of capital) are paid first out of profits, next out of capital and lastly (if necessary) by the partners individually in the proportion in which they are entitled to share profits.

(b) *The assets* (including sums contributed to make up losses or deficiencies of capital) are then applied in the following manner.

  (i) In paying outside creditors.

  (ii) In repaying advances made by partners (distinct from investment of capital).

  (iii) In repaying capital to partners.

  (iv) The residue, if any, is divided among the partners in the proportions in which profits are divisible.

NOTE: Where after paying (i) and (ii) above there is insufficient to repay capital to all the partners in full, deficiencies are shared in the same way as profits: *Nowell* v. *Nowell* (1869). But under the Rule in *Garner* v. *Murray* (1904), if such deficiency is attributable to the insolvency of one of the partners, it must (unless otherwise agreed) be borne by the other partners in the proportion of their last agreed capitals (and not in the proportion in which they share profits or losses).

Thus G, M, & W were partners investing unequal capitals. On dissolution (after paying outside creditors) their balance sheet showed:

Liabilities		Assets		
G. (capital)	£2,500	Cash		£1,891
M. (capital)	£ 314	W. (indebted)	£263	
		Deficiency	£660	
				£ 923
	£2,814			£2,814

HELD: (a) The firm's loss of £660 must be shared by the partners equally, and (b) W's total deficit (£263 + one third of £660 = £483) must be shared between G and M in proportion to their last agreed capitals, i.e. £2,500 and £314 respectively: *Garner* v. *Murray* (1904).

28. Goodwill. This is a partnership asset and means the good reputation and business connections of a firm developed over the years: *Trego* v. *Hunt* (1896).

Unless otherwise agreed in the articles, upon dissolution the goodwill must be sold and the proceeds of sale distributed as capital. Where dissolution is caused by death, the estate of the deceased partner is entitled to share in the proceeds of sale: *Re David & Mathews* (1899).

If the goodwill is not sold and there is no agreement as to its disposal, any partner can carry on the business (even using the firm's name), providing that by so doing he does not expose former partners to liability; *Burchell* v. *Wilde* (1900).

But if by agreement the goodwill is assigned to any person, he can (a) restrain partners from soliciting old customers of the firm, or (b) using the firm's name (but not from setting up a merely competing business): *Boorne* v. *Wicker* (1927).

29. Sale of goodwill. Where goodwill is sold (either to a partner or to an outsider) the value is divisible among the partners in the same manner as they share profits and losses (unless otherwise agreed).

(a) *Purchaser's rights* (unless otherwise agreed). (i) He may represent himself as continuing the former business of the vendors. (*ii*) He has exclusive rights to the firm's name: *Churton* v. *Douglas* (1859); (*iii*) He has the sole right to solicit former customers of the business bought: *Trego* v. *Hunt* (1896), except where the vendor did not sell voluntarily, e.g. where a bankrupt's trustee sells his business, the bankrupt can recommence business after his discharge and can then solicit any former customers: *Walker* v. *Mottram* (1881).

(*b*) *Vendor's rights.* He is entitled to open a competing business, unless restrained by a covenant in the contract of sale: *see* Restraints of Trade, IV, **44–49**.

LIMITED PARTNERSHIPS

30. Limited Partnership Act 1907. This allows a partnership to claim limited liability for some of its members. Limited partnerships are not common, since it is easier and more advantageous to operate a limited registered company.

31. Characteristics of limited partnerships.

(*a*) *Number of partners.* There must not be more than twenty members (ten in the case of banking), of whom at least one must be a general partner: Limited Partnership Act 1907, s. 4(2). But there is no restriction on size if the business of the firm is that of surveyors, auctioneers, valuers, estate agents or estate managers, provided three-quarters of the partners are members of recognised professional organisations and not more than one-quarter are limited partners: Companies Act 1967, s. 121: Limited Partnerships (Unrestricted Size) Regulations 1971.

(*b*) *General and limited partners:* a general partner is fully liable for all debts and obligations of the firm as in an ordinary partnership, and is entitled to participate in management.

A limited partner (*i*) contributes a stipulated amount to the the firm's capital, and is not liable for the firm's debts beyond that amount (which cannot be withdrawn from the business, except on dissolution), (*ii*) cannot participate in management (and if he does so he loses his limitation of liability), (*iii*) has no agency for the firm, and (*iv*) is entitled to inspect accounts, etc.: Limited Partnership Act 1907, ss. 4, 6.

(*c*) *Registration:* a limited partnership must register (*i*) the firm's name, (*ii*) the nature of the business, (*iii*) the principal place of business, (*iv*) the full names of each partner, (*v*) any fixed term for which the partnership is created, (*vi*) a statement that the liability of some of the partners is limited, (*vii*) the sum contributed by each limited partner (in default of registration the firm cannot claim limited liability: s. 5).

(*d*) *Maiority decisions:* in any ordinary partnership the votes of all partners count, but in a limited partnership only the votes of general (unlimited) partners count, unless otherwise agreed.

(*e*) *New partners:* in an ordinary firm admission of new members generally requires consent of existing partners: P.A., s. 24. In a limited partnership, unless otherwise agreed (*i*) a new partner can be admitted without consent of any limited partner, and (*ii*) a limited partner may assign his share to another person (with consent of the general partners, but without the consent of other limited partners): s. 6.

(*f*) *No dissolution by notice:* a limited partner cannot dissolve the firm by notice: s. 6(5).

(*g*) *Death, bankruptcy, or lunacy* of a limited partner does not automatically dissolve the partnership: s. 6(2).

(*h*) *Winding-up:* if a limited partnership is dissolved, the firm's affairs are wound up by the general partners alone, unless the court orders to the contrary: s. 6(3).

(*i*) *General partner becoming limited partner:* if by agreement a general partner becomes a limited partner, such change in status must be notified in the *London Gazette* and the change confers no limitation of liability until notified: s. 10(1).

PROGRESS TEST 2

AGENCY AND PARTNERSHIP

1. Explain how an agency may arise (*a*) by implication, (*b*) by estoppel, (*c*) by necessity.   (VIII, **4, 5, 7**)

2. In what circumstances may a person ratify a contract made on his behalf but without his authority?   (VIII, **6**)

3. A, a minor, hires X as his agent to buy a house. X contracts to buy the house before discovering that A is a minor. A few days later A reaches his 18th birthday and purports to ratify the contract made by X. Is the ratification effective?   (VIII, **6**)

4. "Generally a principal can revoke his agent's appointment at any time." Discuss.   (VIII, **8**)

5. What are the chief rights and duties of an agent, in regard to his principal?   (VIII, **10, 11**)

6. Explain briefly: (a) ostensible authority of an agent, (b) breach of implied warranty of authority by an agent, (c) the doctrine of the undisclosed principal. (VIII, 13–17)

7. In what circumstances may an agent be personally liable on a contract he has made on behalf of his principal? (VIII, 16)

8. Distinguish between factors and brokers, and explain the normal limits of their authority. (VIII, 18, 19)

9. "The limits of a banker's business cannot be laid down as a matter of law." Discuss. (VIII, 21)

10. Define a partnership and state the tests outlined by the Partnership Act 1890 for deciding whether a partnership exists or not. (IX, 1, 2)

11. Explain what is meant by an illegal association. In what circumstances must a business association register a trade name? (IX, 3, 4)

12. To what extent can a partner be regarded as having implied authority to act as agent for his firm? (IX, 5, 6)

13. In what circumstances may a retired partner continue liable for the firm's debts after his retirement? (IX, 7)

14. Explain what is meant by saying that the liability of partners is generally either joint, or joint and several. (IX, 8)

15. "The rights and duties of partners depend on agreement, express or implied, between themselves." How far do you agree? What are the usual rights and duties of partners? (IX, 10–13)

16. Explain what is meant by: (a) partnership property, (b) execution against a partner's share, and (c) goodwill. (IX, 14, 15, 28)

17. In what circumstances may a partner assign his share in a firm, and what is the effect of such assignment? (IX, 16)

18. Explain briefly the circumstances in which a partnership may be dissolved. What is the effect of dissolution? (IX, 17–23)

19. On dissolution of a partnership how, in the absence of contrary agreement, are accounts settled? (IX, 27)

20. Distinguish between, and explain briefly, the rules in (a) *Nowell* v. *Nowell* (1869), and (b) *Garner* v. *Murray* (1904). (IX, 27)

21. A and B, partners, sold their business to X two years ago, for an inclusive price to cover goodwill. X now learns that A, trading under his own name, has opened a competing business and is writing to old customers of the A & B firm, saying: "Please note that A, formerly of A & B, has now opened new premises at 333 New Street." Explain the legal position. (IX, 28, 29)

22. What is a limited partnership? How is such a partnership formed. and how does it differ from an ordinary partnership? (IX, 30, 31)

SPECIMEN QUESTIONS

1. In relation to the law of agency discuss:

(a) the nature of the duties owed by agent to principal;

(b) the legal effect of ratification *C.I.S., December* 1972.

2. (a) Describe with examples what is meant by an "agency by necessity."

(b) P. a university professor at a South American University, has asked A, a London bookseller, to acquire for him a library of scientific books due to be sold by public auction and has made funds available for this purpose. A secures the books but is unable to ship them to P because a revolution has broken out in P's country and all shipping is stopped. A finds that he has difficulties in storing the books and he sells them to C, a *bona fide* buyer, at a price 10 per cent higher than that paid for them at the auction sale. P now seeks your advice concerning his legal rights against A and C. *C.I.S., June* 1970.

3. (a) When, if ever, is an agent personally liable upon contracts made by him on behalf of his principal?

(b) P appointed A his agent to sell radios on his behalf. A sold the radios to X, without disclosing that he was negotiating the contract as an agent. X paid the agreed price but the radios were not delivered to him, so he wishes to sue for the recovery of the purchase price.

In the meantime A has sold the radios to Y, who offered him the gift of a car in return for arranging the deal.

What are the respective rights of X and P in these circumstances? *A.C.A., December* 1971.

4. (a) State and explain the duties owed by an agent to his principal.

(b) E, an estate agent, agreed to find a buyer for S's house. E introduced P, who agreed to buy the house, subject to contract, and left £500 with E as a deposit. P subsequently withdrew from the sale. P was unable to recover the deposit from E, who had gone into liquidation.

Advise P as to his rights against S

What would your answer be if E had accepted the deposit as a "stake holder"? *A.C.A., June* 1973.

5. What rights have (a) a retiring partner and (b) a purchaser of a firm's business in respect of the goodwill of the business? *A.C.A., December* 1969.

6. (a) Explain the distinction between joint and several liability. Why is the distinction important in partnership law?

(b) A and B are in partnership as greengrocers. While negligently driving the firm's van on business. A injures X. X is now suing the firm for damages and it is found that A is insolvent. Advise B on the extent of his own liability and that of the firm. *A.C.A., December* 1970.

7. (a) "The duties of a partner to his firm are fundamentally the same as those of an agent to his principal" Discuss this statement.

(b) L, M and N are partners. Having reached the age of 70, L wishes to retire from the business and to assign his share to his son, who has worked in the business for 10 years. M and N object to the assignment and wish to purchase L's share themselves. Advise M and N. *A.C.A., December* 1971.

8. What is the essential nature of a partnership?

F and G were in process of forming a company to vend garden equipment G without F's knowledge, and in his own name, ordered from E six mowing machines and put them in a shed at the site which had been selected for the company's garden centre. As G is unable to pay the agreed price for the machines, E wishes to claim the money from F.

Advise E. *C.I.S., June* 1972.

9. (a) Explain the way partnership property would be applied on its dissolution.

(b) John has been a partner in a trading firm of repute. He wishes to retire and has agreed to sell his share of the goodwill to Charles and Peter, the continuing partners.

Advise John as to the steps he must take to protect himself against liability in respect of the debts of the partnership incurred while he was a partner and in respect of the firm's future debts. *A.C.A., June* 1973.

10. (a) "There is normally a right in the principal unilaterally to revoke the agency at any time before the agency has been completely performed by giving notice." Explain the rule and indicate whether there are any exceptions to it.

(b) Shaw owes Lamb £700. Shaw has appointed Lamb as his agent to collect certain debts owing to Shaw and to deduct 20 per cent of each amount collected until his loan to Lamb is fully repaid. The agreement also provides that Lamb should receive a commission of 5 per cent of all gross amounts collected.

Lamb has collected £3,000 and thus recovered £600 of his loan. Now Shaw wishes to cancel the arrangement. Advise Lamb as to his rights in the matter both in respect of the unrecovered balance of the loan and of the commission. *A.C.A., December* 1970.

PART THREE

MERCANTILE AGREEMENTS

CHAPTER X

Sale of Goods and Hire-purchase

The law relating to sale of goods is laid down by the Sale of Goods Act 1979, an act which codified the law then existing. The body of law contained in this statute has however been considerably added to by judicial decisions, and by the Supply of Goods (Implied Terms) Act 1973 and the Unfair Contract Terms Act 1977.

The law relating to hire-purchase is laid down by the Hire Purchase Act 1965 and the Consumer Credit Act 1974.

THE CONTRACT FOR SALE OF GOODS

1. Sale of Goods Act 1979, s. 1. This defines the contract as one "whereby the seller (*a*) transfers, or (*b*) agrees to transfer the property in goods to a buyer for a money consideration called the price" (the word property here means rights of ownership).

Two kinds of contract are dealt with in the definition: (*a*) a sale and transfer of property, i.e. an executed contract, and (*b*) an agreement to sell and transfer in the future, i.e. an executory contract.

2. Meaning of "goods." Goods means all chattels and tangible things in possession (chattels personal), but not things in action and money.

"Goods" also means the following.

(*a*) *Industrial growing crops*, once they have been severed from the land. (Until severance they are classed as part of the land itself and are not goods.)

(*b*) *Ships.*

(*c*) *Future goods*, i.e. goods to be made or acquired by the seller after making the contract: S.G.A., s. 61(1). (A sale of such goods operates as an executory contract, i.e. an agreement to sell in the future: s. 5.)

3. An agreement to sell means a contract to transfer property in goods (*a*) at some future time, or (*b*) subject to some condition being fulfilled.

EXAMPLE: S agreed to sell a horse to B if B should be satisfied with it after an eight-day trial. After three days the horse died (without any fault on the part of B). HELD: B was not liable to pay the purchase price, since ownership would not pass to him for another five days. Consequently the contract was discharged by frustration: *Elphick* v. *Barnes* (1880).

4. Sales and Agreements to sell compared.

SALE	AGREEMENT TO SELL
1. An executed contract, operating as an actual transfer of the ownership.	1. An executory contract to transfer ownership at a later date.
2. If the buyer defaults, the seller can sue him for the price.	2. If the buyer defaults, the seller can only sue him for unliquidated damages for breach of contract.
3. If the seller defaults, the buyer can sue for damages and claim delivery of the goods.	3. If the seller defaults, the buyer can only sue for damages.
4. Since ownership passes to the buyer, he bears the risk of loss or deterioration.	4. Since ownership does not pass to the buyer, the risk of loss or deterioration remains with the seller.

5. Contracts for work and materials. The S.G.A. does not apply to these contracts, in which the purchaser is buying the skill of a craftsman and not merely the goods to be produced by him. Whether a particular contract is one for the sale of goods or for the supply of work and materials is sometimes a difficult question of fact.

The test is: Is the essential object of the agreement the provision of goods or the exercise of skill?

EXAMPLE: A dental mechanic, employed to make false teeth, was held to be making a contract for sale of goods: *Lee* v. *Griffin* (1861). But employment of an artist to paint a portrait is a contract for supply of work and materials, since the artist's skill is the main constituent of the contract: *Robinson* v. *Graves* (1935).

In contracts for work and materials there is an implied condition that the work will be carefully and properly carried out, and that the materials used shall be reasonably suitable to the purchaser's requirements, provided these are made known at the time of contracting.

> EXAMPLE: A woman at a hairdresser's was injured by a hair-dye to which she was allergic. She had not told the hairdresser of her allergy. HELD: The hairdresser was not liable: *Ingham* v. *Emes* (1955).

6. Contract of barter. The S.G.A. lays down that a contract for the sale of goods is one in which the consideration is payable in money. Consequently the Act does not apply to barters or exchanges.

But a contract of part-barter, or part-exchange, where part of the consideration is paid in money, is within the S.G.A.: *Simpson* v. *Connolly* (1953).

7. Conditional bills of sale. The S.G.A. does not apply to mortgages in the form of sales of chattels with a provision for resale on repayment of the price or loan. These are governed by the Bills of Sale Acts 1878–82, *see* XVI, **10, 11.**

8. Capacity to contract. Capacity is co-extensive with ordinary contractual capacity, but note the special liability imposed on minors, patients and drunkards to pay a reasonable price for necessaries: S.G.A., s. 2. and *see* Minors, III.

9. Form of contract. Any form suffices, written or oral: S.G.A., s. 3.

10. Price.

(a) *Fixed by parties.* The price (i) may be fixed at the time of contracting by the parties themselves, or (ii) may be left to be determined in the course of dealings between the parties, or (iii) may be left to be fixed in some way stipulated in the contract, or (iv) may be left to be fixed by some third party.

(b) *Fixed by a third party.* Where the contract states that the price is to be fixed by a third party, and he fails to do so, the contract is void: s. 9.

But if the purchaser has by then taken the benefit of the goods, he must pay a reasonable price for them.

If the third party's failure to fix the price is due to the fault of one of the parties, that party is liable to an action for damages: s. 9(2).

(c) *Where no price fixed in any* of the ways listed in (a) or (b) above, the purchaser must pay a reasonable price.

CONDITION AND WARRANTIES

11. Condition and warranties. There is no definition of the former in the S.G.A., but s. 62(1) makes clear that the word "warranty" is to have its normal contractual meaning. It is therefore assumed that the word "condition" also bears the conventional meaning: *see* II, 24–32.

12. Terms implied by the S.G.A. The Act implies several very important conditions and warranties in contracts governed by the Act (unless expressly excluded). These are analysed in detail in 18–23 below.

13. Assessment of terms. Whether a particular term is a condition or warranty is a question of fact in each case, and the terminology used by the parties is not necessarily binding on the courts: *Schuler A. G.* v. *Wickman Machine Tool Sales* (1974).

The importance of the distinction lies in that breach of warranty entitles the injured party to sue for damages for breach of contract, but not to treat the contract as at an end. A breach of condition (a main term) entitles the injured party either (a) to treat the contract as at an end (and to sue for any compensation due to him), or (b) to treat the breach as though it were merely a breach of warranty, go on with the contract and sue for damages for breach: *Wallis* v. *Pratt* (1911). But it appears that, in contracts for the sale of goods, where a particular term is not said by statute or previous decisions to be a condition or warranty, the court may describe it as an "intermediate obligation", the effect of breach then depending on whether or not it goes to the root of the contract: *Cehave N.V.* v. *Bremer* (1975).

> NOTE: Stipulations as to time of payment are not to be regarded as conditions of the contract unless expressly so agreed: S.G.A., s. 10. (But contrast time for performance: in mercantile contracts this is usually regarded by the courts as a condition: *Reuter* v. *Sala* (1879).)

14. Ex post facto warranties. This means conditions which, after breach, are treated as breaches of warranties.

In sales of goods the buyer can treat any breach of condition as breach of an *ex post facto* warranty: s. 11(2).

NOTE: In some cases (unless otherwise agreed) the buyer must treat a breach of condition as breach of an *ex post facto* warranty if the contract is non-severable and the buyer has accepted any part of the goods: s. 11(4). ("Specific goods" means goods identified and agreed upon at the time the contract is made: s. 62(1). A "non-severable" contract means one in which the goods are delivered in one lot which is not easily divisible, e.g. a ton of coal.)

15. Conditions and warranties, express or implied. Terms in a contract of sale of goods may be express or implied (by statute, trade usage, or the course of dealing between the parties), *see* II, 24–32.

Where express terms are added to the contract after it is made, they must be supported by additional consideration otherwise they are not binding.

Terms implied by the S.G.A. may be negatived (*a*) by express terms in the contract, or (*b*) by trade usage.

16. Terms and mere representations. Terms of the contract must be distinguished from mere representations made by a party during the preliminary negotiations. The distinction presents a difficult question of fact in each case, e.g. if in selling a used car A describes it as having done not more than 20,000 miles, is this a term of the contract or merely a representation?

The distinction used to be important because of the different remedies available for misrepresentation and for breach of contract. Now, however, the misrepresentation Act 1967 allows a plaintiff to obtain damages even in cases of innocent misrepresentation (where negligence is present) and the distinction between mere representations and warranties is much reduced in importance. And even if the misrepresentation was entirely innocent (there was no negligence at all), the courts have a discretion to give the injured party damages instead of him being allowed to rescind (*i.e.* put an end to the contract): Misrepresentation Act 1967, s. 2.

17. Dangerous goods. A person selling dangerous goods must warn the buyer of the danger, if he knows of it himself. If he fails to do so (*a*) he is liable for breach of contract to the person with whom he contracted; (*b*) he is liable for the tort of negligence to any person to whom the purchaser transmits the goods: *Donoghue* v. *Stevenson* (1932).

> EXAMPLES: (1) A sold C a tin of disinfectant knowing that it could be dangerous if opened without special care, but failed to warn C. C's sight was damaged by the powder. HELD: A was liable in damages: *Clarke* v. *Army & Navy Co-operative Soc. Ltd.* (1903). (2) Manufacturer of chemical products owes a duty of care to take reasonable steps to see that the product is not injurious to a purchaser's employees: *Wright* v. *Dunlop Rubber Co.* (1973).

TERMS IMPLIED BY THE SALE OF GOODS ACT

18. Implied terms as to title. Section 12, S.G.A. provides as follows.

Subsections 1 and 2: In every contract of sale, other than one to which subsection 3 applies, there is:

(*a*) *an implied condition* in every contract of sale that the seller has the right to sell the goods (or in an agreement to sell, that he will have the right to sell at the time when the property is to pass), and

(*b*) *an implied warranty* that the goods shall be free of any *undisclosed charge or encumbrance* and that the buyer shall enjoy *quiet possession* (subject to any encumbrance disclosed or known to the buyer).

Subsection 3: Where it appears from the contract that the intention is that the seller transfers only such title as he (or some third person) may have, there is:

(*a*) an implied warranty that all known charges or encumbrances have been disclosed to the buyer, and

(*b*) an implied warranty that neither (*i*) the seller, nor (*ii*) any third person to whose claims the sale is subject, nor (*iii*) any person claiming under the seller or such third person, will disturb the buyer's quiet possession.

19. Correspondence with description: s. 13 (condition). That in a sale by description the goods shall correspond with the description and with the sample: s. 13. A sale is not prevented from being a sale by description merely by the fact that the goods are exposed for sale and selected by the buyer himself (as in a self-service store).

NOTE: (1) What is a sale by description? This means that the buyer relies for his information on the description of the goods given by the seller, e.g. in the contract or in preliminary negotiations. Thus where he buys goods which he has not seen, it must be a sale by description. And it may be a sale by description even if he has seen the goods, if he relies on the seller's description and there is some inaccuracy in that description which is not apparent: *Thornet & Fehr* v. *Beers & Son* (1919). (2) This section is construed strictly in favour of the buyer, and covers almost any representation as to the nature, origin or identity of the goods, e.g. the methods of packing the goods: *Re Moore & Co. and Landauer & Co.* (1921). (3) A discrepancy between description and actuality such as could not have been seen on reasonable examination is a breach of this condition, e.g. the buyer examined lace described as seventeenth century and after purchase discovered it was actually eighteenth century. HELD: The discrepancy was not discernible on examination, and he was entitled to rescind the contract: *Nicholson & Venn* v. *Smith Marriot* (1947).

Where the description of the goods is an express term of the contract, another term expressly excluding "all conditions and warranties implied by law" will not protect the seller, e.g. B bought a "new Singer car" from S, and the contract excluded all implied terms. The car was not new. HELD: B could reject the car: *Andrews Bros. (Bournemouth) Ltd.* v. *Singer & Co.* (1934).

20. Merchantable quality: S.G.A., s. 14(2). There is now an implied condition that where the seller sells goods in the course of a business the goods supplied shall be of merchantable quality, except that there is no such condition:

(*a*) as regards defects specifically drawn to the buyer's attention before the contract is made; or

(*b*) if the buyer examines the goods before the contract is made, as regards defects which that examination ought to reveal: S.G.A., s. 14(2)(*b*).

NOTE: (1) Goods are of merchantable quality if they are as fit for the purpose or purposes for which goods of that kind are commonly bought as it is reasonable to expect, having regard to any description applied to them, the price (if relevant) and all other relevant circumstances: S.G.A., s. 14(6). (2) If the goods are defective, it is no defence to the seller to show that the defect could be easily repaired: *Grant* v. *Australian Knitting Mills, Ltd.* (1936).

21. Fitness for particular purpose: s. 14(3) (condition). Where the seller sells goods in the course of a business and the buyer, expressly or by implication, makes known to the seller any particular purpose for which the goods are being bought, there is an implied condition that the goods supplied under the contract are reasonably fit for that purpose (whether or not it is a purpose for which such goods are commonly supplied), except where the circumstances show that the buyer does not rely (or that it is unreasonable for him to rely) on the seller's skill or judgment.

By s. 14(4) an implied condition (or warranty) as to fitness for a particular purpose may be annexed to a contract of sale by usage, e.g. trade custom.

NOTE: (1) It is sufficient if the seller should have realised the intended purpose, even though the buyer did not specifically tell him, e.g. a bottle of milk should be reasonably fit for human consumption: *Frost* v. *Aylesbury Dairies Ltd.* (1905), and if the buyer asks for a hot-water bottle, since the purpose is obvious, the condition will apply: *Priest* v. *Last* (1903). Thus G (aged 6) bought a catapult from P and was injured by its defective condition. HELD: G could recover damages for breach of *ex post facto* warranty from P under s. 14(3) (unfitness for purpose) and under s. 14(2) (merchantable quality). (Also P could recover damages from his supplier under s. 15 (sale by sample), since he had bought by sample and the defect was not apparent on reasonable examination of the sample): *Godley* v. *Perry* (1960). (2) The buyer may be relying on the seller's skill even if the contract is one under which the seller is to manufacture the goods to the buyer's specification: *C. Hill Ltd.* v. *Ashington Piggeries Ltd.* (1969).

22. Sale by sample: s. 15 (condition). That in a sale by sample:

(*a*) bulk shall correspond with sample in quality; and

(*b*) the buyer shall have reasonable opportunity to compare bulk with sample; and

(c) the goods shall be free of any defect rendering them un-merchantable, and which would not be apparent on reasonable examination of the sample.

NOTE: (1) Where part only of the goods are not up to sample, the buyer must still accept or reject all (unless the contract is severable, i.e. in instalments, in which case each instalment may be treated separately). (2) Mere display of a sample during negotiations does not make the contract a sale by sample. There must be definite agreement to this effect. Whether or not it is a term of the contract is a question of fact in each case. (3) Where in a sale by sample goods are sold "with all faults and imperfections," the seller may be relieved from liability under (c) above but may still be liable under (a) and/or (b): *Champanhac Ltd.* v. *Waller Ltd.* (1948).

23. Exclusion of implied terms. The exclusion of the terms implied by ss. 13–15 is governed by the Unfair Contract Terms Act as follows:

(a) The terms implied by s. 12 cannot now be excluded.

(b) In consumer sales any attempt by the seller to exclude the terms implied by ss. 13–15 is void.

A "consumer sale" is one (other than by auction or competitive tender) by a seller in the ordinary course of a business where the goods are of a type usually bought, (i) for private use or consumption, (ii) by a person who is not himself a dealer buying in the course of business, i.e. a person buying for private use.

(c) In other sales, exclusions of ss. 13–15 are valid only if they are reasonable as at the time the contract was made. In assessing what is reasonable the Court will consider:

(i) Whether the buyer should have known of the exclusion.

(ii) Whether in buying the goods the buyer had the opportunity to buy (either from the seller or elsewhere) without the exclusion clause.

PASSING OF OWNERSHIP AND RISK

24. Passing of ownership. The transfer of the legal property in the goods is important for assessing who bears the risk of loss or deterioration, etc.

The position depends (*a*) on whether the contract is a sale or an agreement to sell, and (*b*) on whether the goods are specific and ascertained, or unascertained: *see* below.

25. Specific and ascertained goods.

(*a*) *Specific goods* means goods identified and agreed upon at the time of making the contract: s. 61(1).

Goods are not specific merely because the source of supply has been agreed, e.g. "500 tonnes of coal from stack no. 2."

(*b*) *Ascertained goods* means goods identified and agreed upon after the making of the contract.

(*c*) *Unascertained goods* means goods not yet identified and agreed upon, but merely described, e.g. the coal in (*a*) above.

26. When the property passes.

(*a*) *Specific and ascertained goods:* The property in them passes whenever the parties intend it to pass. The intention of the parties may be (*i*) stated in the contract or (*ii*) left to be ascertained by the court from the circumstances: *see* **27** below.

(*b*) *Unascertained goods:* The property passes only when they become ascertained, i.e. no property can pass in unascertained goods.

27. Tests of intention. Where the contract does not state when the property is to pass, the court will apply the following tests to ascertain the intentions of the parties:

(*a*) *Unconditional contract* for sale of specific goods in a deliverable condition: the property passes when the contract is made (even if delivery is postponed): s. 18(1).

The risk then passes to the buyer, even though the seller retains a lien for unpaid purchase money: s. 20.

(*b*) *Sale of specific goods not in a deliverable state:* the property does not pass until (*i*) the seller puts them into a deliverable state, and (*ii*) the buyer is notified thereof: s. 18(2).

(*c*) *Sale of specific goods in a deliverable state*, but requiring some additional act such as weighing, measuring, testing, etc., to fix the price: the property does not pass until (*i*) the seller has done the required act, and (*ii*) the buyer is notified thereof: s. 18(3).

(*d*) *Goods delivered on approval or on sale or return, etc.:* the property does not pass until (*i*) the buyer signifies acceptance, or adopts the goods (e.g. by using them), or (*ii*) the buyer retains the goods for an unreasonable time or beyond any agreed time limit. What is a reasonable time is a question of fact in each case: s. 18(4).

(*e*) *Contract for sale of unascertained or future goods:* the property passes when (*i*) the seller unconditionally appropriates goods of the required description to the contract, (*ii*) puts them in a deliverable state, and (*iii*) notifies the buyer: s. 18(5).

(Appropriation by the seller includes delivery to the buyer or to a carrier on behalf of the buyer, provided the seller has not reserved a right of disposal: s. 18(5). If a right of disposal is reserved, property does not pass until the seller's conditions are satisfied: s. 19(1). Where the goods are shipped on a Bill of Lading to the order of the seller or his agent, it is presumed that a right of disposal is reserved: s. 19(2).)

28. Perishing of specific goods.

(*a*) *If before the contract is made*, the contract is void: s. 6 (and see *Couturier* v. *Hastie* (1857), IV, 4). This is a simple case of common mistake as to the existence of the subject-matter of the contract.

(*b*) *If after the contract is made*, and before the property passes to the buyer; the contract is void: s. 7. (But if the destruction was due to the fault of either party, the contract would not be void: instead the innocent party could sue for breach of contract.)

(*c*) If after the contract is made, and after the property has passed to the buyer: the buyer bears the loss and must pay for the goods.

"Perished" means destroyed or so changed or deteriorated as to defeat the purpose of the contract. But mere deterioration does not amount to perishing unless it causes the goods to become valueless: *Horn* v. *Minister of Food* (1948).

29. Passing of risk.
Unless otherwise agreed, the risk will pass to the buyer only when the property in the goods passes to him.

Note that passing of risk is independent of possession, e.g. if the property in the goods has passed to the buyer, the risk falls on him even though the seller has not yet delivered the goods.

NOTE: (1) Where performance of the contract is delayed by the fault of one party, the risk of loss or damage falls on that party: *Sterns Ltd.* v. *Vickers Ltd.* (1923). (2) Where delivery involves a sea journey, the goods remain at the seller's risk unless he gives the buyer reasonable notice (so that he can insure the goods): s. 32(3). (3) Where delivery is to a distant place, and the seller agrees to deliver at his own risk, the buyer must nevertheless accept the risk of any necessary deterioration incidental to the long journey: s. 33.

NEMO DAT QUOD NON HABET

There is a general rule of law that *nemo dat quod non habet* ("no one can give what he has not got"). As applied to the sale of goods, the rule means that a seller of goods cannot give a better title to the purchaser than he himself possesses. Thus a purchaser who buys stolen goods from a thief can get no valid title to them, since the thief has no title: *see* 18. (Sales by a hirer of goods under a H.P. agreement are dealt with in 66–74 below.)

The Sale of Goods Act 1979 lays down important exceptions to this general rule and these are stated below.

30. Estoppel. Where the true owner is estopped from denying the actual seller's right to sell the purchaser will get a good title.

EXAMPLE: A allowed some of his property wrongfully to be detained by S, and also allowed B to think that S was entitled to the property. S sold the goods to B. HELD: B got a good title, as A was estopped from denying S's right to sell: *Pickard* v. *Sears* (1837).

31. Orders for sale. Where a person not the owner sells goods (*a*) under a court order, or (*b*) under a legal power of sale, e.g. the power of sale given to a legal mortgagee, the purchaser gets a good title.

EXAMPLE: A deposits goods with B for B to repair them, and then fails to collect and pay for the repaired goods. B has a statutory power to sell the goods: Torts (Interference with Goods) Act, and *see* XIII, 6.

32. Factors Act 1889, s. 2. The purchaser will get a good title if he buys in good faith from a factor, with whom the owner deposited the goods (even though the factor may have no actual authority to sell).

A factor is a mercantile agent whose ordinary business is the buying and selling of goods in his possession: Factors Act 1889, s. 1, *see* VIII, **18** above.

33. Sale of Goods Act 1979, ss. 24 and 25.

(*a*) *Seller in possession after sale.* If the buyer of goods allows the seller to remain in possession of them (or in possession of documents of title thereto) the seller can resell the goods to a second purchaser who will get a good title. The seller can then be sued in damages by the first buyer: s. 24. It is irrelevant whether the buyer has consented to the seller's retention of possession or not: *Worcester Works Finance* v. *Cooden Engineering Co. Ltd.* (1971).

(*b*) *Buyer in possession after sale.* If the seller allows the buyer to get possession of goods (or documents of title thereto) before paying for them the buyer can sell the goods and pass a good title: s. 25(1). (The seller can then only sue the original buyer for damages.)

34. Writs of execution. If a person fails to pay a debt when ordered by the court, a writ may be issued empowering the sheriff to seize his chattels and to sell them in satisfaction of the debt. The sheriff then has power to give a good title, although he is not the owner of the goods sold.

35. Sale under voidable title. The purchaser from a seller whose own title is voidable will get a good title, provided (*a*) he had no knowledge of any defect in the seller's title and (*b*) the seller's title had not been avoided at the time of the sale.

EXAMPLE: A rogue obtained jewels on credit from P by fraud and sold them to B before P discovered the fraud. HELD: P could avoid the rogue's title to the jewels on the grounds of fraud, but since he had not done so before B brought the jewels B got a good title: *Phillips* v. *Brooks* (1919), *see* IV, **6**.

It appears that where the other party cannot be found, avoidance is effective as soon as the victim exhibits clear intention to avoid, e.g. by reporting the fraud to the police: *Car & Universal Finance Co.* v. *Caldwell* (1964).

36. Market overt. The purchaser normally gets a good title if he buys in a market overt (open market).

The term "market overt" covers (*a*) all shops in the City of London, and (*b*) elsewhere, all markets established by statute, charter or custom as open markets.

A bona fide purchaser for value without notice of any defect in the seller's title will get a good title, provided:

(*a*) the sale is in accordance with the customs of the particular market;

(*b*) the sale took place in public, e.g. in the public part of a shop;

(*c*) the market dealer was the seller, not the purchaser;

(*d*) the goods were openly displayed, and were of a class the seller normally deals in;

(*e*) the sale took place in the normal opening hours of the market, e.g. between sunrise and sunset: *Reid* v. *Metropolitan Police Commissioner* (1973).

NOTE: The market overt provisions do not protect a purchaser where: (1) the transaction took place in Scotland; (2) the goods sold belong to the Crown; (3) the sale took place in a private part of the shop or stall, e.g. behind a curtain.

PERFORMANCE OF THE CONTRACT

37. Delivery. It is the duty of the seller to deliver the goods, and of the buyer to accept and pay for them: s. 27. Unless otherwise agreed payment and delivery are normally concurrent: s. 28.

Delivery means voluntary transfer of possession from one person to another. It may be actual or constructive, e.g. by handing over documents of title, or authority for the buyer to obtain the goods from some person in whose possession they are: *Central Newbury Car Auctions* v. *Unity Finance* (1957).

Delivery may also be by the seller agreeing to hold the goods as agent for the buyer: this is known as attornment.

38. Time and place of delivery.

(*a*) *Time for delivery.* Where the seller is to send the goods to the buyer but no time is fixed, they must be sent within a reasonable time and delivery must be at a reasonable hour: s. 29(3).

The seller usually bears the expense of putting the goods into a deliverable condition, and he must take reasonable care to see that they reach the right person: s. 29(6).

(b) *Place of delivery* (unless otherwise agreed) is the seller's place of business, or if he has none then his residence: s. 29(2).

If the sale is of specific goods known by both parties to be lodged at some other place, then delivery is to be made at that place: s. 29(2).

39. Delivery to a carrier. Where the seller is to send the goods, delivery to a carrier (as agent for the buyer) whether named by the buyer or not, is prima facie proper delivery to the buyer: s. 32(1).

In such cases the seller must make a reasonable contract with the carrier, otherwise the buyer is entitled to refuse to be bound: s. 32(2).

40. Delivery of wrong quantities: s. 30.

(a) *If less than ordered* the buyer may reject the lot; if he accepts the lesser quantity he must pay a proportionately reduced price.

(b) *If more than ordered*, the buyer may reject the lot, or may accept the agreed quantity only (if this is possible). He must then pay a proportionate price.

(c) *If goods ordered are mixed* with goods not ordered, the buyer may accept those ordered and reject the others (if it is possible to separate them, otherwise he must accept or reject the lot).

41. Delivery by instalments. Delivery is presumed to be in one transaction, unless it was expressly agreed that it should be by instalments.

If instalments are to be paid for separately on delivery, it is a question of fact whether failure to deliver one instalment justifies repudiation of the whole contract: s. 31.

The test is: Is the breach regarding one instalment sufficiently fundamental to injure the contract as a whole? It is relevant to consider the likelihood of the breach being repeated.

42. Acceptance by the buyer.

(a) The buyer is entitled to examine goods not previously seen, before accepting them: s. 34. Generally the place of delivery is the place of examination, unless otherwise agreed.

(b) The buyer accepts: (i) when he so informs the seller, or (*ii*) when he does some act of ownership, e.g. sells the goods, or (*iii*) keeps the goods an unreasonable time without notifying the seller that he wishes to reject them: s. 35.

(*c*) If the buyer rejects the goods, when entitled to do so, he is not bound to return them to the seller, but only to notify the seller of rejection so as to enable the latter to collect them: s. 36.

(*d*) If the buyer's rejection amounts to repudiation of the contract the seller has an immediate right of action. The same applies when the buyer keeps the goods for an unreasonable length of time without making up his mind.

In such a case the seller's damages will be measured as the amount of loss caused by the wrongful retention: *Long* v. *Lloyd* (1958).

43. Delivery by sea. In contracts for the carriage of goods sold by sea, various special terms are usual. These may be expressly agreed between the parties, but more often they rely on one of the established customary agreements with the implied terms that these contain.

The most common of these standard agreements are f.o.b., c.i.f., and ex-ship contracts: *see* below.

44. F.O.B., (free on board). Under such a contract, the seller's duties (unless otherwise agreed) are as follows.

(*a*) To deliver the goods to a named port of shipment.

(*b*) To put the goods on board ship at his own expense.

(*c*) To negotiate a reasonable Bill of Lading or other contract of carriage, and forward it to the buyer (who pays the freight).

(*d*) To notify the buyer of shipment, so as to enable him to insure the goods at sea. (If the seller fails to do this the goods will travel at his risk; otherwise the goods will be at the buyer's risk.)

Once the goods are shipped the property in them (and usually the risk) passes to the buyer. If the seller is prevented from putting the goods on board, e.g. by a strike, the property and risk remain with him: *Colley* v. *Overseas Exporters* (1921).

45. C.I.F. (cost, insurance, freight). Here the seller's duties go further than in an f.o.b. contract, and are as follows.

(*a*) To deliver the goods to the port of shipment at his own expense, and to see them safely on board.

(*b*) To insure the goods during transit.

(*c*) To negotiate a suitable bill of lading or other contract of carriage and to forward this to the buyer to enable him to claim the goods on arrival at the port of destination. (Purchase money is not normally paid until the documents of title reach the buyer.).

Once the goods are delivered to the ship the risk passes to the buyer (and should be covered by his insurance). The property in the goods passes to the buyer when the goods are shipped, unless the seller reserves a right of disposal in which case property does not pass until the price is paid.

The buyer is entitled to reject (*a*) the documents of title, and/or (*b*) the goods. Acceptance of one does not bind him to accept the other. But the buyer must pay the price when he receives the documents of title, even though he has not yet examined the goods. (It is also the buyer's responsibility to pay unloading charges, and transport from the port of destination to any further inland destination.)

46. Ex-ship. Here the seller is bound to arrange the shipment of the goods to the port of destination, and to such further inland destination as the buyer may stipulate. The buyer is not bound to pay for the goods until they are unloaded from the ship and all freightage charges paid. The goods travel at the seller's risk, but he is not bound to insure them (though of course he usually does).

RIGHTS OF AN UNPAID SELLER
AGAINST THE GOODS

49. Unpaid seller. The term includes any person who is in the position of seller, though not himself the owner, e.g. a factor.

The seller is unpaid as long as any part of the purchase price is outstanding.

Payment by a negotiable instrument is conditional only, i.e. is not effective until the negotiable instrument has been honoured.

48. Differing situations. The seller may have to contend with two different legal situations, (*a*) where the property has not passed to the buyer, and (*b*) where the property has passed to the buyer. His rights differ in these two cases.

49. Property not passed to buyer. Here the seller may (*a*) withhold delivery if the price is unpaid or not tendered, or if the buyer is insolvent, or (b) if part of the goods have been delivered, he may withhold the remainder: s. 39.

50. Property passed to buyer. Here the seller has the following rights.

(a) Lien: *see* **51** below.

(b) Stoppage in transit: *see* **54** below.

(c) Re-sale: *see* **58** below.

51. Lien: s. 41. The seller's lien is a right to retain possession of goods until payment or tender of payment.

A lien arises when:

(a) goods have been sold without any agreement as to credit; or

(b) goods have been sold on credit, but the period of credit has expired; or

(c) goods have been sold on credit and the buyer has become insolvent (whether the period of credit has expired or not).

52. Lien is lost when:

(a) goods have been delivered to a carrier for transmission to the buyer, without the seller reserving a right of disposal; or

(b) the buyer or his agent lawfully obtains possession of the goods; or

(c) the seller waives his lien: s. 43.

53. The seller may exercise a lien:

(a) when in possession merely as agent for the buyer;

(b) where part delivery has taken place (the lien extends over the remainder of the goods);

(c) if the seller breaks his contract while the buyer is solvent, he will still be entitled to claim a lien if the buyer subsequently becomes insolvent.

54. Stoppage in transit: s. 44. This means a right to stop the goods when they are on their way to the buyer (and after they have left the possession of the seller).

The right arises when:

(a) the goods are in transit (*see* **55** below); and

(b) the buyer becomes insolvent. (The buyer is insolvent if he has ceased to pay his debts as they fall due or in the ordinary course of business: s. 62.)

55. Meaning of transit. Goods are in transit until the buyer accepts them, i.e. if in the hands of a carrier prior to delivery, or if rejected by the buyer when delivered: s. 45.

NOTE: Where goods are in the possession of a carrier, the position depends on whether he is agent for the seller or for the buyer (a question of fact in each case). If he is agent for the seller, then the goods are still in the possession of the seller and his right is one of lien, not stoppage. If he is agent for the buyer transit is over, and the seller has no right of stoppage. (The carrier may become agent for the buyer either by appointment as such, or by notifying the buyer that he holds the goods on his behalf, i.e. that they await collection.)

Transit ceases when the goods reach their ultimate destination, but not some intermediate destination (unless further instructions are conveyed to the carrier to send them on, in which case transit has ceased).

56. How stoppage is effected. This is done by the seller (*a*) taking possession of the goods or documents of title thereto, or (*b*) giving notice to the carrier of his exercise of the right of stoppage.

If the seller wrongfully stops the goods, e.g. where the buyer is solvent, he is liable for damages for the tort of conversion if the property has passed to the buyer, or for damages for breach of contract if the property has not yet passed to the buyer.

If a carrier wrongfully delivers stopped goods to the buyer, he is liable for damages to the seller. And if he wrongfully obeys the seller's instructions to stop transit, he is liable for damages to the buyer.

57. Transit ceases when:

(*a*) goods reach their destination and possession is delivered to the buyer or his agent;

(*b*) the buyer or his agent obtains delivery before they reach their destination;

(*c*) a carrier wrongfully refuses to deliver the goods to the buyer or his agent;

(*d*) the goods have reached their destination and the carrier has notified the buyer that he holds them as his agent;

(*e*) goods are delivered to the master of the buyer's ship, or of a ship which the buyer has chartered.

NOTE: Sale by the buyer does not affect the seller's right of stoppage, unless the seller has assented thereto.

58. Resale: s. 48. The contract is not necessarily rescinded by the exercise by the seller of his rights of lien or stoppage, nor does the seller automatically thereby acquire a right to resell the goods to another purchaser.

The seller has a right of resale after exercise of his rights of lien or stoppage in transit where:

(*a*) the goods are perishable; or

(*b*) the price has not been paid within a reasonable time after notice given by the seller of his intention to resell; or

(*c*) such right was expressly reserved by him in the contract.

In addition to the above, the seller may also have a right of action for damages for breach of contract: *Ward* v. *Bignall* (1967).

ACTIONS FOR BREACH OF CONTRACT

59. By the seller: s. 49. He has the following rights of action.

(*a*) For the price.

(*i*) Where the property in the goods has passed to the buyer and he has failed to pay for them.

(*ii*) Where the price is payable on a certain day and has not been paid, the seller can sue for the price notwithstanding that the property has not passed to the buyer or the goods have not yet been appropriated to the contract.

(*b*) Damages for non-acceptance. This action lies where the buyer has refused to accept the goods and the property has not passed to him: s. 50(1).

The measure of damages is the estimated loss directly and naturally resulting to the seller: s. 50(2). Where there is an available market for the goods, the measure of damages will therefore normally be the difference between the contract price and the market price at the date of breach: s. 50(3). Where there is no available market, the seller is entitled to damages for loss of his bargain: *Thompson* v. *Robinson* (1955) and *Lazenby Garages Ltd.* v. *Wright* (1976).

60. By the buyer.

(*a*) *For non-delivery.* The buyer can recover damages calculated in the same manner as in **59** above: s. 51(1).

(b) *For recovery of price*, where this has been paid and the goods have not been delivered.

(c) *For specific performance*, where the contract is for sale of specific or ascertained goods. But such an order is discretionary, and the court may award damages instead: s. 52.

(d) *For tort* (conversion) if the property has passed to the buyer and the seller has wrongfully detained or disposed of the goods. The action for detinue was abolished by the Torts (Interference with Goods) Act 1977.

(e) *For breach of condition* the buyer can reject the goods, or, if he chooses, accept them and sue for damages for breach of an *ex post facto* warranty: *see* II, **28**.

(f) *For breach of warranty*, the buyer can only sue for damages; he cannot reject the goods.

NOTE: The Consumer Protection Acts 1961–1971 and the Consumer Safety Act 1978 give the Government power to lay down standards of safety and manufacture of goods to protect consumers. Any person injured by defects in such goods (whether he is the actual buyer or not) can sue the seller, the manufacturer or any importer—whoever is more appropriate. (Exemption clauses cannot remove this liability.)

AUCTION SALES

61. Auction sales. An auction is a sale at which the auctioneer (as agent for the seller) invites persons present to bid (offer) for goods sold.

The bidder is the offeror, and can withdraw his bid at any time before the auctioneer accepts it, usually by knocking with a hammer.

The general rules laid down by the Sale of Goods Act apply to sales of goods by auction; therefore if the sale is of specific goods the property in them will pass to the buyer as soon as the hammer falls, i.e. as soon as the contract is made: s. 57(2).

Each lot put up for sale becomes the subject of a separate contract.

62. Position of auctioneer. Auctioneers require to be licensed annually: the Auctioneers Act 1845.

(a) *Agent for the seller.* He is primarily agent for the seller, but on accepting a bid he becomes also agent for the buyer. Thus his signature on a memorandum of sale would be binding on both seller and buyer: *Cohen* v. *Roche* (1927).

NOTE: He has a lien on the goods for his charges and has a right of action for the price against a buyer who has taken delivery and has failed to pay. He has implied authority to receive payment in cash, but no implied authority to sell on credit.

(*b*) *Auctioneer's warranties.* Independently of any liabilitity as agent, he impliedly warrants on his own behalf:

   (*i*) that he has authority to sell the goods;

   (*ii*) that he knows of no defect in the seller's title;

   (*iii*) that he will give possession upon payment of the price, and that the purchaser's possession will not be disturbed by the seller or by himself.

(He does not warrant the seller's title in a sale of specific goods, unless he fails to make it clear he is merely acting as agent: *Benton* v. *Campbell, Parker & Co. Ltd.* (1925).)

63. Auctions with and without reserve.

(*a*) *Auctions with reserve.* This means any auction which is announced as being (*i*) subject to a reserve price being reached, and/or (*ii*) subject to the seller himself reserving a right to bid.

If a reserve price has been announced and the auctioneer inadvertently accepts a bid at a lower price, the buyer cannot enforce the sale.

(*b*) *Auctions without reserve.* These are the normal auctions, and in such sales the seller cannot legally bid, either personally or through an agent. If he does so, the buyer can treat the sale as fraudulent.

64. Bidding rings.

It is a criminal offence for any dealer to make an agreement supported by consideration to abstain from bidding at any sale which he attends: Auctions (Bidding Agreements) Act 1969. (A "dealer" is any person who makes it his business to attend auctions for the purpse of buying goods for resale.)

If a dealer is convicted under this enactment, the buyer can claim damages for fraud against any person who is a party to the agreement (and providing the buyer is innocent of any complicity). Also the seller can avoid the sale, unless the goods were bought by an innocent purchaser.

NOTE: The Auctions (Bidding Agreements) Act 1969 attempted to prevent operation of "rings", by enabling the courts to ban participants from auction for from one to three years and to order restoration to the seller of the property sold. (The Act must be displayed at auctions, but is of doubtful value.)

65. Mock Auctions Act 1961. It is a criminal offence to promote or conduct a "mock auction," i.e. an auction at which:

(*a*) articles are sold to a bidder (*i*) for a sum lower than his highest bid, or (*ii*) where part of the price is refunded; or

(*b*) the right to bid is restricted to persons who have already agreed to buy one or more other articles; or

(*c*) an article is offered as a gift by way of inducement.

HIRE PURCHASE ACTS

66. The Hire Purchase Act 1965. The 1965 Act consolidates the law relating to hire purchase and similar transactions. The Act covers:

(*a*) *Hire-purchase*—where a person hires goods for a specified period (by monthly or weekly instalments) and has an option to purchase the goods hired at the expiry of the period of hire (usually with the last scheduled payment). During the period of hire, he is a mere bailee of the goods: *see* Bailment, XIII below.

(*b*) *Credit sale*—where goods are sold to a purchaser (who obtains both possession and title) for more than £30 payable by five or more instalments. (Where the price is less than £30, the H.P. Act 1965 does not apply.)

(*c*) *Conditional sale*—where a person agrees to buy goods and obtains immediate possession, but the transfer of title is postponed until the fulfilment of a condition, e.g. the completion of stated instalments of purchase price.

NOTE: The Act of 1965 is to be repealed from a date yet to be announced under the terms of the Consumer Credit Act 1974.

67. Statutory requirements. The Act provides that all of the above agreements must be made subject to the following requirements.

(*a*) *Statement of cash price.* Before the contract is made the owner (or seller) must notify the hirer (or purchaser) in writing of the cash price of the goods, e.g. by drawing his attention to a price catalogue or price-tab.

(*b*) *Written contract.* The contract is unenforceable by the owner (seller) unless in writing, signed by the hirer (buyer) and by or on behalf of the owner (seller).

In hire-purchase and conditional sale agreements, the contract must state:

(*i*) the total hire-purchase price (or conditional sale purchase price), the amount of each instalment and when payable;

(*ii*) a list of the goods comprised;

(*iii*) a notification of the hirer's (or buyer's) rights.

NOTE: When the Consumer Credit Act repeals the 1965 Act, the above requirements will be substantially repeated.

68. Statutory right of cancellation. Where the hirer/buyer signs any of the three classes of agreement covered by the Acts at a place other than appropriate trade premises, he has a statutory right (which cannot be negated by agreement) to cancel the contract within four days of receiving his (statutory) copy of the agreement.

"Appropriate trade premises" means a place at which the owner (or seller) normally carries on business, or a place where similar goods are normally sold. (Thus the right of cancellation primarily protects those who hire or buy goods at their own homes from door-to-door salesmen.)

69. Implied terms: S.G. (I.T.) A. 1973, ss. 8–12. The terms implied by the H.P. Act 1965 have been effectively replaced by those laid down by the 1973 Act. They can only be excluded in the same ways as terms implied in sales.

NOTE: Exemption clauses excluding liability are void in hire-purchase of "consumer goods" in most circumstances and will be void in other cases unless they are reasonable in all the circumstances: Unfair Contract Terms Act, s. 6.

70. Dealer as agent. In many hire-purchase transactions there are in fact three parties involved. Thus A wishes to buy a car and arranges to take one stocked by B, a dealer, who offers to arrange hire-purchase through C, a finance company. The resulting hire-purchase contract will be between A (the hirer) and C (the owner, who will have bought the car for cash from B).

Formerly there was a danger (particularly with secondhand cars) that B might induce A to enter into the hire-purchase agreement by misrepresentation. After discovering the misrepresentation A would naturally wish to sue either B, the dealer, or C, the

owner. He would then find (*i*) that he had no contractual relationship with B, a mere outsider to the hire-purchase contract,
and could not sue him, and (*ii*) the hire-purchase contract would
contain a clause expressly exempting C from liability for any
misrepresentations made by B.

To combat this situation the courts during the 1950s, pronounced that there might arise, in suitable cases, a "collateral
contract" between A and B entitling A to sue B for his misrepresentation; but A still had no remedy in contract against C because of the exemption clause.

The H.P. Act 1965 and the Consumer Credit Act 1974 (in force
in this regard) have now strengthened the hirer's position by
enacting that in such cases representations made by a dealer
shall be deemed to have been made by him as agent for the owner
or seller (C): ss. 16 and 56 respectively.

The over-all effect of the courts' ruling and the 1965 and 1974
Acts are as follows.

(*a*) At common law: A has a right to sue B for misrepresentation or breach of the collateral contract, i.e. a contract whereby
A agrees to hire (or buy) the car from C, in return for B arranging
the hire-purchase or conditional or credit sale: *Andrews* v.
Hopkinson (1956), *see* II, **32**.

(*b*) Under the H.P. Act 1965: A has a right to sue the owner/
seller (C) for misrepresentation made by his statutory agent (B).

NOTE: A further improvement in the hire-purchaser's position
has come about through the Consumer Credit Act 1974, s. 75.
This came into force on 1st July 1977. Where goods are bought
with money provided by a business which has some existing or
contemplated link with the supplier of the goods, the debtor
has equal rights against both supplier and creditor for any
misrepresentation or breach of contract made or committed
by the supplier. In the event of a misrepresentation by the supplier, the debtor is entitled to rescind the credit agreement:
U.D.T. v. *Taylor* (1980).

71. Right to end the agreement. The hirer or conditional-
purchaser can determine the agreement at any time before the
final instalment is paid by giving written notice to the owner/
seller or his agent: s. 27(1). But he must complete payment of at
least one half of the price: s. 28.

Thus if the hirer has paid less than a half at the date of termination, he can be compelled to make up the difference; if he has paid more than a half, he cannot recover any of the money he has paid. But the court can award less than one half if this more accurately reflects the owner's real loss.

72. Application of the H.P. Acts. The Acts apply to contracts (as specified in **66** above) where the total price payable by the hirer/purchaser does not exceed £5,000 (H.P. Act 1965, ss. 2(2) and (3)). With credit sales there is a minimum of £30: *see* **66** above. The Consumer Credit Act generally applies to agreements where the *credit extended* does not exceed £5,000.

NOTE: If the hirer/purchaser is a corporation it is not protected by the Acts: H.P. Act 1965, s. 3: C.C. Act 1974, s. 8.

73. Hire Purchase Act 1964. This Act protects a person who buys a motor vehicle from a person who has possession of the vehicle (but not ownership) under a hire purchase or conditional sale agreement, e.g. A obtains a car on H.P. from C and then (illegally) sells it to X—the 1964 Act protects X's title to the car (c.f. S.G.A., s. 25 above).

74. Advertisements and quotations. Regulations made under the Consumer Credit Act prescribe the information which must go into an advertisement depending on whether it is a full, intermediate or simple credit agreement. This will often involve a prominent indication of the annual percentage rate of credit (APR). The regulations also set out rules for quotations. *See* the Consumer Credit (Advertisements) Regulations 1980 No. 54 and the Consumer Credit (Quotations) Regulations 1980 No. 55.

CONSUMER CREDIT ACT

75. The Consumer Credit Act 1974. This Act creates a system of controlling all regulated consumer hire and consumer credit agreements.

76. Regulated consumer hire agreement. This is an agreement to hire goods where the rental does not exceed £5,000 and the agreement is capable of subsisting for more than three months: s. 15.

NOTE: Goods hired from public utilities, telephones for example, are not regulated agreements even if coming within the above rules: s. 16(6).

77. Regulated consumer credit agreement. This is an agreement for the provision of credit or any kind of financial accommodation providing that the credit or accommodation does not exceed £5,000: s. 8.

NOTE: An agreement is not regulated if it is exempt: s. 16. Generally, agreements are exempt if they are mortgage loans provided by local authorities and building societies.

78. Regulated agreements. A business providing any kind of regulated agreement must be licensed by the Office of Fair Trading: s. 21. But a local authority does not need a licence nor does a body corporate empowered by a public general Act naming it to carry on a business. A license is either standard or group. A standard licence is issued to a named business. A group licence is issued where it appears to the O.F.T. that the public interest is better served than by obliging the business concerned to apply separately for standard licences. These provisions are in force.

79. Appeal against refusal. Where a licence is refused by the O.F.T. an appeal may be made to the Secretary of State for Trade. An appeal may be further made to the High Court but only on a point of law: ss. 41, 42. These provisions are in force.

80. Unlicensed trading. This is an offence: s. 39. In addition, agreements made by an unlicensed trader cannot be enforced by him unless he has been granted an order by the Director-General of Fair Trading: s. 40. An appeal against refusal of an order can be made exactly as described in **79** above. These provisions are in force.

81. Special rules. Regulated agreements are subject to various special rules.

(*a*) Agreements must be in the specified form: ss. 60, 61.

(*b*) Certain agreements are subject to a cooling-off period: s. 68.

(*c*) The debtors under some agreements are entitled to regular information about the amounts they owe: ss. 77, 78.

(*d*) Default notices are required: ss. 87–89.

(*e*) The debtor under a hire-purchase agreement has a right to pay off his agreement ahead of time and receive a rebate of interest charges: ss. 94, 95.

(*f*) The hirer under a hire agreement can terminate a hire agreement once it has lasted for eighteen months: s. 101.

NOTE: None of these provisions is yet in force.

82. Extortionate credit bargains. The rules relating to extortionate credit bargains apply to all agreements, whether regulated or not. If the court finds that a credit bargain is extortionate, it may reopen the agreement to do justice between the parties: s. 137. A credit bargain is extortionate if:

(*a*) it requires the debtor or a relative of his to make payments which are grossly exorbitant; or

(*b*) otherwise grossly contravenes ordinary principles of fair dealing: s. 138.

NOTE: These provisions are in force and apply retrospectively (i.e. they apply to agreements whenever they were made).

83. Ancillary credit businesses. The Act lists five types of ancillary credit business: credit-brokerage, debt-adjusting, debt-counselling, debt-collecting or the operation of a credit-reference agency: s. 145. All businesses operating an ancillary credit business must be licensed as described in **78** above. The provisions of **79** and **80** also apply.

MISCELLANEOUS CONTRACTS

84. The Unfair Contract Terms Act 1977 makes certain rules about the use of exclusion clauses in contracts (except contracts of sale and hire-purchase) where possession or ownership of goods passes: s. 7. The rules are as follows.

(*a*) As against a consumer, liability for correspondence with description or sample, quality or fitness cannot be excluded or restricted.

(*b*) As against a person who is not a consumer, this liability can be excluded if the exclusion clause can be proved to be reasonable.

(*c*) Liability in respect of the right to give ownership or possession, or the assurance of quiet possession, can be excluded, in the case of consumers and non-consumers alike, where the exclusion clause is proved to be reasonable.

SPECIMEN QUESTIONS

1. Give a short account of the implied terms as to the quality of goods contained in the Sale of Goods Act 1979.

E ordered from F one hundred sacks of potatoes. F delivered the potatoes to E in half-sacks. E had contracted to sell the potatoes to Y by the sack, so, not wishing to have the trouble of repacking them, he rejected F's consignment.

Advise F. *C.I.S., December* 1972.

2. "No one can give a better title than he himself has." Examine this statement in relation to the law of sale of goods. *C.I.S., December* 1972.

3. (*a*) What remedies has the buyer of goods against the seller where the latter has been guilty of a breach of contract?

(*b*) Some months before the investiture of the Prince of Wales, W, a Welsh shopkeeper, orders from M, a manufacturer, a large quantity of commemorative drinking mugs for delivery one week before the investiture. In fact, the mugs are delivered to him one week after the investiture. State with reasons whether W will be legally entitled

(*i*) to refuse to accept delivery of the mugs, and

(*ii*) to claim damages from M. *C.I.S., June* 1970.

4. (*a*) When does the property in the goods sold "on sale or return" pass to the buyer?

(*b*) Jack has been supplied with a colour television set by Televisions Galore Ltd. on two weeks' approval. After a week Jack sold the set to Jim and went abroad. Jim bought the set in good faith and was not aware of the circumstances.

Advise Televisions Galore Ltd. whether they can recover the set from Jim. What is Jack's legal position? *A.C.A., June* 1973.

5. (*a*) James, a client of yours, wishes to introduce hire-purchase facilities in his shop.

Explain to him what a hire-purchase contract is and what formalities are necessary for the creation of a valid hire-purchase contract under the provisions of the Hire Purchase Act 1965. Also explain to him the legal consequences of the failure to comply with these formalities.

(*b*) Joseph bought a car on hire-purchase for £1,000 (total hire-purchase price). He paid £350 but then fell into arrears. Bright Motors Ltd., the owners, took possession of the car without his consent. Realising the "irregularity" of their action they took the car back and left it outside Joseph's house. Bright Motors Ltd.

regard the contract as being still in force and wish to sue Joseph for the outstanding instalments and the return of the car.

Advise Joseph as to his legal position. *A.C.A., June* 1973.

6. What remedies has an unpaid seller of goods against the goods themselves?

A, whose business was in London, had agreed to send a consignment of diamonds to B at Newcastle. A hired a car from an independent firm and gave the diamonds to the driver with instructions to deliver them at B's address. No sooner had the car left London than A heard that B was insolvent and this was in fact the case. A then telephoned X, a friend in Newcastle, and asked X to get the diamonds back for him. X met the car outside B's office and told the driver to give them to him, but at that moment B came out and persuaded the driver to give them to him instead.

The diamonds are now in the hands of B's trustee in bankruptcy from whom A claims them.

Advise A. *C.I.S., June* 1972.

7. (*a*) Define a contract for the sale of goods and explain what is meant by "goods" in this context.

(*b*) A agreed in writing to sell a yacht to B, but when the agreement was signed they had not yet fixed a price. What would be the legal position if:

    (*i*) the agreement stated that "the price shall be mutually agreed at a later date"; or

    (*ii*) the agreement stated that "the price shall be fixed by C"; or

    (*iii*) no price was mentioned in the agreement at all. *A.C.A., December* 1970.

CHAPTER XI

Carriage of Goods

Carriage of goods, whether by land, sea or air, is usually conducted by persons who make carrying their business and who fall within the category of "common carriers."

COMMON CARRIERS

1. Common carriers. A common carrier is one who offers for hire to transport from place to place, either by land, air or water, the goods of anyone wishing to employ him.

The law traditionally imposes special duties on common carriers, above and beyond those imposed on people who casually, for hire or otherwise, carry goods.

NOTE: A private carrier is a person who carries goods for another in pursuance of some special agreement, e.g. a warehouse company delivering goods to a ship: *Consolidated Tea & Lands Co.* v *Oliver's Wharf* (1910). A private carrier's responsibility is that of an ordinary bailee: *see* XIII, **2.**

2. Position of common carriers. The carrier is bound to carry all goods offered to him at a fair price (which may be demanded in advance), unless (*a*) he has no space, (*b*) the goods are of a kind he does not profess to carry, or (*c*) the destination is not on his normal route, or (*d*) the goods are dangerous or are inadequately packed.

If he unjustifiably refuses to carry goods he may be prosecuted and/or sued for damages.

(Many carriers evade classification as common carriers by reserving in advance the right to refuse to carry any goods at will. Thus A offered to carry various types of goods, while reserving the right to reject any, and to charge varying rates according to the kinds of goods carried, the destination, etc. HELD: He was not a common carrier: *Belfast Ropework Co. Ltd.* v. *Bushell* (1918).)

3. Duties of carriers. It is the duty of any carrier (whether common or not):

(*a*) to deliver at the place directed. This is discharged by delivery at the right place, not necessarily to any particular person;

(*b*) to deliver within a reasonable time, allowing extension of time for unforeseeable delays such as unexpected strikes: *Sims* v. *Midland Rly.* (1913);

(*c*) to obey the instructions of the consignor as to alterations of delivery, etc.;

(*d*) not to deviate unnecessarily from his agreed route.

The carrier's rights are: (*i*) to demand reasonable payment (in advance, if desired), (*ii*) to refuse goods not properly packed, and (*iii*) to claim a lien on the goods carried for his charges.

NOTE: A common carrier has at Common Law a particular lien allowing him to retain the particular goods until his charges are paid. He has no right to use or otherwise dispose of the goods in the absence of express agreement.

4. Liability of common carrier. He is an insurer for the safety of the goods he carries, from the moment they are received by him until they are delivered. He is therefore liable for all damage to the goods, whether occasioned by negligence or not, except where the damage is caused by the following.

(*a*) *Act of God:* an act of nature of such extraordinary description or degree that no reasonable person could be expected to guard against or foresee it, e g. lightning, freak winds, earthquake, etc.

(*b*) *Queen's enemies:* the forces of a state with which this country is at war, e.g capture of the carrier's ship by an enemy warship, but not damage by rioters, rebels, etc., since they are not the forces of an enemy state.

(*c*) *Inherent vice in the goods carried:* some latent defect in the goods themselves, over which no one has control and against which the carrier cannot guard, e.g. in animals, disease not visible when consigned, but not mere normal unruliness or stupidity.

(*d*) *Fault or fraud of the consignor:* although the carrier is bound to insure the safety of the goods, he is not liable for harm caused directly by the negligence of the consignor, e.g. through bad packing.

5. Measure of damages. This will be (a) the value of the goods, assessed at destination on the date of scheduled delivery, or (b) loss attributable to delay or depreciation, etc.

Provided that the carrier must not be made liable for damage other than that which: (a) flows naturally and directly from his breach of duty; plus (b) such additional damage as he should reasonably have foreseen at the time of making the contract: *Hadley* v. *Baxendale* (1854), and *see* V, **27**.

6. Modification of carrier's liability. Save where prohibited by statute, common carriers may vary their legal liability by contract; but the courts interpret exemption clauses strictly, and as far as possible to the disadvantage of the carrier. Exemption clauses by private carriers are less strictly interpreted and may even protect the carrier against liability for theft by his servants: *John Carter Ltd.* v. *H. Hanson Haulage* (*Leeds*) *Ltd.* (1965) But no exemption clause will protect any carrier against a fundamental breach (*see* II, **18** above), e.g. where he consigns a valuable cargo to another carrier without the owner's consent: *Garnham, Harris & Elton Ltd.* v. *Alfred W. Ellis* (*Transport*) *Ltd.* (1967).

NOTE: The Unfair Contract Terms Act 1977 controls and invalidates the use of certain exclusion clauses, except where these are authorised by statute. Clauses excluding or limiting liability arising from negligence causing death or personal injury are void. Where negligence results in some other kind of damage, such as damage to personal property, clauses of this kind are only valid if proved to be reasonable. Other clauses valid only if reasonable are (providing the contract is with a consumer or on the other party's written standard terms): those excluding or restricting liability for breach of contract and those which purport to allow no performance of the contract or one which is substantially different from the performance which was reasonably expected. The first Schedule to the Act states, however that the provisions on negligence resulting in death or personal injury apply to contracts for the carriage of goods by ship or hovercraft, but that the other provisions only apply in favour of a person dealing as a consumer. Furthermore, the same Schedule makes special provision for the carriage of goods by ship or hovercraft in pursuance of a contract which either specifies that as the means of carriage over part of the journey to be covered, or makes no provision as to the means of carriage and does not exclude that means. The position here is that the above provisions concerning negl'gence resulting in death or personal injury apply. The other provisions do not extend to the contract as it operates for and in relation to the carriage of the goods by that means, except in favour of a person dealing as a consumer.

7. Liability of consignor. The consignor must notify the carrier if goods are dangerous, e.g. explosives or combustibles. He is also deemed to warrant the fitness of goods to be carried, and is liable for damages for breach of warranty even if ignorant of an unfitness which causes harm to the carrier.

CARRIAGE BY LAND

8. Two principal statutes. The Carriers Act 1830, and the Transport Act 1962, are the principal statutes governing carriage by land. Otherwise, the applicable rules are those of common law, stated in the preceding section.

9. Carriers Act 1830. This applies only to common carriers (but not to British Rail or carriage of goods by sea). The main provisions of the Act are:

(*a*) The carrier is under no liability for loss or damage to packages containing certain articles, worth all told more than £10, unless at the time of consignment the consignor notified the carrier of the true value and contents of the package. (The carrier may then charge a higher fee for the increased risk. The carrier must post notice of such extra charges at his office; otherwise he is not allowed to charge them. When such higher fee is charged, the consignor may demand a receipt for any payment made.)

Articles covered include: gold, silver, gems, watches, bills and securities, paintings and engravings, title deeds and some other documents, glass, china, furs, etc.

(*b*) A notice alone cannot limit or reduce the carrier's liability: there must be express agreement to that effect.

(*c*) The Act gives no protection to the carrier for loss or damage caused by the crime of the carrier's servants, or the carrier's own negligence. (But the burden of proof is on the consignor.)

(*d*) A carrier is only liable for the real value (of which he may require proof), i.e. he need not accept the consignor's assessmen.

10. Carriage by rail. This is governed by the various Transport Acts, and the Act of 1962 stipulates that British Rail is not to be regarded as a common carrier (and is therefore not subject to the Carriers Act 1830). Contracts for carriage of goods by rail are governed by the B.R. Rules, which envisage two main types of agreement:

(*a*) *Board's risk conditions.* The Board is liable for any loss, misdelivery or damage, unless it can prove Act of God, seizure under legal process, default of consignor (e.g. bad packing, or inherent vice in goods), or wastage through normal conditions.

It may also evade liability for casualty if it can prove it has exercised reasonable care, or there has been fraud by the consignor.

The Board is also usually liable for loss caused by deviation from the scheduled route causing delay unless it can prove that the deviation was not caused by any negligence.

The Board has a general lien for carriage charges and expenses, and other charges outstanding against the owners. Goods may be sold if not claimed within a reasonable time.

(*b*) *Owner's risk conditions.* The Board's liability is lower, so are the carriage charges. The Board is not liable for loss, damage, deviation, misdelivery, delay or detention, save where such is proved to have been caused by wilful misconduct of the Board's servants, including gross negligence.

Negligence is presumed where loss arises through non-delivery of the whole consignment.

NOTE: Damageable goods improperly packed. The Board may refuse such goods, and where it agrees to carry them it is only liable if (*a*) there is wilful misconduct, or (*b*) damage would have occurred even though the goods have been properly packed, and (*c*) the Board would have been liable under Board's risk conditions.

11. Termination of rail transit. Transit ceases when (*a*) the goods are delivered, or (*b*) the sender exercises his right of stoppage in transit, *see* X, **54**, or (*c*) where it is agreed to take goods to a particular depot to await collection—here transit ceases one day after notice of arrival.

12. Notice of claims must be served on the Board within three days of termination of transit, and any claim must be made within

seven days. (If the claim is for non-delivery, the times are
extended to twenty-eight days and forty-two days from commencement of transit.)

13. Passengers' luggage. To make the Board liable, the passenger
must prove (*a*) that the Railway assumed control of the luggage,
and (*b*) that the luggage was "personal luggage," i.e. for the
personal use of the passenger.

Assumption of control is a question of fact in each case.
Putting luggage in the guard's van is indicative of assumption
of control, but the fact that the passenger took the luggage into
the compartment with him does not of itself rule out the possibility that the railway has assumed control.

14. Railway passengers. The Board is not a common carrier of
passengers and therefore (*a*) may refuse any passenger, and (*b*)
does not insure passengers' safety.

The Board can lay down any limitation on contractual or
other liability for the safety of passengers, save that it cannot
impose conditions which (*i*) negative liability for death or
injury, or (*ii*) prescribe a time limit for the enforcement of claims
therefor. This was laid down in the Transport Act 1962, s. 43 (7).
This was repealed and replaced with identical provisions by the
Unfair Contract Terms Act 1977.

15. Carriage by road. Where a passenger is carried by road
transport, in public service vehicles, the contract cannot negative
in any way claims for bodily injury or death of the passenger:
Road Traffic Act 1960, s. 151.

Ordinary common carriers are under the usual liabilities of
common carriers. Private carriers are liable only for negligence,
or as otherwise agreed.

Carriage of goods by road within Britain is largely free of
statutory restrictions, save those laid down by the Carriers
Act 1830, and the various Road Traffic Acts. Where goods are
to be transported internationally within the E.E.C. and some
other countries, carriage is governed by the detailed provisions
of the Carriage of Goods by Road Act 1965. Reference should
also be made to the Carriage by Air and Road Act 1979.

CARRIAGE BY AIR

16. Carriage by air. The Carriage by Air and Road Act 1979
governs international carriage between the United Kingdom and
countries which are parties to the various international con-
ventions dealing with carriage by air.

Under the Act the carrier is liable for loss of goods or injury
to passengers, unless he can establish one of the specified defences, e.g.:

(*a*) that all reasonable precautions were taken for safety of
goods;

(*b*) that loss or injury was due to negligent pilotage or navigation.

Maximum liability (*i*) for death or injury is 250,000 francs,
and (*ii*) for loss or damage to goods is 250 francs per kilo (unless
agreed otherwise). The maximum liability for goods may be
increased by Order in Council, up to 25,000 francs per kilo.

The Carriage by Air Acts (Application of Provisions) Order
1967, applies similar rules to carriage by air within the United
Kingdom, i.e. "non-international" carriage.

CARRIAGE BY SEA

17. Carriage by sea. The owner of a ship may be a common
carrier, and as such (if not protected by contract) is an insurer
of goods carried, subject to the usual general defences, e.g. Act
of God.

Carriage by sea is arranged under a contract called a contract
of affreightment, either in the form of a charterparty or a bill of
lading.

NOTE: Carriage by sea is governed by the normal common law
rules relating to common carriers, save as amended by the
Hague Rules as enacted for Britain by the Carriage of Goods
by Sea Act 1971.

18. Contracts of affreightment. These are normally of two kinds.

(*a*) *Bills of lading.* Usually the shipper arranges with the
owner or master of the ship the amount of freight (the carriage

charge) and the terms of carriage. He gets a receipt for the goods consigned (the mate's receipt) on delivery to the ship, and a bill of lading signed by the master when the goods are actually put on board.

The bill of lading contains the terms of the contract, and must be stamped. The bill usually states that the goods were received in good order and condition (if such was the case), the weights and measures of the goods (if known) and the conditions of carriage.

(b) *Charterparties.* Sometimes a shipper hires a ship for his own sole purposes, i.e. charters it. Under such a charterparty he may take over control of the ship and crew, in which case master and crew become his servants. Such a contract is not really a contract of carriage so much as a lease of the ship.

More usually the shipper charters the ship for a definite voyage, agreeing to take all its freightage space for the voyage or series of voyages, and the master and crew remain the servants of the owners.

19. Implied undertakings by shipowners.

(a) That the ship is seaworthy, i.e. is fit for the particular voyage contemplated. This is an absolute warranty, and breach of it renders the owners liable irrespective of any question of fault or negligence on their part, unless liability is modified by the contract.

Bad stowage may amount to unseaworthiness if it endangers the safety of the ship (not merely the safety of the cargo): *Elder Dempster* v. *Zochonis & Co.* (1924).

If the shipper discovers unseaworthiness before the voyage commences, he may repudiate the contract.

(NOTE: The warranty is not absolute in bills of lading governed by the Carriage by Sea Act 1971.)

(b) That the ship will be ready (i) to load cargo and (ii) to sail, on the agreed date. (If delay is fundamental, the shipper may repudiate the contract; otherwise he can only sue for damages.)

(c) That the ship will not deviate unnecessarily. Deviation to save life is permissible, but deviation to save property is not (except in bills of lading governed by the Carriage of Goods by Sea Act 1971).

Most contracts contain a deviation clause allowing the ship

to call at agreed ports in any order, and to make other necessary
and pre-agreed deviations. But such clauses are strictly construed.

20. Liability of shipowners. The Merchant Shipping Acts
1894–1979, provide that, regarding British ships, no owner,
charterer, manager, or operator, etc., shall be liable for damage
for which he is not personally or jointly responsible in the following cases.

(*a*) *Loss or damage by fire* (even though caused by unseaworthiness).

(*b*) *Loss caused by robbery* of such articles as jewels, watches,
gold, silver, etc., unless the true value was declared by the
consignor at the time of contracting.

(*c*) *Where loss of life or bodily injury* is caused to passengers,
or damage to goods (or to persons other than passengers), by
negligence or default in navigation, the damages payable by
the owners are limited to (*i*) 3,100 gold francs per ton of the
ship's weight for injury to persons, and (*ii*) 1,000 gold francs for
injury to goods.

(*d*) *The dangerous nature of any goods* must be notified to the
shipowner, who may refuse to carry dangerous goods, or charge
additional sums, etc.

21. Freight. The shipowner's carriage charges are called freight
and usually become payable only when (*a*) he has delivered the
goods, or (*b*) he is prevented from delivering them by some fault
of the consignor. Unless otherwise agreed, the person responsible for paying freight is the consignor.

Freight may take the following forms.

(*a*) *Advance freight*, payable before the goods will be delivered.
If through no fault of the shipowner the goods are lost (e.g.
through one of the excepted perils), liability to pay freight
remains.

(*b*) *Lump sum freight*, i.e. a sum payable by a charterer for the
use of the ship. If the ship is ready on the agreed date but no
cargo is loaded, the charterer still becomes liable to pay the
freight.

(*c*) *Pro rata freight*, i.e. a reduced sum payable where (by
agreement) the cargo is delivered at some port other than that
originally agreed.

(*d*) *Dead freight*, i.e. a sum payable by way of compensation for loss of revenue where a charterer fails in a promise to provide a full and complete cargo.

22. General and particular average. Three types of proprietary interest are risked in sea voyages: the ship (owner's interest), the freight (charterer's interest), and the cargo (cargo owner's interest). Loss sustained by any one interest must usually be borne by that interest alone, and is called a particular average loss, e.g. cost of damage to the ship, falling on the owner alone.

But if one interest suffers loss by reason of damage or expense incurred on behalf of the whole venture (i.e. on behalf of all three interests), such loss must be averaged out over all three interests, and the other two must contribute compensations to the interest which has sustained loss, i.e. a general average assessment is made. (*See also* Marine Insurance: XII, **26**.)

General average contributions can only be claimed where:

(*a*) the danger was common to all, and was real danger, e.g. not a false alarm;

(*b*) the party claiming contribution must not have caused the danger;

(*c*) the interest against which contribution is claimed must have been saved.

23. The Athens Convention 1974. This Convention has been effectively brought into force by the Unfair Contract Terms Act 1977, s. 28. In effect, a shipowner can limit his liability in negligence for personal injury to approximately £30,000 for each passenger, and is further able to apply a total limit to each incident which may give rise to claims other than passenger claims. Where both limits apply, the total limit for the incident may effectively reduce the limit for each passenger to a figure below £30,000.

BILLS OF LADING

24. Bill of lading. A document signed by the master, the shipowner, or his agent, specifying the goods shipped and setting out the terms of carriage.

Such a document is a receipt, evidence of contract, and a document of title to the goods. A bill of lading is not a negotiable instrument, but does entitle the holder to delivery of the goods; and property in the goods passes to the transferee of a bill on indorsement of the bill to him.

25. Carriage of Goods by Sea Act 1971. This Act (based on the international Hague Rules) govern all bills of lading for the carriage of goods from any port in Great Britain or Northern Ireland.

The 1971 Act provides the following.

(*a*) There is no absolute warranty as to seaworthiness: s. 3.

(*b*) Bills governed by the Act must contain (*i*) particulars of identification of the goods (by "leading marks" stamped upon them), (*ii*) the number of pieces shipped, (*iii*) the condition of the goods as they appear on inspection. This statement is evidence of their receipt in the stated condition.

The shipper is deemed to guarantee the accuracy of particulars furnished by him to the carrier.

(*c*) Statements as to apparent condition of goods refer only to external appearance, i.e. defects apparent on reasonable inspection.

(*d*) A bill of lading is prima facie evidence of receipt by the carrier of the stated goods, but the master's signature does not estop the owner from proving (*i*) that the goods were not in fact shipped, or (*ii*) that the owner's agent acted without authority—where this happens the agent himself may be liable to breach of warranty of authority: *V/o Rasnoimport* v. *Guthrie and Co. Ltd.* (1966).

(*e*) The Act implies that the shipowner will (*i*) use reasonable diligence to make the ship seaworthy, (*ii*) properly man and equip it, (*iii*) provide adequate hold storage, refrigeration plant, etc., and (*iv*) use reasonable care in loading and unloading, or that his agents will do so. (The burden of proving compliance with these requirements is on the shipowner.)

(*f*) Excepted perils. The shipowner is not liable for damage due to (*i*) negligence or default by the master, crew, etc., in navigating or managing the ship at sea (not in dock), (*ii*) fire, (*iii*) accidents of navigation, (*iv*) Act of God, (*v*) war, (*vi*) strikes and lock-outs, (*vii*) riots and civil commotion, (*viii*) saving life or property at sea, (*ix*) wastage due to inherent vice in the goods, (*x*) inadequate packing, or other fault of the consignor, (*xi*) latent defects not discoverable by careful inspection.

These exemptions only apply provided that loss is not occasioned by the negligence or default of the carrier or his servants
or agents, including stevedores: *Leesh River Tea Co. Ltd.* v.
British India S.N. Co. Ltd. (1966).

(g) The carrier cannot contract out of or reduce his liability
under the Act. However when the value of the goods is declared
beforehand the carrier may limit his liability to 10,000 gold
francs per kilo whichever is the higher. There are special provisions for containers.

The defences given to the carrier are extended to his servants
or agents. Neither he nor they are entitled to limit the damage if
it resulted from acts *or* omissions done with intent to cause
damage, or recklessly, and knowing damage would probably
result.

CHARTERPARTIES

26. Charterparties. A charterparty is a contract whereby a
charterer hires a ship for the carriage of cargo on a particular
voyage (a voyage charter) or for a period of time (a time charter).
Possession of the ship and control of the crew usually remain
with the owner, but occasionally the ship is completely leased to
the charterer (a charter by demise), and he may provide his own
crew.

A charterparty differs from a bill of lading in that it deals with
the whole ship, while a bill does not.

27. Form of charterparty. It must be in writing and usually
contains the following.

(a) A statement of the ship's tonnage (so that its cargo capacity
can be assessed). A substantial inaccuracy in tonnage gives rise
to a right of action for breach of warranty.

(b) A statement of the ship's whereabouts, which is a condition
of the contract and if untrue entitles the charterer to repudiate
the contract: *Behn* v. *Burness* (1863).

A charterparty may also contain a paramount clause, i.e.
one which stipulates that the liability of the shipowner shall be
limited in the manner provided by bills of lading covered by the
Carriage of Goods by Sea Act 1971.

28. Usual terms. In a voyage charter the following terms are
usually included.

(a) An undertaking by the owner that on the agreed date the ship will be seaworthy, fully provisioned and ready to sail when loaded, to the agreed port of destination.

(b) An "excepted perils" clause, protecting the owner from liability for loss caused by Act of God or the Queen's enemies, restraint of princes (interference by a foreign state), barratry (wilful default by the master, mutiny by the crew, etc.) and perils of the sea, e.g. natural disasters, storms, icebergs.

(c) An undertaking by the charterer to complete loading and unloading within a certain number of days (called lay days) and to pay compensation (called demurrage) for undue delay.

Sometimes the charterparty also provides that if the charterer completes loading and unloading more quickly than agreed, the freight charge shall be reduced; the reduction is called dispatch money.

29. Shipowner's implied undertakings. The following undertakings by shipowners are implied by law in all charterparties.

(a) That the ship will be seaworthy.

(b) That it will be ready to load and sail on the agreed dates (substantial delay may amount to breach of condition; trifling delay is merely breach of warranty).

(c) That the ship will not deviate from its route except for good cause, or as agreed in the contract.

Good cause usually means where necessitated by (i) the safety of the ship, or (ii) for the purpose of saving life (not merely property).

30. Full and complete cargo. A charterparty sometimes binds the charterer to provide the ship with a full and complete cargo, i.e. as much as the ship can safely carry (excluding deck loading, unless otherwise agreed). If a particular quantity of cargo is agreed (usually measured in tons), the charterer discharges his obligation if he provides approximately that quantity, even though he fails to take all available space.

If the charterer fails to provide the agreed full and complete cargo, the shipowner (unless otherwise agreed) can:

(a) charge the charterer dead freight, i.e. damages for loss of revenue for the unoccupied space; or

(b) deviate from his route to collect supplementary cargo.

31. Cesser and lien clauses. These are usually inserted and provide the following.

(*a*) *Cesser clause:* the charterer's liability under the charter-party is to cease as soon as the agreed cargo is loaded.

(*b*) *Lien clause:* the master and owners are given a lien on the cargo for the unpaid freight and for demurrage charges.

SPECIMEN QUESTIONS

1. State the forms which a contract of affreightment may take, and mention what undertakings by the shipowner or carrier are implied in every contract of affreightment.

Explain what is meant by "deviation" and state the effect thereof. In what circumstances is deviation allowable by statute or otherwise? *C.I.S., Final, December* 1961.

2. (*a*) Who is a "common carrier" and how does his position in law differ from that of a "private carrier"?

(*b*) Miss E contracted with G, a local removal man, that he move her furniture from London to Brighton. One of the conditions of the contract was that G would not be responsible for loss or damage by fire. During transit one of the removal men carelessly dropped a cigarette in the van. The van caught fire and Miss E's furniture was lost. Consider with reasons whether Miss E will be able to recover damages from G. *C.I.S., Final, December* 1963.

3. (*a*) What is a bill of lading and what are its functions? What is the legal effect of a statement in a bill of lading that the goods are "in apparent good order and condition?"

(*b*) What provisions are implied in a bill of lading to which the Carriage of Goods by Sea Act 1924 applies? *C.I.S., June* 1970.

4. The K Shipping Co. agreed to carry a cargo of pig iron for the J Co. from the United Kingdom to Australia. It was within the terms of the charterparty that the ship should call at a port in the Island of Rebellia. Upon approaching that island the ship's captain was warned by a radio message from Rebellia that there was a revolution in progress, and that shipping should avoid the port. The captain, nevertheless, entered the harbour whereupon the vessel was seized by the rebels. When it was released six months later the voyage was continued. At the time of delivery of the cargo at Sydney, the price of pig iron having fallen heavily,

interest, without invalidating the policy. Thus the assignee of a policy, who has no insurable interest, may still be able to enforce it: for this reason life policies can be assigned as securities—*see* below.

7. Assignment by way of mortgage. A life policy can be used as security for a loan (e.g. by a bank). The methods by which this can be achieved are as follows.

(*a*) Legal assignment to the creditor (who must then give the notice to the insurer required by the P.A.A. 1867).

NOTE: (1) The assignment must be under seal; (2) the assignee can sue in his own name; (3) the insurer holds the policy moneys for the benefit of the assignee; and (4) the assignee gains priority from the date of registration.

(*b*) Equitable assignment to the creditor, by deposit of the policy plus a memorandum of the reasons for deposit.

On redemption of a legal mortgage of a policy, the mortgagee reassigns the policy to the mortgagor. When an equitable mortgage is redeemed, no formal reassignment is necessary: the lender merely cancels the memorandum of deposit and returns the policy.

8. Life policies as securities. They have several advantages and disadvantages as securities.

(*a*) *Advantages:* (*i*) methods of mortgaging are simple; (*ii*) the surrender value of the policy is increased by each payment of premium, so that the value of the security will appreciate as long as premiums are paid; (*iii*) the policy can be realised immediately (if, for instance, the insured fails to pay his premiums when due) by surrender to the insurer; (*iv*) death of the insured makes the moneys assured immediately available.

(*b*) *Disadvantages:* (*i*) the mortgagee is to some extent at the mercy of the person paying the premiums, and his default may invalidate the policy; (*ii*) the insurer may be able to avoid the policy if the proposer failed to disclose all material facts; (*iii*) suicide of the insured may invalidate the policy; (*iv*) the policy may contain provision for avoidance by the insurer on breach of various covenants by the insured.

FIRE INSURANCE

9. The contract. A contract of fire insurance is one providing for indemnification of the insured up to a certain amount in the event of injury or loss by fire, caused to a specified property during a specified time.

The insured can only recover for actual loss: *Castellain* v. *Preston* (1883).

The proposer must have an insurable interest in the property insured: Life Assurances Act 1774, s. 1. Owners, tenants, trustees, and mortgagees have insurable interests, but a shareholder in a company has no insurable interest in the property of the company.

NOTE: To discourage people setting fire to their own property in order to get insurance money, the Fire Prevention (Metropolis) Act 1774, s. 83, provides that any person interested in the property (such as a tenant, mortgagee, etc.) can compel the insured to use the money in repairing and reinstating the damaged premises.

10. Average clauses. A fire policy often contains an average clause which provides that the insured can only recover such proportion of the loss caused by fire as the value of the policy bears to the value of the property insured.

Thus, if property worth £5,000 is insured for only £2,500 and fire damage is caused to the extent of £2,500, the insurer can refuse to pay more than half this amount.

11. Subrogation. On payment of all moneys due under the policy, the insurer is entitled to be subrogated to the rights of the insured, i.e. to pursue any remedies available in the insured in contract or tort in respect of the loss. Thus if the fire was caused by the negligence of X, the insurer (after paying out on the policy) could sue X for his negligence.

If the insured forestalls this right of subrogation by discharging or waiving any claim against such third parties, the insurer is likewise discharged from liability under the policy to the same extent: *Phoenix Assurance Co.* v. *Spooner* (1905).

Subrogation is only available where the insurer has paid the whole claim of the insured, and any action can only be brought in the name of the insured.

12. Excepted perils. Risks covered include loss by fire (even though caused by the insured's own negligence, but not if caused by his wilful default), and loss occasioned by a fire brigade in putting out the fire.

Excepted perils include riot, civil commotion, war, explosion, and sometimes Act of God.

A policy will not cover consequential loss (such as loss of profits of a business), unless expressly so agreed.

ACCIDENT, BURGLARY, AND OTHER FORMS OF INSURANCE

13. The contract. The same general rules apply as with life and fire insurance. Note that burglary insurance is a form of indemnity insurance (i.e. compensation for actual loss), while accident insurance is often lump sum insurance (i.e. stipulating for the payment of a lump sum on the occurrence of a specified event).

Policies in this class usually provide that notice of the burglary, accident, etc., must be given to the insurer within a specified time, failing which the insurer may be discharged from liability: *Re Williams & Thomas* (1902). The Unfair Contract Terms Act 1977 does not apply to contracts of insurance: Schedule 1.

EXAMPLE: Diamond merchants insured their wares but failed to disclose a fact they considered immaterial, i.e. that their sales manager had been convicted of smuggling diamonds in the U.S.A. eight years previously. Later they were robbed of diamonds and claimed under the policy. HELD: Even though the manager was not involved in the robbery, his conviction was a material fact and should have been disclosed in the proposal—the claim was dismissed: *Roselodge Ltd.* v. *Castle* (1966).

14. Burglary insurance. The policy usually provides cover against house-breaking and theft from the premises insured. Cover is restricted to the premises agreed.

15. Accident policies. These usually provide for the payment of a lump sum in the event of death by accident, and of smaller sums in other eventualities. Provision may also be made for payment of weekly sums during disability, sickness, etc.

The policy usually covers only accidents (or sickness) to the insured alone, though other persons may be included if so desired.

(*a*) *Accidents to the insured.* Cover is for personal injury or death, caused by chance or by the negligent or intentional act of any third person, e.g. assault. It will not cover injuries deliberately self-inflicted.

(*b*) *Accidents to third parties*, e.g. to passengers in the insured person's car, or a visitor to his premises, etc. Such cover gives the injured person a right to sue the insurer for the sum assured if (*i*) the insured becomes bankrupt, or makes any composition with his creditors, or (*ii*) is a company which goes into liquidation. Otherwise only the insured can sue: Third Parties (Rights against Insurers) Act 1930.

NOTE: All motorists must be insured against injury to third parties and in addition passengers must be covered by the driver's insurance (even if they have agreed to travel at their "own risk"): Road Traffic Act 1972. A person injured by a car who obtains judgment against the motorist can recover the damages awarded in that action from the motorist's insurer: Road Traffic Act 1972, ss. 149, 150. In such policies, restrictions on the insurer's liability because of the age or condition of the assured or of the car (provided the car is roadworthy), or of the load carried, are void.

MARINE INSURANCE

16. The contract. This is a contract whereby the insurer (underwriter) promises to indemnify the insured against loss caused by maritime perils: Marine Insurance Act 1906, s. 1.

Maritime perils means perils at sea, but the policy may be extended to cover inland navigation: M.I.A. 1906, s. 2.

17. Insurable interest. The insured must have an insurable interest in the vessel, or in the maritime venture at the time of the loss: s. 5.

Persons having insurable interests include mortgagees of a ship, lenders of money on security of the ship and/or freight ("bottomry"), or on the security of the cargo ("respondentia"), the master and crew to the extent of their wages, the owners of the ship, cargo, etc.; the underwriter himself (who can thus re-insure against his own risk as insurer).

18. Duty of disclosure. The contract, like all insurance contracts, is *uberrimae fidei* and full disclosure must be made of facts which materially affect the risk.

Matters need not be disclosed if: (*a*) they diminish the risk, or (*b*) are waived, or (*c*) may be deemed to be known in the ordinary course of trade.

Where the contract is made by an agent, he must disclose all facts which are known (or should be known) to his principal.

19. Kinds of policy.

(*a*) *Voyage policies*, to insure for a voyage from one place to another, i.e. a particular voyage.

(*b*) *Time policies*, which provide cover for a stated period. (This must not be longer than twelve months, subject to any renewals at the end of the twelve months.)

(*c*) *Mixed policies*, i.e. a combination of Voyage and Time cover.

(*d*) *Valued policies*, where the value insured is specified.

(*e*) *Unvalued policies*, where the value insured is not specified but is left open for assessment in accordance with customary usage if the occasion arises.

(*f*) *Floating policies*, where the name of the ship is left blank so that the policy is available for any ship owned by the insurer.

(*g*) *Open cover*. This is not an actual insurance policy, but a contract to issue a policy at a given time or on the occurrence of a particular event.

(*h*) *Re-insurance*, where the underwriter himself insures against his own liability under a marine insurance policy.

20. Measure of indemnity. The assured can only recover for actual loss. If the loss is total, he is entitled to the maximum sum assured by the policy whatever that may be.

In the case of partial loss the position is as follows.

(*a*) *Partial loss to ship*. The insured can recover the cost of repairs, or the amount of depreciation if the ship is not repaired.

(*b*) *Partial loss of goods*. The insured can recover the value of goods lost, or if the policy is a valued policy the loss calculated as a proportion of the total amount assured.

21. Warranties. In marine insurance the word warranty is largely used in the same sense as the word condition in ordinary contracts, and means that the assured undertakes absolutely that something shall be done or some requirement fulfilled, or affirms or denies the existence of particular facts.

Such a warranty must be exactly complied with, otherwise the policy will be avoided: M.I.A. 1906, s. 33.

Warranties may be expressed or implied by the Marine Insurance Act 1906.

22. Implied warranties.

(*a*) In a voyage policy (*i*) that the ship shall be seaworthy at the start of the voyage: s. 39, (*ii*) that the ship is normally fit to carry any goods insured: s. 40.

(*b*) Generally, (*i*) that the adventure is legal: s. 41, (*ii*) if cover is granted for the ship in port, that she shall be reasonably fit to meet the hazards of the port: s. 39.

(There are no implied warranties covering (*i*) the nationality of the ship, or the seaworthiness of a ship covered by a time policy, or (*ii*) that goods insured are seaworthy.)

23. Premiums.
These must normally be paid before the policy is issued, and are returnable as and when agreed, or where the policy is void for any reason, or where in an unvalued policy the venture has been over-insured: s. 84.

24. Risks covered.
These include all the normal risks of sea journeys, loss from fire, pirates or thieves, barratry (wilful misconduct by master or crew), and collision (up to three-quarters of the damage sustained).

The insurers are only bound to compensate for direct loss, and consequential loss (e.g. loss of profits) requires express cover.

25. Loss may be total or partial.
Total loss may be either actual or constructive.

(*a*) *Actual*. The property covered is destroyed or is so changed as to have changed its character entirely, or where the assured is deprived of its use. (Actual loss may be presumed if a ship is missing for an unreasonable time, and no information can be obtained as to its whereabouts).

(*b*) *Constructive*. The property covered is reasonably abandoned in circumstances which make it appear that total loss is inevitable, e.g. where the crew leaves a sinking ship, of which no more is heard.

(Where there is constructive total loss, the insured may treat it as partial loss if he wishes, or may relinquish his property to the insurer who may salvage it if possible. In the latter case he must give notice of abandonment to the insurer, and acceptance of such notice is conclusive evidence that the insurer admits liability.)

26. General average loss. Where a general average loss has occurred, the assured may recover the total value assured from the insurer who may then (by subrogation) recover his due contribution from the other parties' liability.

(For meaning of general average, *see* Carriage of Goods, XI, **22**.)

27. Assignment of policy. Unless prohibited by the contract, a marine policy can be assigned by indorsement: s. 50. The assignment is subject to equities in the normal way. It may be made either before or after loss.

28. Discharge of insurer. In a voyage policy the insurer is automatically discharged if the ship (*a*) sails from a port other than specified in the policy, or (*b*) deviates unreasonably from the scheduled route (in which case discharge dates from the time of deviation).

Deviation is excused (*i*) where authorised by the policy, or (*ii*) where for the purpose of saving life (not property), or (*iii*) where necessary to obtain medical aid for any person aboard the ship, or (*iv*) where necessary for the safety of the ship, or (*v*) otherwise where caused by circumstances beyond the control of the master or his employer.

STATE SUPERVISION

29. Insurance Companies Act. The activities of insurance companies are regulated by the Insurance Companies Act 1974. Incorporated bodies and most that are unincorporated require Government approval before transacting insurance business. Members of Lloyds and other associations approved by the Government need no prior authorisation. No new business will obtain authorisation unless assets exceed liabilities by at least £50,000. Existing businesses need wider margins. An insurance company must have at least £100,000 paid up capital. Every director, controller and manager of an insurance company must be a "fit and proper person". Advertisements and statements must not mislead; and from 1st January 1980 long-term assured persons will have a ten-day cooling-off period. The Insurance Companies Act 1981 further amends the law relating to insurance companies by restricting the carrying on of insurance business and contains provisions for the regulation of insurance companies.

30. Policyholders' protection. If an insurance company fails, the

Policyholders' Protection Board, appointed under the Policy-holders' Protection Act 1975, takes over. The Board is financed by levies on insurance companies authorised to conduct business in the United Kingdom under the Insurance Companies Act 1974. The Board ensures that insured persons are not left without cover.

31. Brokers. These are required to be registered under the Insurance Brokers (Registration) Act 1975.

SPECIMEN QUESTIONS

1. Explain the expression "insurable interest" in connection with a contract of marine insurance; and state what persons possess an insurable interest in such a contract.

What duty of disclosure rests on the assured? *C.I.S., Final, December* 1962.

2. (*a*) What is the nature of a contract created by a fire insurance policy?

(*b*) A is insured with several companies in respect of the same property to an amount exceeding the value of the property. In the event of a loss through fire what are the rights of A and the insurance companies? *I.C.A., Final, May* 1962.

3. Adam made a proposal to an insurance company for an insurance on his life for £5,000. On the proposal form he answered various questions truthfully and disclosed all relevant facts. A few days later, but before the proposal was definitely accepted, Adam was taken ill with pneumonia. Subsequently the company accepted the proposal and the first premium was paid. Two days later Adam died of pneumonia and the company learned for the first time of his illness. Is the company liable to pay the £5,000? *I.C.A., Final, November* 1962.

4. (*a*) What is meant by a warranty in a contract of marine insurance? How does it differ from a warranty in a contract for the sale of goods?

(*b*) What warranties are implied in a contract of marine insurance? *C.I.S., Final, December* 1964.

5. In respect of a contract of insurance explain what is meant by

(*a*) an insurable interest;

(*b*) subrogation.

Give examples of the former and illustrate the operation of the latter by reference to a set of facts which you may devise for this purpose. *C.I.S., June* 1972.

CHAPTER XIII

Bailment

NATURE AND KINDS OF BAILMENT

1. Definition of bailment. A bailment is a delivery of goods by one person to another for some limited purpose, on condition that when the purpose has been accomplished the goods shall be returned.

The bailment may be simple or exclusive. In an exclusive bailment the bailee (the person to whom the goods are bailed) can during the continuance of the bailment retain the goods against anyone, including the bailor, e.g. a pledge or pawn of goods: *see* XVI, **9** below. In a simple bailment the bailee can defend his possession against anyone, except the bailor.

2. Duties of bailee. These are defined by common law, though the duties of an "involuntary bailee" are now regulated by the Unsolicited Goods & Services Acts 1971 and 1975: *see* **3** below.

(*a*) To take reasonable care of the goods bailed to him. If goods are lost or damaged the onus is on the bailee to prove that he did exercise reasonable care, irrespective of whether the bailment was for reward or was gratuitous: *Houghland* v. *R. R. Low* (*Luxury Coaches*) *Ltd.* (1962).

(*b*) To return the goods in accordance with the contract. If he fails to do so, he is liable for loss or damage notwithstanding the exercise of reasonable care. If he entrusts goods to a servant who steals them, the bailee is liable in conversion to the bailor: *Shaw & Co.* v. *Symmons & Sons Ltd.* (1917).

(Contracts of bailment frequently contain a clause restricting the duty of care or excluding it, but if the bailee returns the goods to the wrong person he has no protection from such a clause: *Alexander* v. *Rly. Executive* (1951), and *see* **5** and **11** below.)

NOTE: (*i*) The burden of proving exercise of reasonable care is on the bailee. Therefore if he has lost the goods or they are damaged when returned, it is for the bailee to prove that loss or damage was not due to his negligence.

(*ii*) If goods are lost or damaged while in his custody, and the bailee cannot show how this happened, he is liable: *Houghland* v. *R. R. Low Ltd.* (1962): *Levison* v. *Patent Steam Carpet Cleaning Co. Ltd.* (1977); *Port Swettenham Authority* v. *T. W. Wu & Co.* (1978); *Mitchell.* v. *London Borough of Ealing* (1978).

(*iii*) If goods are lost while in his custody it is not enough for the bailee to show that he was reasonably careful to protect them; he must show also that he made reasonable efforts to recover them: *Codman* v. *Hill* (1919).

(*iv*) The bailee is liable for the negligence or dishonesty of his servants, if he did not use reasonable care in selecting them, e.g. where he entrusts goods bailed to a known thief: *Williams* v. *Curzon Syndicate Ltd.* (1919). But he is not generally liable for wrongs committed by his independent contractors, or by servants if he can show he was reasonably careful in his selection of them.

(*v*) If the bailee professes a particular skill, he is liable if he fails to exercise that skill, even if the bailment is gratuitous: *Wilson* v. *Brett* (1843).

(*vi*) The bailee is not liable for loss or damage occasioned by Act of God (inevitable and unforseeable accident), robbery with violence, or war.

(*vii*) Where there is no express contract between the parties, the duties of the bailee arise from the law of tort: *Chesworth* v. *Farrar* (1966).

3. Involuntary bailees. By the Unsolicited Goods & Services Acts 1971 and 1975, where a person becomes an involuntary bailee e.g. has unsolicited goods delivered to him by post, so that he can not easily refuse to take delivery) the following rules apply.

(*a*) The goods become the property of the recipient:

(*i*) after thirty days, if he has served notice on the sender with a demand for removal of the goods, or

(*ii*) after six months, if no notice has been given to the sender.

(*b*) These rules do not apply if the goods were sent for the purposes of the recipient's trade or business.

4. Duty of bailor. If the goods are bailed for a particular purpose of which the bailor knows, e.g. hire of a car, he is under a duty to disclose any defect rendering the goods unsuitable for that purpose.

He impliedly warrants the fitness of the goods hired, and owes a duty of reasonable care, i.e. he is not liable as regards defects of which he had no knowledge or reasonable opportunity of knowledge.

(In other types of bailment the bailor generally owes no duty of care, except a duty to warn the bailee if goods are dangerous, e.g. where explosives are deposited in a cloakroom.)

5. Particular contracts. The bailee may by express terms seek to exclude liability for negligence, particularly in bailments for reward. Such terms must be clear and unambiguous and are generally construed against the bailee as far as possible, under the *contra proferentem* rule: *Morris* v. *C. W. Martin & Sons Ltd.* (1965): *Levison* v. *Patent Steam Carpet Cleaning Cleaning Co. Ltd.* (1977).

Thus the bailee loses the protection of such exemption clauses if he breaks the contract in some other way, e.g. by delivering goods to the wrong person: *Alexander* v. *Rly. Executive* (1951).

EXAMPLES: (*a*) If the bailment is a contract for personal service, the bailee loses the protection of exemption clauses if he breaks his contract by delegating performance to another, e.g. where a laundry accepted articles "at owner's risk entirely" and then delivered them for cleaning to another firm which lost them: *Davies* v. *Collins* (1945). (*b*) The bailee is liable if he deviates from the contract, and cannot then rely on exemption clauses, e.g. where he undertakes to store goods at a certain warehouse but in fact warehouses them elsewhere and they are lost: *Lilley* v. *Doubleday* (1881). (*c*) The bailee also loses the benefit of exemption clauses if he or his agent misrepresents the effect of the clauses: *Curtis* v. *Chemical Cleaning & Dyeing Co.* (1951).

NOTE: *See* further **11** below.

6. Bailee's power of sale. A bailee cannot sell or otherwise dispose of goods bailed unless:

(*a*) the contract so provides; or
(*b*) a right of sale is conferred by statute.

Otherwise if he sells goods bailed he is liable for damages for the tort of conversion, i.e. converting to his own use and disposition goods to which another is entitled.

A statutory power of sale of uncollected goods is given by the

Innkeepers Act 1878, The Pawnbrokers Acts and the Torts (Interference with Goods) Act 1977.

For the 1977 Act to apply, the goods must be in the control or possession of the bailee, where:

(a) the bailor is obliged to take delivery or could give directions as to their delivery; or

(b) the bailee could impose such an obligation, but cannot trace or communicate with the bailor; or

(c) the bailee can reasonably expect to be relieved of any duty to safeguard the goods on giving notice, but cannot trace or communicate with the bailor.

The Act makes special provision for goods accepted for repair or other treatment, goods accepted for valuation or appraisal, and the storage, warehousing and the like, of goods.

If the bailor fails to collect his goods after the prescribed notice has been given (or after the bailee has made reasonable attempts, but failed, to give such notice) the bailee may sell the goods. He must account over to the bailor less the costs of sale and sums outstanding.

7. Types of bailment.

(a) *Deposit* (*depositum*), means goods are deposited for safe custody, e.g. in a cloakroom. The bailee cannot use the goods and must (subject to any terms of the contract) exercise reasonable care of them while in his possession. He must return them to the bailor, and no exemptionary clause will protect him if he delivers them to the wrong person: *Alexander* v. *Railway Exec.*

(b) *Loan for use* (*commodatum*). The bailee is entitled to use the goods loaned and is not liable for fair wear and tear, unless he deviates from the conditions of the loan.

(c) *Hire* (*locatio rei*). Here the bailor impliedly warrants the fitness of the goods bailed for the purpose hired. The bailee must take reasonable care of the goods and use them in accordance with the terms of the contract. He is not liable for loss by robbery, accidental fire occasioned without negligence, etc. In a hire for reward the owner cannot usually reclaim the goods save in accordance with the terms of the contract, i.e. the bailment is exclusive.

Hiring is automatically determined (even in hire-purchase contracts) if the hirer attempts to sell the goods: *Helby* v. *Matthews* (1895).

(*d*) *Innkeepers.* They are bailees of their guests' luggage in certain circumstances: *see* **8, 9** below.

(*e*) *Deposit for work to be done* (*locatio operis faciendi*), e.g. deposit for repair or alteration. The bailee must take care of the goods and hand them to the true owner or his agent when requested, but he has a lien over the goods for his charges and need not return them until his charges are paid.

(*f*) *Pawn or pledge* (*vadium*) of chattels as security for a loan: *see* XVI, **9**.

(*g*) *A consumer hire agreement.* This is an agreement capable of lasting for more than three months and where the rental does not exceed £5,000: Consumer Credit Act 1974, s. 15. When this Act is fully in force, various formalities will attach to make such agreements. The hirer (the bailee) will also have the right to terminate most agreements after eighteen months: s. 101.

NOTE: A hire-purchase agreement is *not* a consumer hire agreement.

8. Innkeepers and guests. A hotel or innkeeper is one who holds himself out as ready to receive all travellers who: (*a*) are willing to pay a reasonable price for accommodation offered, and (*b*) come in a condition fit to be received: Hotel Proprietors Act 1956, s. 1.

An innkeeper must accept all travellers provided he has enough room and they are willing to pay and are in a reasonably fit condition to be received. Failure to accept *bona fide* travellers renders him liable to an action for damages: *Browne* v. *Brandt* (1902), and possibly to prosecution.

Any person is a traveller who calls for a meal or a drink: *Williams* v. *Linnitt* (1951). But he is only entitled to protection for his luggage if he stays to take sleeping accommodation.

9. Innkeeper's liability. The inn or hotel keeper is an insurer of his guests' luggage (but not of their pet animals, cars, etc.), and can only evade liability for loss or damage by showing that it was caused by: (*a*) Act of God, (*b*) war, (*c*) guest's own negligence (though leaving luggage in an unlocked room is not usually such negligence: *Brewster* v. *Drennan* (1945)), or (*d*) inherent vice in the goods themselves.

By the Hotel Proprietors Act 1956, the innkeeper's liability is restricted to £50 for any one article or a total of £100 for any one guest, unless:

(*a*) loss or damage was caused by the wilful default or negligence of the innkeeper or his servants; or

(*b*) the goods were expressly deposited with the innkeeper for safe custody in some place specially provided, e.g. the hotel safe.

A notice of these restrictions on liability must be given to the guest before or at the time of registering (when the contract is made), and a notice placed in the room is therefore inadequate: *Olley* v. *Marlborough Court Hotel* (1949).

Such notice must be prominently displayed at or near the reception office and/or in the main hall of the hotel. If not so displayed the innkeeper loses the protection of the Act.

10. Innkeeper's lien. The innkeeper has a right to retain all a guest's luggage for non-payment of his charges. The lien does not extend to things over which the innkeeper owes no duty of care, e.g. the guest's car or pet animals.

The lien is lost if the guest is allowed to remove the goods; there is no power to detain the guest himself.

By the Innkeepers Act 1878, the hotelier is given a statutory right to sell such goods as are subject to his lien, and reimburse himself for his charges out of the proceeds of sale. The right to sell becomes exercisable when the goods have been retained for six weeks; and one month's notice of the sale must be given to the guest to give him a final chance to pay the bill.

11. Exclusion clauses. Where goods are received under a bailment (but not a hire-purchase agreement), exclusion clauses are ineffective against a consumer to exclude or restrict liability in relation to correspondence with description, quality or fitness for purpose. As against someone who is not a consumer, such clauses are valid if they can be shown to be reasonable. Liability in respect of the right to give possession and the assurance of quiet possession can be excluded if the clause is shown to be reasonable. This applies to consumers and non-consumers alike. These provisions are all contained in the Unfair Contract Terms Act 1977, s. 7.

SPECIMEN QUESTIONS

1. To what extent is the borrower of goods loaned to him for use under a duty to take care of the goods?

B deposited a motor van with a firm of garage proprietors for sale on commission upon the terms of a printed document which stated that "customers vehicles are driven by our staff at customers' sole risk." While the van was being demonstrated to a prospective buyer, it was damaged through the negligence of one of the staff. Discuss the legal position. *C.I.S., Final, December* 1962.

2. Explain the nature of a bailment. Mention three forms which bailment may take, and explain the nature of the consideration which will support a contract of bailment.

B contracted to warehouse D's furniture at B's depository in Chelsea, but B warehoused a part of the furniture at a depository in Fulham. The furniture warehouse at Fulham was destroyed by fire. Discuss the legal position. *C.I.S., Final, June* 1961.

3. (*a*) Define the term "bailee." What are the duties of a bailee of goods?

(*b*) Fred has received an unsolicited parcel of goods from Innertia Sales Ltd. Fred has written to Innertia Sales Ltd. informing them that he does not wish to buy the goods sent and that he wishes them to be removed from his premises as soon as possible.

For six weeks Fred did not hear from Innertia Sales Ltd. and eventually decided to sell the goods.

Now Fred has received a letter from Innertia Sales Ltd. demanding payment and threatening legal proceedings if the payment is not made by return of post.

Advise Fred.

Would your answer be different if Fred had not written to Innertia Sales Ltd. requiring them to remove the goods? *A.C.A., June* 1973.

CHAPTER XIV

Arbitration and Awards

ARBITRATION

1. Reference to arbitration. Arbitration in mercantile disputes
is now mainly governed by the Arbitration Act 1950, the Arbitration Act 1975 and the Arbitration Act 1979. A dispute may be
referred to arbitration in the following ways.

(*a*) *By Order of the Court.* The Rules of the Supreme Court
provide that the court may refer settlement of disputes to
official referees, Masters of the Court, registrars, district registrars, etc. The reference may relate to a specified issue (e.g. the
costs in an action before the court), or to the whole dispute.
Reference by the court usually occurs in cases where some
special technical or local knowledge is required, and all the parties
consent to the dispute going before a specially qualified arbitrator.

(*b*) *By certain statutes* which may provide that disputes arising
under the statute are to be settled by arbitration. The statute
may then lay down special rules for the conduct of the arbitration
(otherwise the Arbitration Act 1950 will normally apply).

(*c*) *By consent of the parties,* out of court, e.g. under an arbitration clause in a contract. An arbitration agreement is "a *written*
agreement to submit present or future differences to arbitration,
whether an arbitrator is named therein or not": *A.A.*, 1950, s. 32.
An agreement to submit to arbitration is not an exclusion clause:
Unfair Contract Terms Act 1977, s. 13. Oral agreements are valid
but are not covered by the Arbitration Act.

(Contrast a Valuation, which is made before any dispute
arises and in order to forestall disagreement.)

(*d*) The Arbitration Act 1975 provides for the recognition of
arbitration agreements with an international element, and the
consequent staying of court proceedings concerning disputes
which should be arbitrated, and the recognition and enforcement
in the United Kingdom of arbitral awards made in other countries party to the New York Convention on the Recognition of
Foreign Arbitral Awards.

190

2. Arbitration agreements. If in a contract there is an arbitration clause, the court may stay any proceedings respecting the agreement and refer the dispute to arbitration: A.A., s. 4 and 1975 Act, s. 1.

The court may stay proceedings if:

(*a*) The dispute is within the scope of the arbitration clause.

(*b*) The applicant has not in any way consented to proceedings being brought before the court, e.g. by filing a defence.

(*c*) The applicant is willing to do anything necessary to assist arbitration.

(*d*) The contract stipulates that no right of action is to accrue under the contract until the arbitration procedure described therein has been resorted to: *Scott* v. *Avery* (1856).

(*e*) There is no reason in the interests of justice to refuse the application.

NOTE: Reasons for refusing the application (A.A., s. 24) include (*i*) suspected bias of the arbitrator, e.g. where he is an associate or relative of one of the parties to the dispute, (*ii*) the fact that allegations of fraud are being made against one of the parties to the dispute, (*iii*) the fact that the dispute involves a point of law and is therefore best left to the court.

Refusal to enforce Convention awards is permissible, e.g. where the party to the arbitration agreement is under some incapacity: Arbitration Act 1975, s. 5.

3. Construction of arbitration agreements. The Act of 1950 implies the following clauses in arbitration agreements, unless expressly excluded by the parties:

(*a*) Reference is to a single arbitrator, unless otherwise stated. (If reference is to two arbitrators, they must appoint an umpire to decide between them, by a casting vote.)

(*b*) Parties to arbitration must submit to examination on oath, must produce necessary documents if ordered, etc. Witnesses may also have to submit to examination on oath.

(*c*) The arbitrator's award is final and binding, but he can always make an interim award, pending final decision.

(*d*) Arbitrators can apportion costs, and any provision in the agreement that any party must pay his own costs however the arbitration is decided is void.

(*e*) Arbitrators can order specific performance, except in contracts relating to land.

(*f*) The parties may alter the arbitration agreement by mutual consent, but the arbitrator cannot. (The court may rectify the agreement at any time, but not so as to introduce new matter: as to rectification, *see* IV, **9**.)

(*g*) The time for making the awards may be fixed by the agreement; if not, then a reasonable time is implied, and can be extended by the courts.

(*h*) If the contract itself is assignable and is assigned, any arbitration clause in it is also assigned: *Shayler* v. *Woolf* (1946).

(*i*) Death or bankruptcy of any party to the agreement does not affect the validity of the agreement or the arbitrator's appointment.

(*j*) An arbitration agreement may be revoked by the court if (*i*) the arbitrator shows bias, or (*ii*) there is any question of fraud involved in the dispute.

CONDUCT OF PROCEEDINGS

4. The arbitrator. Any person can be an arbitrator, even though personally interested in the subject-matter of the dispute.

Reference to an arbitrator is presumed to mean a single arbitrator, unless otherwise stated. If a dispute is referred to a single arbitrator and none is appointed (or the one appointed refuses to act), and the parties fail to agree on a replacement, any party can serve seven days notice demanding appointment. If then no appointment is made, he can appeal to the court: A.A., 1950 s. 10; *Tritonia Shipping Inc.* v. *South Nelson Forest Products Corpn.* (1966).

If reference is to two arbitrators and one is not appointed, the appointor of the other arbitrator can serve similar seven days notice and on expiry of the notice can make his own appointment (subject to the court's power to invalidate such appointment).

If reference is to three arbitrators, an award by two of them is binding.

An arbitrator's authority is irrevocable (unless otherwise agreed). But the court may revoke his appointment, or remove him, or nullify the arbitration agreement entirely. Grounds for removal would include misconduct, bias, fraud, or failure to act with reasonable speed: s. 23. When removing an arbitrator, the court may appoint a replacement: s. 25. Only exceptional circumstances (such as misconduct) will justify the court allowing revocation of the appointment: *City Centre Properties Ltd.* v. *Tersons Ltd.* (1969).

An arbitrator or valuer in a commercial dispute is presumed to be entitled to reasonable remuneration, unless otherwise agreed. And he has a lien for his fees on the subject-matter of the award. An arbitrator (unlike a valuer) is not liable for negligence in making his award: *Sutcliffe* v. *Thackrah* (1974); *Arenson* v. *Casson Beckman* (1975); *Campbell* v. *Edwards* (1976).

NOTE: A judge of the Commercial Court may act as a sole arbitrator (or as an umpire) with permission of the Lord Chief Justice. Appeals from such judge/arbitrator are to the Court of Appeal, not to the High Court: Administration of Justice Act 1970, s. 4.

5. Conduct of proceedings.

(*a*) The arbitration agreement may provide rules for governing proceedings, e.g. the customs of a particular trade.

(*b*) The arbitrator is entitled to call for examination on oath, discovery of documents, presentation of pleadings in writing, etc., unless otherwise agreed.

(*c*) At the hearing the arbitrator may exclude persons other than the parties.

(*d*) The arbitrator fixes the time and place of the hearing and must notify the parties. If any party fails to attend, the arbitrator can proceed in his absence but must first give reasonable notice of his intention to do so.

(*e*) The arbitrator must hear both sides, and obey the ordinary rules of evidence. Improper rejection of evidence is grounds for setting the award aside, but not if it was caused by mere honest mistake as to its value: *Falkingham* v. *Victorian Rly. Commissioners* (1900).

(*f*) Attendance of witnesses can be compelled by writ of *sub poena* issued by the High Court, at the arbitrator's request. Any witness giving false evidence on oath is guilty of the crime of perjury: Perjury Act, s. 1.

(*g*) In commercial cases where an umpire is appointed, arbitrators may appear before him and give evidence as witnesses: *Bourgeois* v. *Weddell & Co.* (1924).

(*h*) The arbitrator can state his award in the form of a "special case" for the opinion of the court, and can be ordered to do so if the court thinks fit: s. 9. The special case may state a question of law for the court's decision, or may relate to the award itself. A clause in the arbitration agreement prohibiting the stating of a special case is void: *Czarnikov* v. *Roth, Schmidt & Co*. (1922). The court does not construe special cases rigidly, and may draw inferences from the facts: *Universal Cargo Carriers Corpn*. v. *Citati* (1958). Statement of the special case renders the arbitrator *functus officio* and terminates his jurisdiction.

NOTE: Where there is a clear-cut point of law involved arbitrators must "state a case" on request by a party to the abritration: *Halfdan Grieg & Co. A/S* v. *Sterling Coal & Navigation Corp*. (1973).

(*i*) The Arbitration Act 1979 places strict limits on the judicial review of arbitration awards.

6. The award.

(*a*) The arbitrator can make his award at any time, unless otherwise stated in the agreement. If a time is fixed by the Arbitration Act 1950 or any other statute, the court generally has power to extend the time limit.

(*b*) The award may be verbal or in writing, or in such form as the agreement expressely requires.

(*c*) An award of money (unless otherwise agreed) carries interest like a judgment debt, and the arbitrator has the same powers as a High Court judge to award interest on any debt. Interest is payable at 10 per cent on any sum awarded unless it is specifically withheld: *Timber Shipping Co. S.A.* v. *London & Overseas Freighters Ltd*. (1971).

(*d*) Costs are generally in the discretion of the arbitrator, which must be fairly exercised but need not be supported by reasons: *Perry* v. *Stopher* (1959).

7. Requisites of a valid award.

(*a*) It must be certain in meaning (though the court may assist interpretation where necessary, and may rectify mistakes in expression).

(*b*) It must be final (though this does not prohibit the making of interim awards, pending final decision of the dispute).

(*c*) It must be possible and reasonable.

(*d*) It must settle all the points referred to arbitration, but must not deal with matters outside the reference.

(If part of the award is valid and part void, the court may apply the Doctrine of Severance to separate the good from the bad and enforce the valid parts.)

8. Remission to arbitrator. The award is final, but the court has power to remit any matter back to the arbitrator for reconsideration any time within three months of the award being made: s. 22.

Grounds for remission are (*a*) defect in the award, sufficient to justify setting it aside, (*b*) serious omission through inadvertence, (*c*) formal defect, (*d*) mistake by the arbitrator, (*e*) technical misconduct by the arbitrator, (*f*) discovery of new and material evidence.

9. Setting awards aside. An award may be set aside because of (*a*) misconduct of the arbitrator, (*b*) uncertainty or lack of finality in the award, (*c*) illegality of the contract on which the award was made.

(In a reference by consent of the parties, mistake is rarely grounds for setting aside the award unless it is a mistake of law.)

10. Enforcement of awards. Enforcement is as follows: (*a*) in the same manner as a judgment of a court, (*b*) by action in the court to enforce the award, (*c*) by court order for specific performance.

Arbitration agreements are subject to the Limitation Act 1980, and rights of reference or enforcement of any award may lapse thereunder.

SPECIMEN QUESTIONS

1. (*a*) In what ways may a reference to arbitration be made? What is the effect of an oral submission?

(*b*) What are the main advantages and disadvantages of arbitration? *C.I.S., Final, December* 1963.

2. Define an arbitration agreement, and state to what arbitration agreements the Arbitration Acts 1950 and 1979 apply.

Where one party to an arbitration agreement commences legal proceedings concerning the subject-matter of the agreement, mention the circumstances in which the court may stay the proceedings.

R rendered services to a sanitary authority under an agreement whereby disputes were to be referred to the authority's surveyor. Disputes arose which would probably lead to a conflict of interest between E and the surveyor. If E commences proceedings against the authority, ought the court in your opinion to stay the proceedings? Adapted from *C.I.S., Final, June* 1961.

3. A contract provided for any dispute between the parties to it to be referred to arbitration. A dispute has arisen and been properly referred to a single arbitrator, who has made a valid award.

(*a*) Can either party appeal against the award?

(*b*) How can the award be enforced? *I.C.A.*, *Final*, *May* 1962.

4. State FIVE of the provisions which, unless a contrary intention is expressed, are included in every arbitration agreement. *I.C.A.*, *Final*, *May* 1964.

5. State the conditions upon which an award obtained in an arbitration conducted in a foreign country may be enforced in England. *I.C.A.*, *Final*, *November* 1961.

6. A contract between a British subject and a French company provided that disputes arising under it should be determined by arbitration in France. An arbitration held in France has resulted in an award being made in favour of the British party to the contract, and he desires to enforce the award in England. Can he do so, and if so, subject to what conditions? *I.C.A.*, *May* 1967.

7. Explain the difference between an arbitrator and an umpire. In what circumstances may an arbitration award be set aside? *C.I.S.*, *June* 1972.

8. State the main requisites of a valid arbitration award and examine the grounds upon which an award may be set aside. *C.I.S.*, *June* 1971.

PROGRESS TEST 3

MERCANTILE AGREEMENTS

1. Distinguish between an agreement to sell, and a contract for the sale of goods. How do such contracts differ from contracts for the supply of work and materials? (X, **1**, **3**, **5**)

2. In what circumstances must the injured party treat a breach of condition in a contract for the sale of goods as though it were a breach of warranty? (X, **14**)

3. Summarise briefly the conditions and warranties implied by the Sale of Goods Act and explain how such terms can be excluded from contracts covered by the Act. (X, **18–23**)

4. Explain the meaning of the following phrases in connection

XIV. ARBITRATION AND AWARDS 197

with the sale of goods: (*a*) sale by sample; (*b*) sale by description; (*c*) merchantable quality. (X, **19–22**)

5. "Generally in a sale of goods there is no term implied that goods shall be of any particular quality or that they shall be fit for any particular purpose." How far do you agree? (X, **19–22**)

6. A enters B's shop and asks for soap. B, who runs a general store, sells him soap intended for washing poodles. A uses the soap to wash his own hair and as a result goes bald. Has A any remedy under the Sale of Goods Act? (X, **21**)

7. A buys a car from B in reliance on B's assertion that the car has not done more than 20,000 miles. At the time of purchase A signs a contract which states: "This contract overrides and excludes all conditions and warranties implied by the Sale of Goods Act, and all representations made by the seller." A now finds that the car has done 100,000 miles. What is his legal position? (X, **23**)

8. Distinguish between specific, ascertained and unascertained goods and explain why the distinction is important. (X, **24–29**)

9. When, if ever, may a purchaser of goods get a better title than was possessed by the person from whom he bought the goods? (X, **30–36**)

10. Explain briefly the rules laid down by the Sale of Goods Act regarding: (*a*) delivery of wrong quantities, (*b*) delivery by instalments, and (*c*) time and place of delivery. (X, **38, 40–41**)

11. Summarise the duties of the seller in f.o.b., c.i.f. and ex ship contracts and explain the meaning of these technical terms. (X, **44–46**)

12. What are the rights of an unpaid seller, and what does this term mean? (X, **47–58**)

13. What is the position of an auctioneer as agent for the seller and the buyer of property? (X, **62**)

14. "Hire-purchase is much more hire than purchase." Discuss. (X, **66**)

15. What conditions and warranties are implied by the Hire Purchase Acts and to what contracts do these Acts apply? (X, **66–69**)

16. A is persuaded to take a car on hire-purchase through the misrepresentation of B, the dealer. The car is sold by B to a finance company, which then lets the car to A on hire-purchase. Later A discovers the misrepresentation, and wishes to know whether he can sue B for damages. Explain the legal position. (X, **70**)

17. What is a common carrier, and what are his duties and liabilities at Common Law? How far can such duties and liabilities be modified by contract? (XI, 1–6)

18. Explain briefly the main provisions of: (a) The Carriers Act 1830, and (b) The Transport Act 1962. (XI, 9, 10)

19. How far is a railway company liable for the safety of (a) passengers, and (b) passengers' luggage? (XI, 13, 14)

20. Explain briefly the meaning and significance of the following: (a) bill of lading, (b) charterparty, (c) freight, (d) demurrage, (e) general average. (XI, 18–22)

21. State briefly the main provisions of the Carriage of Goods by Sea Act 1971, with regard to bills of lading. (XI, 24)

22. Write short explanatory notes on the following: (a) voyage charter, (b) paramount clause in charterparty, (c) full and complete cargo. (XI, 25, 26, 29)

23. How does an insurance contract differ from a wager? What is meant by "insurable interest" (a) in life insurance, and (b) marine insurance? (XII, 1, 2, 5, 17)

24. State the main provisions of the Policies of Assurance Act 1867, with regard to the assignment of life insurance policies. Explain how such a policy can be used as security for a loan. (XII, 6, 7)

25. Explain the significance of the average clause in a fire insurance policy. In what circumstances can the insurer claim subrogation to the rights of the insured? (XII, 10, 11)

26. What is meant by a warranty in a marine insurance contract, and what warranties are implied under the Marine Insurance Act 1906? (XII, 21, 22)

27. In connection with marine insurance, explain the following terms: (a) bottomry, (b) respondentia, (c) constructive total loss, (d) general average loss. (XII, 17, 25, 26)

28. Explain how the state supervises insurance businesses. (XII, 29, 30).

29. Explain briefly the following: (a) *depositum*, (b) *locatio rei*, (c) Torts (Interference with Goods) Act 1977, (d) innkeepers' lien. (XIII, 6, 7, 10)

30. What are the duties of a bailee? How far is a bailee liable for loss occasioned by the negligence of his employees? (XIII, 2)

31. Explain the main provisions of the Hotel Proprietors Act 1956. (XIII, 8, 9)

32. How may reference to an arbitrator occur? (XIV, 1)

33. In what circumstances may the court stay proceedings, and

refer a dispute to arbitration under an arbitration agreement?
(XIV, 2)

34. What are the principal powers of an arbitrator under the
Arbitration Act 1950 as amended by the Arbitration Act 1979?
How may an arbitration award be enforced? (XIV, 3, 4–6, 10)

PART FOUR
NEGOTIABLE INSTRUMENTS

CHAPTER XV

Negotiable Instruments

NEGOTIABILITY

1. Meaning of negotiability. Certain classes of chose in action, called "negotiable instruments," can be transferred (or negotiated) without the formalities necessary in assignments of choses in action under s. 136 the Law of Property Act or the rules of Equity.

A negotiable instrument is a document evidencing an obligation, which (*a*) is transferable by mere delivery (or by delivery plus indorsement), (*b*) such delivery operating to transfer all legal rights to the obligation evidenced, (*c*) free of any defects in the transferor's title.

(A negotiable instrument payable to bearer, such as a bank note, is transferable by delivery alone. One payable to the order of a specified person, such as most cheques, is transferred by delivery of the instrument indorsed (signed) on the back by the payee or other transferor.)

2. Characteristics of negotiable instruments.

(*a*) Title passes by delivery (or by delivery + indorsement); whereas a legal assignment of an ordinary chose in action must be in writing under s. 136, L.P.A., and any assignment not in writing is merely equitable: *see* VI, **8**.

(*b*) No notice is necessary to the debtor or other obligee; whereas ordinary assignments must be notified under s. 136, L.P.A. or the Rule in *Dearle* v. *Hall*: *see* VI, **8, 10**.

(*c*) The holder can sue in his own name; whereas an equitable assignee of an ordinary chose in action cannot.

(*d*) A bona fide transferee for value takes free of any defects in the transferor's title; whereas an assignee of an ordinary chose gets no better title than his assignor had.

(*e*) A transferee in due course (*see* **38** below) takes free of any defences which could have been raised by the debtor against the transferor; whereas any defence available against an assignor of an ordinary chose in action can be raised against the assignee.

3. Examples of negotiable instruments.

A chose in action may become negotiable either (a) by statute, or (b) by mercantile custom judicially recognised.

Instruments negotiable by statute include Bills of Exchange and Promissory Notes. Instruments negotiable by custom include bank notes, share warrants, bearer debentures, and exchequer bills.

NOTE: The following are not negotiable instruments, though they are freely transferable: bills of lading, Post Office orders, share certificates, IOUs and receipts.

EXAMPLE: A postal order and a £1 note are stolen from X. The thief sells both to Z. (i) The bank note is a negotiable instrument payable to bearer and Z becomes the legal owner of it: X cannot recover it from Z and can only sue the thief. (ii) The postal order is transferable, but not negotiable; therefore the seller of it cannot give a better title than he has himself. The thief has no title, therefore Z can get no title; X can recover the postal order or its value from Z (who can only sue the thief for damages).

4. Who can sue on a negotiable instrument?

If a negotiable instrument is dishonoured (i.e. not paid when due), a holder for value can sue any person who signed the bill before it came into his possession.

The persons who may be liable are: (a) the drawer, i.e. the person who first issued the instrument, (b) the acceptor, i.e. the person (if any) who has accepted liability on the instrument, and (c) any indorser, i.e. any person who has transferred the instrument to another and indorsed it to effect the transfer (he will also have a right of action against accommodation parties, i.e. persons who have signed an instrument merely to lend the credit of their names to the instrument).

EXCEPTIONS: A signatory may avoid liability in the following cases: (i) where he signed under a fundamental mistake as to the nature of the document: see IV, 1–7; (ii) where his signature was forged (since, then, he has not signed it himself), unless he is estopped from denying the genuineness of the signature, e.g. where he facilitated the forgery; (iii) where he signed *sans recours* ("without recourse"), indicating that he accepted no liability on the instrument; (*iv*) where for some reason the law will not allow him to be sued, e.g. minors, bankrupts, enemy aliens.

BILLS OF EXCHANGE

5. Bills of Exchange Act 1882. This Act codified the law relating to cheques and other bills of exchange, the most important kinds of negotiable instruments.

(Most of the rules laid down by the Act as applying to bills of exchange generally apply also to cheques, which are bills of exchange drawn on a banker. But since cheques are bills payable on demand, the rules relating to presentation for acceptance do not apply to them.)

6. Bills of exchange defined. A bill of exchange is "An unconditional order in writing, addressed by one person to another, signed by the person giving it, requiring the person to whom it is addressed to pay on demand, or at a fixed or determinable future time, a sum certain in money to or to the order of a specified person or to bearer": Bills of Exchange Act 1882, s. 3(1).

The person issuing the order is called the drawer, and the person to whom it is addressed is the drawee. If the bill is made payable to a named person, or to his order, it is an Order Bill and he is the payee. Otherwise a bill may be payable to bearer, and such a bearer bill is transferable by mere delivery (without any indorsement). An Order Bill, however, requires to be indorsed by the payee to effect transfer.

(The definition of bills of exchange should be memorised, and the comments on the definition (below) studied carefully.)

7. "Unconditional order." It must be a positive order to pay, not a mere request or authorisation. The usual wording is "Pay X . . .", though "Please pay X . . ." is also regarded as unconditional.

An order is not unconditional if:

(*a*) it gives the drawee a discretion whether to pay or not, e.g. "Pay X, if satisfied with goods consigned";

(*b*) it orders payment from a particular fund, e.g. "Pay X out of my current account." (But where an unconditional order to pay is merely coupled with mention of a particular fund, for the guidance of the drawee, this is sufficiently unconditional);

(c) it requires the drawee to do something more than to pay money, e.g. "Pay X and notify me in writing".

8. Parties to a bill. The three necessary parties are the drawer, the drawee, and the payee (or bearer). One person may fulfil two different capacities, e.g. where he draws a bill payable to himself, or payable to the drawee (such as a cheque on X Bank and payable to the bank in payment of a debt). In such cases the bill is fully valid and can be negotiated in the normal way.

But where the drawer and drawee are the same legal person (e.g. where a branch of a company draws a bill on its head office), the order is not strictly a bill of exchange, but a promissory note in favour of the payee: B.E.A , s. 5(2).

A bill is also treated as a promissory note if the payee is a fictitious person or lacks contractual capacity: B.E.A., s. 5(2).

9. Addressed to drawee. He must be identified with reasonable certainty (depending on the circumstances).

A bill can be addressed to joint drawees (e.g. to X, Y, and Z), but not to alternate drawees (e.g. X, Y, or Z).

NOTE: An instrument made payable to "cash" is not payable "to the order of a specified person or to bearer" and therefore is not a bill of exchange: *Orbit Mining & Trading Co. Ltd.* v. *Westminster Bank Ltd.* (1963).

10. Dating a bill. If a bill is undated the holder may insert what he believes to be the correct date of issue (which may be necessary for calculating time for payment).

If an incorrect date is inserted the bill is nevertheless enforceable by a holder in due course as though the date were correct: B.E.A., s. 12.

A bill should bear the correct weekday date, but is not invalid merely because it is post-dated, ante-dated, or Sunday dated.

Any date appearing on a bill is presumed to be the correct one unless the contrary is proved: B.E.A., s. 13.

(NOTE: By B.E.A., s. 45, the drawer and indorsers are discharged from liability if the bill is not presented for payment on the due date. B.E.A., s. 12 (above) therefore protects a holder in due course against s. 45, where he has in good faith relied on an incorrect date.)

11. Consideration and capacity.

(*a*) *Consideration.* Bills of exchange require to be supported by consideration like other simple contracts, but note the following.

(*i*) *Consideration is presumed, in favour of a holder.* Thus the normal burden of proof is reversed; in other contracts the person seeking to enforce the contract must prove that he has given consideration, in bills of exchange it is for the defendant to show that no consideration has been given.

(*ii*) *Past consideration suffices,* i.e. any antecedent debt or other obligation: B.E.A., s. 27.

(*b*) *Capacity to contract* by bill of exchange is generally co-extensive with ordinary contractual capacity: *see* III. Thus a minor incurs no liability by signing a bill, but adult signatories to the same bill would be fully liable.

12. Sum payable. A bill must order the payment of a "sum certain in money," i.e. not in goods or services, etc. (Note also that the words used are "sum certain," not "a certain sum" which could mean an unspecified sum.)

(*a*) A sum may be certain within the meaning of the Act even though it is to be paid:

(*i*) with interest (usually calculated from the date of the bill);

(*ii*) by instalments; or

(*iii*) according to some indicated rate of exchange, e.g. where a bill drawn in pounds in Britain is payable in dollars in the U.S.A.: B.E.A., s. 9(1).

(*b*) *Words and figures.* Where the sum payable is stated in both words and figures (though this is not legally necessary) which do not agree, the sum denoted by the words is the amount payable: B.E.A., s. 9(2).

13. Order and bearer bills. A bill may be drawn payable to bearer, or to the order of the drawer, payee, or (sometimes) drawee: B.E.A., s. 3(1).

(*a*) *Order bills* are those payable to a named payee or some person designated by him.

A bill is an order bill if:

(*i*) the bill itself so states; or

(*ii*) it is payable to a specified person without further words prohibiting transfer e.g. "Pay X" or "Pay X or order." (But a bill payable to "X only" is not an order bill and in fact is not really a negotiable instrument at all, but an ordinary chose in action. Such a bill is enforceable by X, but if X sells it to Y, Y cannot enforce it against the drawer or drawee except through the agency of X.)

(*b*) *Bearer bills* are those transferable by mere delivery.
A bill is a bearer bill if:

    (*i*) the bill itself so states;

    (*i*) the last or only indorsement is in blank (*see* **27**, (*g*)); or

    (*iii*) the bill is payable to a fictitious or non-existent person: B.E.A., s. 7(3) and 8,

(A non-existent person is one of whose existence the drawer is unaware, or who does not exist at all. A fictitious person is one of whose existence the drawer is aware, but who was not intended by the drawer to receive payment: *Bank of England* v. *Vagliano Bros.* (1891).)

14. Inland and foreign bills.

(*a*) *An inland bill* is one which is or purports to be (*i*) both drawn and payable within the British Isles, or (*ii*) drawn within the British Isles upon some person resident therein: B.E.A., s. 4(1).

(*b*) *Foreign bills* are all other bills. But unless the contrary appears on the face of the bill the holder may treat it as an inland bill.

15. Bills in a set.
A set of bills means a bill executed in duplicate, triplicate, etc. The payment of one part of a bill in set discharges the other parts also: B.E.A., s. 71.

But if the drawee mistakenly accepts two or more parts of the same bill he will be liable on each part accepted as if it were a separate bill. Similarly a holder who indorses several parts is liable on each.

16. Inchoate instruments.
Where a person signs a blank piece of paper and (*a*) delivers it to another, (*b*) intending it to be converted into a bill, it operates as authority to fill it up as a complete bill for any amount, using the signature already upon it as that of drawer, acceptor, or indorser: B.E.A., s. 20(1).

Such a bill can only be enforced against the original signer if it is:

    (*a*) filled up within a reasonable time of delivery, and

(*b*) completed strictly within the limits of the authority given: s. 20(2).

But after completion the bill is fully enforceable in the usual way. Thus where S signs an inchoate instrument and delivers it to X with authority to complete it for not more than £100, if X fills it up for £1,000 he cannot force S to accept liability for that amount. But if X sells (negotiates) the bill to H, who takes it in good faith and without notice of the £100 limit, H as a holder in due course could enforce the bill for the full £1,000 against S. (As to the meaning of "holder in due course," *see* **38**.)

17. Material alterations: s. 64.

(*a*) What alterations are material: amount, date, payee's name, terms of acceptance, place for payment, crossings on a cheque, altering order to bearer. (Alteration of the place where drawn is material if it changes an inland bill into a foreign bill, or vice versa.)

(*b*) Effect. An unauthorised alteration discharges from liability all persons who became party to the bill before the alteration, unless they expressly or impliedly assent to the alteration: B.E.A., s. 64.

(*c*) Apparent and non-apparent alterations. The effect of s. 64 differs slightly where the alteration is not apparent.

(*i*) *Alteration is not apparent:* a holder in due course can enforce as if it had not been altered, i.e. with the alteration deleted: s. 64.

(*ii*) *Alteration apparent:* all parties prior to the alteration are discharged from liability (even against a subsequent holder in due course). But the bill will be valid and enforceable as between persons who became parties subsequent to the alteration.

EXAMPLE: S draws a cheque for £100 in favour of X, who fraudulently alters the amount to £1,000 and sells (negotiates) it to Y who negotiates it to Z. Here: Z can enforce it against Y and X, even if the alteration is apparent; but he has no remedy against S unless he is a holder in due course and the alteration was not apparent (when he can make S liable for the unaltered amount).

(*d*) *Cheques:* The provisions of s. 64 apply to cheques, but note if a cheque is altered and the drawer later authorised the alteration (usually by initialling it) the effect is (*i*) the drawer is bound by the cheque as altered, (*ii*) other parties are protected by s. 64 unless they too have assented to the alteration.

18. Overdue bills. A bill is deemed to be overdue in the following circumstances.

(*a*) Bills payable on demand are overdue when they have been in circulation for an unreasonable time.

(*b*) Other bills are overdue when the date fixed for payment has passed without the bill being presented: B.E.A., s. 36.

Effect of a bill being overdue is (*i*) that it can still be negotiated, but (*ii*) a transferee can get no better title to it than his transferor had, i.e. he cannot be a holder in due course.

(A holder in due course is one who takes a bill in good faith and for value before it is overdue, and he gets a perfect legal title to the bill irrespective of any defects in his transferor's title.)

19. Lost bills. If a bill is lost before it is overdue, the holder can compel the drawer to issue a replacement (though he cannot compel any other parties to sign the copy): s. 69.

Where this happens the drawer can demand security from the holder, to guard against the possibility of having to pay twice over, i.e. on the original bill and on the replacement.

20. Bills as conditional payment. A creditor who receives a cheque or other bill in settlement of his debt is not regarded as finally paid, since he has not received cash but merely a contractual right to obtain cash under the terms of the bill.

Payment by bill of exchange therefore is conditional, i.e. subject to a condition that if the bill is dishonoured the creditor shall have a right of action for the debt against the debtor.

SIGNATURE, DELIVERY AND INDORSEMENT

21. Meaning of negotiation. A bill is negotiated when it is transferred in such a way as to constitute the transferee the holder of the bill, i.e. by delivery of a bearer bill, or by delivery plus indorsement of an order bill: B.E.A., s. 31.

Negotiation may be prohibited by clear words written on the face of the bill, e.g. by marking the bill "not negotiable."

NOTE: The addition of the words "not negotiable" has differing effects in cheques and other bills. (*i*) A cheque crossed "not negotiable" remains transferable, but the transferee gets no better title than his transferor possessed, i.e. the instrument descends to the status of an ordinary assignable chose in action: *see* **52** below. (*ii*) Any other bill marked "not negotiable' ceases to be transferable altogether: *Hibernian Bank* v. *Gysin & Hanson* (1939). (*iii*) A cheque or other bill marked "not transferable" ceases to be transferable altogether (and therefore is not really a bill of exchange).

22. No liability without signature. Liability on a bill is incurred only by a person who has signed it, either as drawer, acceptor or indorser: s. 23.

(*a*) *Signature in an assumed name*, or on behalf of a firm, confers full liability: s. 23.

(*b*) *Transferor by delivery*. A person who transfers a bill by delivery without indorsement (i.e. a bearer bill), is not liable upon it (except to his immediate transferee): s. 58.

(*c*) *Indorsement by a stranger*. A person who is not a party to a bill but who signs it for any reason, is fully liable on the bill by reason of his signature, to a holder in due course: s. 56.

(*d*) *Agent's signature*. Any agent signing a bill incurs full personal liability unless he makes it clear that he signs merely on behalf of someone else e.g. by signing "*per pro*" or "for and on behalf of" his principal: s. 26. Thus a company director who signs a cheque merely as "director" or "manager" will be personally liable on the cheque: he should sign "J. Jones, director, *per pro* X Co. Ltd."

EXAMPLE: Directors of a company signed a cheque on which the ampersand was omitted from the name "X. & Co. Ltd." HELD: The company was not properly named and the directors were personally liable on the cheque: *Hendon* v. *Adelman* (1973).

23. Signature sans recours. The drawer or any indorser can negative or limit his liability by clear words accompanying his signature on the bill: s. 16.

(*a*) Signature *sans recours* ("without recourse") negatives all liability of the signer on the bill.

(*b*) Signature *sans frais* ("without expenses") limits the signer's liability to the actual value of the bill, i.e. excludes liability for any expenses arising through dishonour and subsequent action for enforcement.

24. Forged signatures: s. 24. "Where a signature on a bill is forged or placed thereon without the authority of the person whose signature it purports to be, the forged or unauthorised signature is wholly inoperative" and no rights can be acquired by reason of such signature (unless the party against whom enforcement is sought is for some reason estopped from denying the genuineness of the signature).

NOTE: (*a*) Forged or unauthorised. A forged signature is one which is false or altered, e.g. where X signs S's name to a cheque, or alters a signature to that of another person. An unauthorised signature is where X signs his own name, but without authority to do so, e.g. where an agent without authority to do so signs a cheque on behalf of his principal. (*b*) Ratification of unauthorised signatures. An unauthorised signature can be ratified by the person by whose authority it purports to be made, thus validating it. (A forgery cannot be ratified in any circumstances since falsely making or altering any document is a criminal offence, and as such can never be validated: Forgery Act 1910. (*c*) Estoppel. If a person knows that his signature to a bill has been forged, but leads others to believe that the signature is genuine he will be estopped from denying the genuineness of the signature and will be fully liable on the bill, e.g. where S habitually lets his wife forge his signature to cheques and obtain cash thereon, he may be estopped from denying the genuineness of such signature if a dispute later arises.

25. Effect of forged signatures.

(*a*) *Forgery of drawer's signature:* the bill is void since it fails to satisfy the definition in B.E.A., s. 3(1) of an order 'addressed by one person to another, signed by the person giving it".

(But the bill will remain valid as between subsequent parties to it, e.g. X draws a cheque in favour of himself on S's bank and forges S's signature as drawer. He then negotiates the cheque for value to Y. Here S incurs no liability on the bill (unless estoppel applies), but Y has full rights of action against X.)

(*b*) *Forgery of the acceptor's signature:* the acceptor incurs no liability, but a holder has full rights against other persons whose signatures are genuine, i.e. the drawer and indorsers.

(*c*) *Forgery of indorsement:* If the bill is an order bill indorsement is vitally necessary to effect legal transfer; therefore any forgery of such indorsement nullifies transfer. Thus the transferee gets no title to the bill, and has no claims against persons who became parties to it before the forgery. (But by s. 55 the bill will be valid and enforceable as between parties subsequent to the forgery.)

EXAMPLE: S draws a cheque in favour of A, who negotiates it to B. X steals it from B and negotiates it (by forging B's indorsement) to Y who negotiates it to Z. Z can enforce the bill against Y (and X), and Y can claim compensation from X. But neither Y nor Z have any claims against S, A, or B. (But B could compel S to issue another cheque, on giving adequate security.)

NOTE: In cases (*a*) and (*c*) above no person who takes the bill subsequent to the forgery can be a holder in due course (though by ss. 54, 55 he may have the legal rights of such a holder against persons who became parties subsequent to the forgery).

26. Delivery of bills. No person is liable upon a bill unless he has (*a*) signed it, and (*b*) delivered it. An order bill must have the signature of the transferor on it in order to effect a valid transfer; but a bearer bill is transferable by delivery without indorsement.

NOTE: (*a*) Importance of delivery. No person is liable on a bill even if he has signed it, if he can prove positively that he did not deliver it, either actually or constructively. Delivery means deliberately and unconditionally transferring possession to another: B.E.A., s. 21(1). Thus if a bill is stolen from X, he has not delivered it and he (and prior parties) incur no liability except under (*b*) below. (*b*) Delivery presumed. (*i*) Delivery is conclusively presumed in favour of a holder in due course, who can thus enforce a bill even against a person who can show that he did not deliver it: s. 21(2). (*ii*) Delivery is also rebuttably presumed in favour of any holder (though here it can be disproved so as to avoid liability): s. 21(3). (*c*) When delivery is rebuttably presumed. Delivery is not presumed conclusively where (*i*) the bill was not complete or was irregular when it left the possession of the party to be charged, e.g. an inchoate instrument, or (*ii*) where the person seeking to enforce it is not a holder in due course. (*d*) Conditional delivery. Where a bill is delivered subject to the fulfilment of some condition, delivery is incomplete until the condition is satisfied, and the bill is not enforceable between the parties to the conditional delivery. (But such bill is fully enforceable by a holder in due course: *see* (*b*) above.) (*e*) When deliverer liable. Although a person who delivers a bill without signing it is not generally liable on the bill, he impliedly warrants (*i*) that he will indemnify his immediate transferee (but no one else), (*ii*) that the bill is genuine, and (*iii*) that he is entitled to transfer it. (This warranty does not apply if the transferee has not given value for the bill.)

27. Valid indorsements. An order bill requires the indorsement (signature) of the transferor in order for the transfer to be effective.

Requirements of valid indorsements.

(*a*) It must be written (on the back of the bill). The signature of the indorser is sufficient, without further words indicating transfer: s. 32(1).

Indorsement may be in ink, print, pencil, etc. (but banks discourage indorsements in pencil, since they are easily obliterated; and indorsement by rubber stamp on a cheque will not usually be accepted by a bank).

(*b*) Partial indorsement is ineffective. The indorsement must relate to the full value of the bill: s. 32(2).

(*c*) Where there are several payees, all should indorse (unless one has authority to indorse on behalf of the others, e.g. in a partnership): 32(3).

(*d*) Manner of indorsement should correspond exactly with the drawing, e.g. if the payee's name is misspelt he should indorse in the misspelt version (adding the correct spelling if he wishes): s. 32(4).

(*e*) Allonge. Where there is insufficient space on the bill for further indorsements, an additional piece of paper (called an allonge) may be glued to the bill to receive further indorsements.

(*f*) Indorsement by agent. An agent is personally liable as indorser unless he makes it clear that he indorses only on behalf of another, e.g. by indorsing "per pro" his principal

(*g*) Blank and special indorsements. If the indorser merely signs his own name (without adding that of the transferee), the indorsement is said to be in blank and the bill becomes payable to bearer (so that it can be further negotiated by mere delivery).

If the indorser adds the name of the transferee the bill is specially indorsed, and is payable to order, i.e. if the transferor wishes to negotiate it further he must himself indorse the bill.

(Thus by means of its indorsements, an order bill may be converted into a bearer bill at any time, and vice versa.)

28. Restrictive and conditional indorsements.

(*a*) A restrictive indorsement is one which prohibits further transfer or limits transferability, e.g. "Pay X only, signed J. Smith," or an indorsement indicating that the indorsee is to receive payments only as agent for the indorser: s. 35(1).

By this means an indorser can deprive the bill of its negotiability. This will not affect the rights of the transferee as against the indorser, but will prevent him passing a full title to any further transferee: s. 35(2).

(*b*) Conditional indorsement is one which makes payment or transfer subject to some condition, e.g. "Pay X, after his marriage to Z."

Such a condition can be ignored by the payer: s. 33.

(*c*) Indorsement *sans recours*. If the indorser seeks to restrict his liability to the transferee by indorsing *sans recours*, or *sans frais* (*see* 23 above), the transferee can refuse to accept the bill with this indorsement. If he does take the bill so indorsed, he is bound by the restriction.

(*d*) Falculative indorsement is one in which the indorser waives some of his legal rights in favour of the transferee, e.g. indorsement with "notice of dishonour waived": s. 16(2). In such a case the transferee and subsequent transferees can enforce the bill against the indorser without giving notice of dishonour, etc.

LIABILITY OF PARTIES

29. Parties to a bill. A party means a person who is liable on the bill, i.e. the drawer, acceptor, and indorsers.

However, the payee (before he indorses the bill) has rights under it, and can also be described as a party.

30. Order of liability.

(*a*) *Before acceptance* the drawer is the principal debtor and primarily liable.

(*b*) *After acceptance*, the drawee takes over primary liability (and the drawer and indorsers are merely sureties for him).

(*c*) *After indorsement*, the indorser becomes liable as a surety for the value of the bill.

The holder can thus enforce the bill against the drawer, the acceptor (primarily) and any indorsers. He can sue any one or he can sue any combination of them, and each is liable for the full value of the bill.

(As between themselves the parties have no right of contribution: contrast guarantors, *see* XVII, 9–10. But any party who has been made to pay the full amount on the bill has a right of action for that amount against his immediate transferor.)

31. The drawer: s. 55.

(*a*) *Liability.* He engages that (*i*) on due presentment it will be paid according to its tenor, and (*ii*) if dishonoured, he will compensate the holder or any indorser who has suffered loss thereby (provided necessary proceedings on dishonour are taken).

(*b*) *Estoppel.* He is precluded from denying to a holder in due course the existence and capacity of the payee.

32. The drawee/acceptor.

He is the person to whom the order is addressed. He is under no liability on the bill unless and until he accepts it, after which he assumes primary liability (and is called the acceptor).

Where a bill is not payable on demand it must be presented to the drawee for him to signify his acceptance of liability (or to reject it), and later presented to him again for payment. A bill payable on demand, such as a cheque, is merely presented for payment without any prior presentation for acceptance.

(*a*) *Acceptor's liability.* He engages that he will pay the bill on due presentment for payment according to its tenor.

(*b*) *Estoppel.* He is precluded from denying (*i*) the existence, capacity and signature of the drawer, (*ii*) the existence and capacity of the payee of an order bill (though he may deny the validity or genuineness of the payee's indorsement): s. 24.

33. Indorsers.

They are people (including the payee) who indorse an order bill in order to transfer it.

(*a*) *Liability.* They engage (*i*) that on due presentment the bill will be accepted and paid according to its tenor, and (*ii*) that if it is dishonoured they will compensate the holder (or any indorser who is compelled to pay it) providing necessary proceedings for dishonour are taken: s. 66.

(*b*) *Estoppel.* An indorser is precluded from denying (*i*) to a holder in due course—the genuineness of the drawer's signature and of all indorsements prior to his own, (*ii*) to a later indorser—the validity of the bill or his own title when he indorsed it.

(Remember that any person signing a bill otherwise than as drawer or acceptor incurs the full liability of an indorser.)

34. Accommodation party. This means a person who has signed a bill as drawer, acceptor or indorser without receiving value therefor.

An accommodation party is liable on the bill to any holder for value, but not to the person whom he has accommodated, i.e. the person to whom he lent the credit of his name.

An accommodation bill is one of which the acceptor is an accommodation party: s. 59(3), i.e. a person who accepts for the honour of the drawer or some other party. (When a bill is not accepted by the original drawee, some other person may step in to accept the bill to save the drawer or any indorser from being sued for dishonour. This is called "acceptance for honour.")

35. Referee in case of need. The drawer or any indorser who fears that a bill may not be accepted by the drawee may designate some other person in addition to the drawee as "referee in case of need," to whom the holder may apply for payment (if he wishes) in the event of dishonour by the drawee: s. 15.

If the referee accepts liability, the bill becomes an accommodation bill and he is said to be accepting for honour of the drawer or any indorser on whose behalf he intervenes: ss. 65–68.

36. Fictitious and non-existing payees: s. 7. Where the payee of a bill is a fictitious or non-existing person, the bill may be treated as payable to bearer (and can be negotiated without the indorsement of such payee): s. 7(3).

(*a*) Fictitious payee means someone whom the drawer did not intend to receive payment, though he may be an existing person and may be named by the drawer as payee.

EXAMPLES: (*i*) V's clerk G obtained V's acceptance of bills G had forged, and apparently drawn by a customer of V in favour of X, a person known to V. G then forged X's indorsement to the bills and obtained their value. HELD: The clerk was the real drawer of the bills, and he knew of X's existence but did not intend him to obtain payment, therefore X was a fictitious payee and the bills were payable to bearer: *Bank of England* v. *Vagliano Bros.* (1891). (*ii*) A clerk induced his employer to draw cheques payable to X, to whom the employer owed money. The employer intended X to be the payee, but the amounts of the cheques were forged by the clerk, who later forged X's indorsements and obtained payment. HELD: The cheques were not payable to a fictitious payee since the drawer intended X to receive payment, though not of the amounts stated. Thus the cheques were order bills, needing a valid indorsement by X to effect transfer, therefore the forged indorsements by the clerk were ineffective and the transferee obtained no title: *Vinden* v. *Hughes* (1905).

(*b*) Non-existing payee means someone (living or not) of whose existence the drawer is unaware, even though he may have intended him to receive payment.

EXAMPLE: A clerk induced his employer to draw cheques in favour of X (an actual person), by pretending that the money was owing to X. The clerk then forged X's indorsements and obtained the value of the cheques. HELD: X was a non-existing payee, and these cheques were therefore bearer bills. Consequently transfer would have been effective without indorsement at all: *Clutton* v. *Attenborough* (1897).

37. Position of holder.

(*a*) *Meaning of holder.* He is the payee or indorsee of a bill, who is in possession of it, or the bearer of a bearer bill: s. 2.

Thus a person who takes an order bill by means of a forged indorsement is not a holder, since he is neither the indorsee of it, nor the bearer of a bearer bill.

(*b*) *Position of holder.* He can enforce the bill (*i*) against any person who has signed it, and (*ii*) against the transferor from whom he obtained it, whether that person signed it or not.

To have full rights of enforcement he should (*i*) have given value himself (in which case he is probably a holder in due course: *see* below), or (*ii*) have obtained it from a person who has given value for it (in which case he is a holder for value: *see* 39 below).

But in any case the law presumes in favour of any holder that his possession is supported by valuable consideration, and in any action brought by the holder it will be for the defendant to disprove this presumption (not for the holder to prove the existence of consideration): *see* 11 above.

38. Holder in due course: s. 29.

(*a*) *Meaning.* He is a holder who has taken a bill (*i*) complete and regular on the face of it, (*ii*) before it was overdue and without notice that it had been dishonoured (if such was the case), (*iii*) in good faith and for value and (*iv*) without notice of any defect in the transferor's title: s. 29(1): *see* **67** below.

NOTE: (*i*) That the payee cannot be a holder in due course, since he did not take the bill by the process of negotiation, i.e. he was one of the original parties to the issue of the bill: *R. E. Jones Ltd* v. *Waring & Gillow, Ltd.* (1926). (*ii*) A person who derives his title through a forged indorsement cannot be a holder in due course, since a holder is a person who derives his title through a valid indorsement (s. 2) and a forgery is an invalid and inoperative indorsement (s. 24).

(*b*) *Rights.* A holder in due course can (*i*) sue on the bill in his own name, and (*ii*) defeat any defences arising from defects of title or arising from the relations of the parties before he took the bill.

Thus the only defences that can be raised against his claims are (*i*) that he does not satisfy the definition given in s. 29(1), e.g. that the bill was overdue when he took it, or had some patent defect (such as disagreement of words and figures of the amount), (*ii*) that a forged indorsement vitiates his title, (*iii*) that issue, acceptance or negotiation of the bill were produced by fraud, coercion or illegality (in which case the holder in due course can still enforce the bill but only if he can prove positively that, subsequent to the alleged fraud, coercion or illegality, value has in good faith been given for the bill, i.e. the burden of proof shifts to the holder): s. 30(2).

(*c*) *Presumption in favour of holder.* Every holder of a bill is presumed to be a holder in due course until the contrary is proved.

(*d*) *Good faith.* Negligence of the holder (e.g. failure to make reasonable enquiries) does not preclude him from being a holder in due course, i.e. does not necessarily amount to bad faith.

39. Holder for value.

(*a*) *Meaning.* He is a holder of a bill for which value has at some time been given; he need not have given value himself.

(*b*) *Rights.* He can enforce the bill against all persons who became parties prior to the giving of such value. (Remember also the presumption in favour of all holders that value has been given for the bill.)

He can sue on the bill in his own name, but he obtained no better title than his transferor possessed. Thus if a holder in due course gives the bill as a present to V, V is a holder for value (since value has been given by the holder in due course) and has a good a title as his transferor, i.e. in this case, a perfect title.

EXAMPLE: S draws a cheque in favour of A, who indorses it for value to B, who gives it gratuitously to C who gives it gratuitously to D. Presuming all indorsements are valid, D is a holder for value (even though he did not himself give value) and can enforce the cheque against all persons who became parties prior to value being given, i.e. against S and A, but not against B or C.

ACCEPTANCE, PAYMENT AND DISHONOUR

40. Acceptance of bills of exchange. Bills not payable on demand must be accepted by the drawee as a pre-requisite to payment. (Bills payable on demand, including cheques, bypass this intervening stage and proceed straight to payment.)

(a) *Drawee's liability.* The drawee is under no liability to holders of the bill until he accepts liability, by signing across the face of the bill. (Though he may be liable to damages for breach of contract to the drawer if he improperly refuses to accept a bill which he was contractually bound to accept.)

Acceptance is signified by the drawee signing across the face of the bill, with or without addition of the date or such words as "accepted": s. 17.

(b) *When made.* Acceptance may be made at any time, even before the drawer's signature of the bill (though usually after). A bill may be accepted when overdue or when previously dishonoured: s. 18.

If a bill payable after sight is dishonoured by non-acceptance but the drawee later changes his mind and accepts it, the holder is entitled to have the acceptance back-dated to the date when it was first presented for acceptance: s. 18(3). This may be important, e.g. where a bill is payable 3 months after sight by the drawee.

(c) *Kinds of acceptance.* Acceptance may be either general (unqualified acceptance of the bill as drawn) or qualified. The holder is entitled to general acceptance, and may treat the bill as dishonoured if only a qualified acceptance is offered: s. 44(1). If he takes a qualified acceptance he loses his right of recourse against prior parties to the bill (except such of them as authorised him to do so): s. 44(2).

(*d*) *Kinds of qualified acceptance.*

(*i*) Conditional, e.g. "Accepted subject to deduction for expenses."

(*ii*) Partial, e.g. for part only of the sum specified.

(*iii*) Local, i.e. payable only at a particular place. (Merely naming a place for payment is general acceptance, unless it is to be made only at the place named.)

(*iv*) Qualified as to time, e.g. "accepted payable in six months" where the bill specified three months.

(*v*) Acceptance by some only of several joint drawees.

41. Presentment for acceptance. A bill payable after sight must be presented for acceptance within a reasonable time, and if not so presented the drawer and all indorsers prior to presentation are discharged from liability: s. 40(1).

Presentment is only necessary where:

(*a*) The bill is payable after sight or after demand (since presentation will enable calculation of the period after which the bill shall be payable).

(*b*) There is an express stipulation for presentment.

(*c*) The bill is payable elsewhere than at the residence or place of business of the drawee, e.g. at a bank. (But the drawee for his own convenience may nominate his bank or some other place as the place for payment, in which case the bill is said to be domiciled. Domiciling a bill is not qualified acceptance, unless it is done in such a way as to prohibit the holder from seeking payment anywhere else.)

42. Presentment for acceptance is excused, and the bill may be treated as dishonoured where:

(*a*) The drawee is dead, bankrupt, lacks capacity or is a fictitious person.

(*b*) Presentment is impossible, e.g. because the drawee cannot be found.

(*c*) Acceptance is refused: s. 42(2).

43. Presentment for payment. A bill not payable on demand must be presented for payment on the due date (as fixed by the bill, e.g. three months after acceptance, or "after sight").

(*a*) Presentment must be at a reasonable hour on a business day, and at the proper place: s. 45(3).

(*b*) Delay in presentment is excused if due to circumstances beyond the holder's control: s. 46(1).

(*c*) A bill not presented within due time is not invalidated, but it cannot be enforced against persons who drew or indorsed it unless such person's signature was added within a reasonable time. (Compare the position of the drawer of a cheque, who is discharged by delay only to the extent he has suffered damage: s. 74 and *see* **48**.)

(*d*) Presentment for payment may be excused where: (*i*) after reasonable diligence it cannot be effected, e.g. because the acceptor cannot be found; (*ii*) the drawee is a fictitious person; or (*iii*) presentment has been waived: s. 45(2).

(*e*) A bill is dishonoured by non-payment when (*i*) it is properly presented but payment is refused or cannot be obtained, or (*ii*) presentment is excused: s. 47(1). An offer of partial payment can be treated as dishonoured, or it can be accepted and the bill treated as dishonoured for the balance.

NOTE: Formerly three "Days of Grace" were added to the due date for the benefit of the drawee but to bring English law into line with international usage these were abolished by the Banking and Financial Dealings Act 1971.

44. Procedure on dishonour. The holder of a dishonoured bill must notify the fact of dishonour to all prior parties against whom he reserves a right of action; persons not so notified are discharged.

Similarly any indorser must reserve his rights of action by notifying parties prior to himself.

But even where it is known that a bill will be dishonoured on presentation on maturity (because, e.g., of the drawer's insolvency) notice of dishonour must not be given until dishonour has actually occurred: *Eaglehill Ltd.* v. *Needham Builders Ltd.* (1972).

(*a*) *Inland bills:* Notice of dishonour can be in any form, oral or written, providing it clearly identifies the bill: s. 49(5). Return of a dishonoured bill is sufficient notice to the drawer: s. 49(6). Notice must be given within a reasonable time of dishonour: s. 49(12).

(*b*) *Foreign bills: Noting and Protesting.* Formal notice of dishonour is required in the case of foreign bills (and is optional in the case of inland bills).

Formal notice is achieved by getting the bill re-presented by a notary public (or, if none can be found, by a householder in the presence of witnesses), who notes on the bill the answer obtained, if any.

The notary or householder then issues a formal certificate of dishonour (called the Protest), setting out the circumstances of dishonour. The Protest and a copy of the noted bill are then sent by the holder to the person or persons he intends to make liable.

45. Circumstances under which notice of dishonour is dispensed with.

(a) When after exercise of reasonable diligence it cannot be given, e.g. where the address cannot be found.

(b) When waived, expressly or by implication, by the person entitled to notice.

(c) As regards the drawer: (i) where drawer and drawee are the same person, (ii) where the drawee is a fictitious person or lacks capacity, (iii) where the drawer is the person to whom presentment for payment was made, (iv) where the drawee was under no obligation to the drawer to accept the bill, or (v) where the drawer has countermanded payment.

(d) As regards the indorser: (i) where the drawee is a fictitious person or has no capacity, and the indorser was aware of this when he indorsed, (ii) where the indorser is the person to whom the presentment was made, or (iii) where the bill was accepted or made only for the indorser's accommodation.

46. Discharge of bills. This occurs by the following means.

(a) By payment in due course, i.e. to a bona fide holder without the payer having notice of any defect in the holder's title: s. 59.

Note that by s. 60 where a banker, in reliance on a forged indorsement, pays a bill drawn on him (i) in good faith and (ii) in the ordinary course of business, the bill is effectively discharged and the bank incurs no liability. (The Cheques Act 1957, s. 1, reduces the importance of this rule by providing that indorsements are no longer necessary in most cases.)

(b) By an acceptor becoming the holder of all rights on the bill at or after its maturity: s. 61.

(c) By renunciation by the holder of all rights against the acceptor: s. 62. (Renunciation must be in writing, or the bill must be delivered up to the acceptor.)

(d) By intentional cancellation by the holder or his agent: s. 63. (Unintentional cancellation is ineffective.)

(e) By material alteration of the bill or its acceptance, without the consent of all parties liable upon it, e.g. by alteration of date, amount, etc.: s. 64.

CHEQUES

47. Definition. A cheque is a bill of exchange drawn on a banker and payable on demand: B.E.A., s. 73.

It is not necessary that the words "on demand" should appear on a cheque, since all bills are treated as payable on demand where no time is specified for payment: s. 10.

48. Stale and overdue cheques.

(a) A stale cheque is one which has been in circulation for a considerable period of time. Banks generally refuse to honour a cheque more than six months old.

(b) An overdue cheque is one which has been in circulation for an unreasonable time: s. 36. (A person who takes an overdue cheque cannot be a holder in due course.)

NOTE: (i) What is a reasonable time? This depends on all the circumstances of each case. Thus where a cheque is intended by the drawer to be presented within two or three days, failure to present within that time might amount to unreasonable delay: *Wheeler* v. *Young* (1897). By contrast, if a cheque was issued overseas for payment in Britain time would have to be allowed for its transmission to Britain in computing what is a reasonable time. (ii) Discharge of drawer. If not presented within a reasonable time the drawer is discharged to the extent of any damage he suffers from the delay. In the absence of such damage he remains fully liable for 6 years, after which his liability is statute-barred: Limitation Act 1939. (iii) Summary on delay in presentation. (a) Bills other than cheques—drawer and indorsers completely discharged: B.E.A., s. 45; (b) Delay re cheques: (i) indorsers discharged under s. 45; (ii) drawer discharged only to extent of damage suffered: s. 74. (iv) Damage suffered by drawer. Example: A drew a cheque for £100 in favour of B, who failed to present it for some time. When drawn, A's account had funds to meet the cheque, but during the intervening time the bank went into liquidation. HELD: B could claim for the money as a creditor of the *bank*, but A was under no liability and B had no claim against him: *Wheeler* v. *Young* (1897).

49. Undated and post-dated cheques.

(a) Undated cheques. A banker is not bound to honour such a cheque, but it must be remembered that any holder is entitled to fill in the correct date: s. 20(1). Any date appearing on a bill is presumed to be the correct date.

(b) Post-dated cheques. These are not really cheques, since they are not payable on demand. However, a banker is entitled to pay a post-dated cheque when it falls due. If he pays it before its date he cannot debit the customer's account, and must bear the loss if the customer stops the cheque before its due date.

(Post-dated cheques are frequently used today instead of bills of exchange payable at some time after sight, e.g. where a purchaser of goods issues a post-dated cheque for goods to be delivered later, thus being entitled to stop the cheque if the goods are not delivered when agreed.)

50. Payment by cheque.

(a) *Conditional payment.* Payment by any bill is conditional only. A creditor is entitled therefore to refuse payment by cheque, and in any case payment is not effective until the cheque is honoured. (But a creditor who takes a cheque in payment may be estopped from action against the debtor if the cheque is dishonoured because he negligently failed to demand payment himself. But the cheque will remain enforceable by other parties against the drawer for six years: Limitation Act 1939.)

(b) *Cheques through the post.* If a cheque is sent through the post and is lost, the loss falls on the sender, unless the creditor requested this method of payment. Such a request will not be implied; it must be express: *Pennington* v. *Crossley & Sons* (1897).

(c) *Cheques as evidence of payment.* An unindorsed cheque which appears to have been paid by the banker on whom it was drawn is prima facie evidence of receipt by the payee of the sum stated on the cheque, even without the payee's indorsement: Cheques Act 1957, s. 3.

51. Crossings on cheques. The object of crossing a cheque is to convey instructions that it is not to be paid otherwise than through a bank, or to make some other stipulation as to the manner of payment: s. 76.

A crossing is a material part of a cheque and any unauthorised alteration of a crossing is unlawful (s. 78) and discharges the cheque: s. 64.

The drawer or any holder may cross a cheque, or add to an existing crossing, e.g. where the holder of a cheque crossed generally adds the words "not negotiable."

Crossings are usually intended as instructions to the paying banker, but a crossing "account payee" is an instruction to the collecting banker.

52. Types of crossing.

(a) *General crossing:* indicated by drawing two transverse lines across the face of the cheque, thus / /, with or without the addition of the words "& Co." between the lines (or such other words as "not negotiable": *see* below).

The effect of such a crossing is to make the cheque payable only to a collecting banker, i.e. it precludes the paying banker from paying cash for the cheque across the counter.

(b) *Special crossing:* indicating the name of a particular banker, with or without the addition of two transverse lines. The effect is that the paying banker must pay the cheque only to the collecting banker named on the crossing, and to no other.

(c) *"Not negotiable":* this general crossing deprives the cheque of its negotiability, and it becomes an ordinary transferable chose in action, i.e. it can be assigned, but the assignee obtains no better title than was possessed by his assignor: s. 81.

Thus where a clerk took a blank cheque from his employer, which was already crossed "not negotiable," and fraudulently made it payable to P, it was HELD that the employer could recover the value from P (who had obtained cash), since the clerk had no title to the cheque and P could get no better title than the clerk had: *Wilson & Meeson* v. *Pickering* (1946).

(d) *"Account payee"* (or *"Account payee only"*): this is not a statutory crossing but is recognised and obeyed by banker's custom. A collecting bank which collects for some person other than the payee named may therefore be liable for negligence. (A paying banker is not generally affected by this crossing.)

53. Alterations on a cheque.

Any material alteration of a cheque or other bill discharges from liability any party to the bill who did not assent to the alteration. On a cheque, alterations of date, amount, name of payee, or of any crossing would be material.

Bankers therefore should not pay a cheque unless any alteration is initialled by the drawer, and where the words "or order" have been altered to "bearer" the normal practice is to insist on the drawer's full signature by way of assent.

(Note the distinction between apparent and non-apparent alterations: *see* **17** above.)

54. Indorsements. The general rules about indorsements apply to cheques.

Note that the Cheques Act 1957, s. 1, dispenses with the need for an indorsement where the apparent payee or indorsee of a cheque is paying it into his own account. But the Committee of the London Clearing Banks has listed the following instruments as still requiring indorsement.

(*a*) Cheques with receipt forms attached.

(*b*) Bills other than cheques.

(*c*) Promissory notes

(*d*) Drafts drawn on H.M. Paymaster, etc.

(*e*) Cheques cashed over the counter.

55. Duty of bankers as to crossed cheques. The banker is liable to the true owner for any loss occasioned where:

(*a*) he pays a cheque which is crossed specially to more than one banker (unless the additional special crossing merely indicates that one of the bankers named is to collect merely as agent for the other);

(*b*) he pays a cheque crossed generally otherwise than to a bank, i.e. treats it as an open cheque;

(*c*) he pays a cheque crossed specially otherwise than to the banker named in the crossing or his agent: s. 79.

56. Protection of paying banker. The drawee bank is statutorily protected against liability if it pays in the following circumstances.

(*a*) *Cheques with forged indorsements:* provided they are paid (*i*) in good faith and (*ii*) in the ordinary course of business: B.E.A., s. 60.

(*b*) *Crossed cheques:* provided the bank pays a cheque drawn upon it, (*i*) in accordance with the crossing, (*ii*) in good faith, and (*iii*) without negligence: B.E.A., s. 80.

(*c*) *Cheques not indorsed or irregularly indorsed:* provided the cheque is drawn on the bank and is paid (*i*) in good faith, (*ii*) in the ordinary course of business: Cheques Act 1957, s. 1.

57. Protection of collecting banker. A collecting banker, that is one who presents a cheque to the drawee bank on behalf of a customer, is protected from liability where he receives payment for a customer who has no title or defective title, provided he does so (*i*) in good faith and (*ii*) without negligence (whether or not the cheque is crossed): Cheques Act 1957, s. 4.

NOTE: (*a*) The section applies only to customers. A person becomes a customer as soon as he opens an account, i.e. where the bank obliges someone, not having an account, by cashing his cheques from time to time, this does not make such person a customer: *Commissioners of Taxation* v. *English, Scottish & Australian Bank Ltd.* (1920). (*b*) The following have been held to amount to negligence by a collecting bank.

(*i*) Opening an account for someone without making adequate enquiries about him: *Hampstead Guardians* v. *Barclays Bank* (1923).

(*ii*) Collecting payment for a customer of a cheque made out to the customer's employer without making enquiries: *Underwood Ltd.* v. *Martins Bank* (1924).

(*iii*) Paying into a customer's private account a cheque payable to him in an official capacity: *Ross* v. *London County Bank* (1919).

(*iv*) Receiving payment for a customer of cheques clearly indicating they are payable to him only as agent for someone else: *Bute* (*Marquess*) v. *Barclays Bank* (1955).

(*v*) Where a bank uses a computer to identify the branch on which a cheque is drawn and a customer with accounts at two branches alters a cheque from branch A to draw it on branch B and the computer fails to recognise the change, if the customer then stops the cheque by notice to branch B and the computer directs the cheque to branch A which pays the cheque, the bank may be liable for negligence: *Burnett* v. *Westminster Bank, Ltd.* (1966).

(*c*) Where a collecting banker is negligent he may be sued for damages for the tort of conversion by the true owner of the cheque.

(*d*) Where the customer's own negligence in drawing cheques contributes to the loss the amount recoverable from the banker is reduced under the Law Reform (Contributory Negligence) Act 1945: *Lumsden & Co.* v. *London Trustee Savings Bank* (1971).

NOTE: There is no corresponding duty of care imposed on the drawer or acceptor of any bill: *Scholfield* v. *Londesborough* (1896).

58. Termination of banker's authority: s. 75. A banker's authority to pay a cheque drawn by his customer is terminated by the following.

(*a*) *Countermand of payment*, written or oral, though if oral countermand is made, it is the practice to insist on written confirmation and merely to postpone payment pending receipt of confirmation.

(*b*) *Notice of the customer's death.* Observe that it is not the death which terminates the authority, but notice of the death.

(*c*) *Notice of the mental incapacity* of the customer.

(*d*) *Notice of the presentation of a bankruptcy petition against* the customer.

Note that if the bank receives notice of an act of bankruptcy committed by the customer, it can still pay out to the customer himself but should not pay out cheques drawn by him in favour of third parties (otherwise it may be liable to make good such payments to the trustee in bankruptcy): *Re Keever* (1966).

(*e*) *The making of a receiving order* in bankruptcy against the customer.

(*f*) *The service of a garnishee order* attaching the balance of the customer's account, i.e. a court order addressed to a debtor commanding him not to pay the stated debt to his creditor but to hold the money pending further orders from the court (which may eventually direct that the money shall be paid to some other person).

(*g*) *Notice of a breach of trust*, i.e. when a customer is about to use trust funds for his own purposes.

(*h*) *Notice of a defect in the presenter's title.*

(*i*) *Insufficient credit* in the customer's account, or where payment would increase the customer's indebtedness beyond some agreed limit.

The bank is entitled to refuse to pay a cheque if it exceeds the customer's entitlement by as little as a penny, and it cannot pay part of a cheque. If it wrongly refuses to honour a cheque properly drawn it is liable to the customer for damages for breach of contract, but is not liable to the holder. A bank may also be liable for damages for libel if it makes a defamatory comment unjustifiably on a cheque, e.g. where it wrongly marks a cheque "No funds."

(*j*) *Where money is paid into a trust account*, a bank is liable if it knowingly assists in a dishonest and fraudulent design on the part of the trustees: *Rowlandson* v. *National Westminster Bank Ltd.* (1978).

PROMISSORY NOTES AND MISCELLANEOUS INSTRUMENTS

59. Promissory note: s. 83. This is an unconditional promise in writing by one person to another, signed by the maker, and engaging to pay on demand or at a fixed or determinable future time a sum certain in money to or the order of a specified person or to bearer.

A promissory note is inchoate and incomplete until delivery to the payee or bearer: s. 83.

60. Differences from bills of exchange.

(*a*) Acceptance of a note is never necessary, since there is no drawee.

(*b*) A promissory note (unlike a bill) cannot be drawn in a set.

(*c*) The maker is the person liable to pay. (In a bill; the drawer is only liable until the drawee accepts.)

(*d*) A promissory note must contain an unconditional promise to pay. (The acceptor of a bill may make a conditional promise to pay.)

(*e*) A promissory note is a promise to pay; a bill is an order to pay.

(*f*) A bill may be treated as a promissory note where (*i*) drawer and drawee are the same person; (*ii*) the drawee is fictitious or lacks capacity: s. 5(2).

61. Bank notes. These are promissory notes payable to bearer. When presenting a note for payment it is not necessary for the bearer to reveal how he came by the note, but if the circumstances arouse suspicion the bank would be entitled to refuse payment until satisfied of good faith; if, however, the bearer sued the bank for its refusal, the burden of proving bad faith would rest on the bank.

62. Joint, and joint and several notes. Where a note is issued by two or more persons, their liability may be joint or joint and several, depending on the circumstances.

(a) *On a joint note*, each maker is fully liable for the whole amount, but a person suing to enforce the note has only one cause of action and can sue all, or one or any combination, but cannot later bring a second action against parties not sued in the first.

If the maker of a joint note dies, his estate ceases to be liable on the note.

(b) *On a joint and several note*, each maker is fully liable but a holder has several rights of action, e.g. he may sue all, or any one, or bring successive actions against the makers. And the death of a maker does not relieve his estate from liability on the note.

NOTE: Where a note runs "I promise to pay" and is signed by two or more makers, it is deemed to be a joint and several note: s. 85.

63. Miscellaneous banking instruments.

(a) *Bankers' Drafts.* These are drafts to order payable on demand, drawn by an office of a bank upon itself or upon some other office of the same bank: Bills of Exchange Act (1882) Amendment Act 1932.

Drafts may be crossed, and the crossing has the same effect as the crossing on a cheque. The Cheques Act 1957 extends the protection given bankers by the B.E.A. to cover bankers' drafts.

(b) *Conditional orders.* These are documents ordering payment of money subject to the fulfilment of some stated condition. They may be crossed like cheques, and the Cheques Act 1957 extends the provisions of the B.E.A. protecting bankers to conditional orders.

Note that a document apparently a cheque may in fact be a conditional order, e.g. a cheque stating on it that payment is not to be made unless an attached receipt form is signed. But the mere fact that a cheque contains a receipt form does not make it a conditional order, unless payment is made conditional on the signing of the receipt.

(c) *Dividends and interest warrants.* These are drafts issued by a company and ordering its bank to pay the stated sum to a named person. They can be crossed like cheques, and are covered by the protections given by the Cheques Act 1957.

(d) *Deposit receipts.* These are acknowledgments by a banker that he holds funds to a certain amount for the depositor. They are not negotiable instruments.

64. Quasi-negotiable instruments. The following documents have some of the qualities of negotiability, but not all, and are therefore not negotiable instruments.

(*a*) *Bills of lading:* receipts for goods shipped, signed by the carrier or his agent. A bill of lading is a document of title to the goods specified therein, and possession of the bill entitles the holder to delivery of the goods. But it is not a negotiable instrument, so that a transferee gets no better title than was possessed by his transferor.

(*b*) *Dock warrants:* documents issued by a dock or warehouse company acknowledging that it holds certain goods on behalf of the person named, or his indorsee. They are documents of title assignable by delivery plus indorsement, but they are not negotiable instruments and the indorsee gets no better title than his transferor.

(*c*) *American share certificates* usually have a transfer form printed on the back, and the owner can sign this form leaving the name of the transferee blank. This then operates as a power of attorney to a subsequent transferee to fill in his own name or the name of another, the person named being entitled to apply to the company for registration as a shareholder. Such transferee gets no better title than his transferor.

(*d*) *I.O.U.s.* These are merely written admission of the existence of a debt (with an implied promise to pay at some future date). They are not negotiable but can be assigned under s. 136, L.P.A., 1925.

Note that if the document contained an express promise to pay, it would be a promissory note.

65. Consumer Credit Act 1974. When they come into force, sections 123–125 of C.C.A. will place restrictions on the taking and negotiating of negotiable agreements. A creditor or owner will not be entitled to take a negotiable instrument in payment, other than a bank note or cheque, in discharge of any sum payable by a debtor, hirer or surety under or in relation to a regulated agreement. Where any cheque is taken, it can only be negotiated to a banker. It will also be unlawful for a creditor or owner to take a negotiable instrument as security.

66. Non-compliance with these provisions. Section 124 of C.C.A. sets out the consequences of not complying with these provisions. If a negotiable instrument has been improperly taken, the agreement under which the sum is payable is enforceable against the debtor or hirer on an order of the court only If contravention of these provisions has occurred in relation to a sum payable by a surety, the security is only enforceable on a court order. And if the application is dismissed on other than technical grounds, the security becomes ineffective.

67. Holders in due course. Section 125 states that where a negotiable instrument is wrongly given, the person taking it is not a holder in due course, and is not entitled to enforce the instrument. A cheque, it will be remembered, can be taken but must be negotiated to a bank. If the cheque is not negotiated to a bank, a defect in title arises within B.E.A., s. 29 (*see* **38** above). This means that the person receiving the cheque is prima facie a holder in due course: B.E.A., s. 30(2). It will be for the person liable on the cheque to prove that. when the cheque was negotiated the holder knew of the defect. If a person becomes liable to a holder in due course on a negotiable instrument unlawfully given, or on a cheque unlawfully negotiated, the creditor or owner must indemnify the injured party.

But remember that none of these provisions in the Consumer Credit Act is yet in force.

PROGRESS TEST 4

NEGOTIABLE INSTRUMENTS

1. How would you define a negotiable instrument? What are the characteristics of such an instrument, and how does it differ from other choses in action? (XV, **1–3**)

2. What persons are liable on a negotiable instrument and to whom? (XV, **4**)

3. Define a bill of exchange. Explain what is meant by saying that a bill must be unconditional. What is a conditional order and what is its effect? (XV, **6, 7, 63**)

4. What is meant by saying that there must be three parties to a bill of exchange? What is the effect where the drawer and drawee are one and the same person? (XV, **8, 60**)

5. X is the holder of an undated cheque, and when he presents it to his bank the bank refuses to take it. Explain why the bank refused it and what X can do to remedy the situation. (XV, **10, 49**)

6. "A cheque is an exception to the rule that past consideration is no consideration." Discuss. (III, **18**; XV, **11**)

7. What is meant by saying that a bill must order the payment of a "sum certain" and not a "certain sum" of money? (XV, **12**)

8. Distinguish between order and bearer bills, and explain how each can be negotiated. Distinguish also between non-existing and fictitious payees. (XV, **13, 36**)

9. Explain briefly the meaning of: (a) Inland and foreign bills; (b) Bills in a set; (c) Inchoate instruments. (XV, **14–16**)

10. What is, and what is the effect of, a material alteration of a bill? Why is it important to distinguish between apparent and non-apparent alterations? (XV, **17, 53**)

11. What is meant by an overdue bill? How does an overdue cheque differ from a stale cheque? (XV, **18, 48**)

12. X owes Y £100 and draws a cheque for that amount in favour of Y. The cheque is lost or stolen before Y is able to present it to his bank. Y now maintains that he has not been paid. What is the legal position? (XV, **19, 20, 50**)

13. What is meant by the negotiation of a bill? Explain the effect of marking a bill or a cheque "not negotiable." (XV, **21**)

14. X negotiates a bearer bill to Y for value and later, when the bill is dishonoured, X maintains that he is under no liability (a) to Y, or (b) to any person to whom Y has negotiated the bill. What is the legal position? Would it make any difference to Y's position if he had not given value? (XV, **11, 22**)

15. Explain the effect of the following signatures on a bill of exchange: (a) signature of a stranger; (b) agent's signature; (c) signature *sans recours*; (d) signature *sans frais*. (XV, **22, 23**)

16. "A forged or unauthorised signature is wholly inoperative on a bill of exchange." Discuss this statement, distinguishing between forged and unauthorised signatures and explaining how estoppel may operate to prevent a person whose signature has been forged from denying that he signed the bill. (XV, **24**)

17. Distinguish carefully between the effect of forgery of the signature on a bill of: (a) the drawer; (b) the drawee; (c) an indorser. (XV, **25**)

18. What is meant by the delivery of a bill? What is conditional delivery and what is its effect? (XV, **26**)

19. "Delivery is presumed in favour of any holder of a bill of exchange." Explain this statement, and state the cases where delivery is not presumed conclusively. (XV, **26**)

20. "An order bill is transferable by delivery plus indorsement.

Explain this statement, and explain also what is meant by a valid indorsement. (XV, **26, 27**)

21. Explain the following terms: (*a*) Blank and special indorsements; (*b*) Restrictive indorsements; (*c*) Conditional indorsement; (*d*) Indorsement *sans recours*. (XV, **27, 28**)

22. In what order are the parties to a bill liable upon it? Explain carefully the liability of: (*a*) the drawer; (*b*) the drawee; (*c*) an indorser. (XV, **30–33**)

23. Explain the significance of the following terms: (*a*) Referee in case of need; (*b*) Accommodation party; (*c*) Accommodation bill; (*d*) Fictitious payee; (*e*) Non-existing payee. (XV, **34–36**)

24. Distinguish carefully between the following terms in relation to bills of exchange: (*a*) holder, (*b*) holder for value, (*c*) holder in due course. (XV, **37–39**)

25. What are the rights of a holder in due course and of a holder for value? (XV, **38, 39**)

26. What is meant by saying that neither a payee of a cheque nor the paying banker can be a holder in due course? (XV, **38, 56**)

27. When does a bill of exchange require acceptance by the drawee in order to render it payable? What is, and what is the effect of, qualified acceptance? (XV, **40, 41**)

28. When is presentment for acceptance (*a*) neccessary, (*d*) unnecessary? (XV, **41, 42**)

29. Explain the following: (*a*) Days of Grace, (*b*) Noting and Protesting, (*c*) Presentment for payment. (XV, **43, 44**)

30. When is presentment for payment excused? (XV, **43**)

31. When is a bill dishonoured (*a*) by non-acceptance, and (*b*) by non-payment? (XV, **40, 44**)

32. When is notice of dishonour necessary and when is it unnecessary? What form should such notice take (*a*) in the case of Inland Bills, and (*b*) in the case of Foreign Bills? (XV, **44, 45**)

33. What is a promissory note and how does it differ from a bill of exchange? What is the distinction between (*a*) joint notes and (*b*) joint and several notes? (XV, **59, 60, 62**)

34. Define the following, and explain how far they are subject to the provisions of the Cheques Act 1957: (*a*) Bankers' draft, (*b*) Conditional order, (*c*) Dividend warrant, (*d*) Deposit receipt. (XV, **63**)

35. Some instruments are negotiable by statute, and others are negotiable by custom; others again have some of the characteris-

tics of negotiable instruments, but not all. Explain this statement. (XV, 3, 64)

36. Define a cheque. How does a cheque differ from an ordinary bill of exchange? (XV, 6, 47)

37. An overdue cheque is one which has been in circulation for an unreasonable time. What is meant by "unreasonable time" in this context? (XV, 48)

38. The effect of delay in presenting a cheque differs from the effect of delay in presenting other bills. How? (XV, 48)

39. "A banker is not bound to honour an undated or post-dated cheque." Do you agree? (XV, 49)

40. On 1st June X sent to his insurance company a cheque to cover the insurance on his car. The cheque arrived on the 2nd June. On the 2nd June X was charged by the police with driving an uninsured vehicle, since his insurance expired in May. Explain why the prosecution would succeed. (XV, 50)

41. What is the object of crossing a cheque, and what types of crossing are legally recognised? (XV, 51, 52)

42. When does a banker's authority to pay a cheque drawn upon him cease? (XV, 58)

43. State and explain briefly the protections given to paying bankers by statute. (XV, 56)

44. A collecting banker who collects a cheque for the wrong person may be liable in tort to the true owner. What form does this liability take, and when does it arise? (XV, 57)

45. Explain the significance of the Consumer Credit Act 1974. (XV, 65–67)

SPECIMEN QUESTIONS

NOTE: In answering these questions, you will *ignore* the possible effect of the Consumer Credit Act 1974.

1. As a general rule, a bill of exchange must be presented for payment in order to retain the liability of the drawer and of the indorsers.

You are required to state:

(a) those circumstances which excuse delay in presentment for payment; and

(b) those circumstances which make it unnecessary to present the bill at all. *Inst. of Bankers, Part II, April* 1970.

2. (a) How does the Bills of Exchange Act 1882 define the following terms:

(*i*) a general acceptance;

(*ii*) a partial acceptance;

(*iii*) a local acceptance?

(*b*) The holder of a bill for £1,000 drawn at one month after date presents it to the drawee for acceptance. The drawee accepts the bill payable two months after date. What type of acceptance have been given, and what steps should the holder take? *Inst. of Bankers, Part II, April* 1972.

3. (*a*) What condition must be fulfilled before a person may be regarded as a "holder in due course"? How does his legal position differ from that of the "holder"?

(*b*) Ivor has received the following cheques, in good faith and for value, from John:

(*i*) A cheque crossed "A/c payee only" payable to Stephen Cole and endorsed by him;

(*ii*) A cheque crossed "Not negotiable" payable to and endorsed by P. Offerman, who had obtained it by fraud;

(*iii*) A crossed cheque payable to "Christine Dickens or order," on which Christine Dickens' endorsement had been forged.

Ivor had no knowledge of the history of these cheques when he received them. Advise him as to whether he has a good title to them. *A.C.A., June* 1973.

4. L drew a cheque for £300 payable to M in payment for a motor cycle. M specially endorsed the cheque to N in payment for a picture, and N specially endorsed it to O, telling him that the money was to be used for O to have a holiday. Instead of using the cheque as directed O specially endorsed it to P as a gift.

As the cheque has been dishonoured, P wishes to know his rights against all the parties concerned. Advise him. *C.I.S., June* 1972.

5. L drew a cheque for £100 in favour of X and gave the cheque to Y (L's secretary) to remit to X. Y endorsed the cheque by forging X's signature, and negotiated it to M in return for goods.

Advise L as to his rights. *C.I.S., December* 1972.

6. Jones transferred the following cheques to Brown:

(*a*) An uncrossed cheque payable to Smith whose endorsement had been forged by Jones.

(*b*) A cheque crossed "not negotiable" payable to Jones and endorsed by him, which Jones had obtained by fraud.

(*c*) A cheque crossed "account payee" payable to Jones and endorsed by him.

Brown had no knowledge of the history of the cheques and gave value to Jones for them. Advise Brown whether he has a good title to any of these cheques. *A.C.A., December 1971.*

7. (*a*) What is meant in the law relating to bills of exchange by a holder in due course? Why is it important to ascertain whether the holder of a bill is a holder in due course?

(*b*) D owed £100 to C for goods supplied. When payment fell due, D drew a cheque for £100 in C's favour and sent it to him. Subsequently, however, D stopped payment of the cheque before C had cashed it. Will C have a right of action on the cheque against D? Would your answer be the same if the cheque had been drawn in C's favour by D's friend, F, acting at D's request and F had stopped payment? Would, in this case, C have a right of action against F? Give reasons. *C.I.S., June 1970.*

8. Williams sells goods to Thomas at the price of £100 and Thomas gives Williams a cheque for the amount, payable to Williams or order. What are Williams' rights and liabilities in each of the following situations:

(*a*) Williams loses the cheque and asks Thomas for another, but Thomas declines to give one.

(*b*) Williams endorses the cheque to Rees to satisfy a debt of £85 which he owes to Rees. The cheque is subsequently dishonoured and Thomas cannot be traced. Rees claims the sum of £100 from Williams. *I.C.A., Final, November 1962.*

9. A buys goods from B and asks B to accept C's cheque for part of the money and the balance in cash. He explains that he has no banking account of his own and that C's cheque is crossed. B agrees to this and the goods are given to A and he hands B the cheque and cash as arranged. The cheque is payable to "A or order," but B omits to obtain A's endorsement. He subsequently discovers his mistake.

(*a*) Is B entitled to ask for A's endorsement?

(*b*) Will B's rights against C be affected if he finds A obtained the cheque by fraud? *I.C.A., Final, May 1962.*

10. (*a*) Allen sells a typewriter to Baker, an infant, who pays for it by his cheque. Allen endorses the cheque to Cook who takes it in good faith and for value. The cheque is dishonoured on presentation. Can Cook enforce payment of the cheque against A or B?

(*b*) Davis, by mistake, draws a cheque payable to Evans, who does not exist. The cheque is negotiated by Franks by a forged endorsement to Green, who takes it in good faith and for value. Can Green enforce payment of the cheque? *I.C.A., Final, May* 1964.

11. (*a*) Explain the rights and duties of a paying banker and a collecting banker in relation to cheques.

(*b*) How is a banker's authority to pay a cheque drawn on him by his customer terminated? *A.C.A., December* 1967.

12. (*a*) What is a bill of exchange? How does a cheque differ from other bills of exchange?

(*b*) What is meant by the "negotiation" of a bill of exchange? How does the addition of the words "not negotiable" affect the transferability of (*i*) bills of exchange generally, and (*ii*) cheques? *A.C.A., December* 1971.

PART FIVE

SECURITIES

CHAPTER XVI

Securities

SUMMARY OF PROPERTY LAW

1. Understanding of property law. Students who are required to study the subject of securities need at least a background knowledge of the law of property. This section is intended to provide a superficial outline to facilitate understanding of the law relating to securities, but students who have no prior knowledge of the subject would be well advised to make a more detailed study of property law.

2. Ownership and possession. The owner of property is the person who has the maximum legal rights over the property (including the right to actual possession). He may however part with possession, without surrendering ownership, e.g. where the owner lends property to another.

Ownership is a legal concept; possession is a state of fact, and involves actual control over the property. When the owner of land leases it to a tenant, the tenant acquires legal possession and can assert his right of control against anyone (even against the owner, if the owner in breach of the lease attempts to regain possession).

3. Transfer of ownership.

(*a*) *Personal property.*

(*i*) Chattels can be transferred by mere delivery, with intention to pass ownership (and not merely possession).

(*ii*) Choses in action require to be assigned either in accordance with the method laid down by s. 136 L.P.A. or Equity or in accordance with some particular method laid down for particular choses, e.g. share transfers.

(*b*) *Real property.* Freehold land (and also leasehold) should be transferred by deed if legal ownership is intended to pass.

Any attempted conveyance which is not by deed operates to transfer only an equitable interest in the property.

A deed is not necessary in the following cases.

(*i*) Leases for a term not exceeding three years.

(*ii*) Assents by personal representatives. A deceased person's land vests in his personal representatives and they can transfer it to the beneficiaries under the deceased's will (or upon his intestacy) by a mere written assent.

(*iii*) Disclaimers by a trustee in bankruptcy need only be in writing.

(*iv*) On redemption of a mortgage of land, the land revests in the mortgagor as soon as the mortgagee signs a receipt for the mortgage moneys.

SECURITIES GENERALLY

4. Meaning of "security." A security is some right or interest in property given to a creditor so that, in the event of the debtor failing to pay his debt as and when due, the creditor may reimburse himself for the debt out of the property charged.

Both real and personal property may be charged with repayment of a debt in this way. (Real property means freehold land, and personal property includes leasehold land and all moveable property, such as chattels and choses in action.)

5. Forms of security.

(*a*) *Mortgages.* A mortgage is an assurance to the creditor of the legal or equitable interest in property as security for the discharge of debt, subject to a proviso that on repayment of the debt the property shall revert to the borrower.

The characteristic of a mortgage is that possession of the property remains vested in the mortgagor (the borrower), while the mortgagee (the lender) obtains some or all of the rights of ownership, or the right to obtain ownership if the debtor defaults.

Land is the form of property most usually mortgaged, but chattels can be mortgaged by Conditional Bill of Sale (*see* **10** below), and choses in action (such as insurance policies) can be mortgaged by assignment subject to a condition that on repayment the chose shall revert to the borrower.

(*b*) *Pledges or pawns.* A pledge is a deposit of chattels with a lender as security for a debt. If the pledgee is a professional lender upon this type of security (a pawnbroker) the pledge is called a pawn.

A pledge differs from a mortgage in that the lender obtains possession of the chattel, while the borrower retains ownership.

(c) *Liens.* A lien is a right to retain property until a debt is paid (a possessory lien) or to seek a court order for sale of the property (equitable lien).

A lien differs from mortgages and pledges in that it arises by implication of law from certain situations, while mortgages and pledges are the result of express agreement between a borrower and a lender.

6. Appropriate Formalities. The Consumer Credit Act 1974 lays down various requirements concerning formalities for securities provided in relation to regulated agreements. But note that none of these controls is yet in force.

(a) Any security must be in writing and must conform to requirements laid down in regulations yet to be made as to form and content: s. 105.

(b) A security instrument must be properly executed (i.e. signed in the prescribed manner; embodying all the terms of the security; its terms are readily legible; and a copy is provided at the proper time): s. 105.

(c) Failure to observe the requirements of (a) or (b) means that the security is enforceable against the surety on an order of the court only: s. 105.

(d) If an application for an order is dismissed other than on technical grounds, the security is to be treated as ineffective: ss. 105 and 106.

(e) Regulations yet to be made may provide for any matters relating to the sale or other realisation of securities: s. 112.

(f) The Consumer Credit Act cannot be avoided by the use of a security: s. 113. For example, where a hire-purchase agreement is terminated under s. 100 C.C.A., the hirer is not liable for more than 50 per cent of the total purchase price. The C.C.A., s. 113, would make it impossible for a security to be used so as to obtain more than 50 per cent.

7. Land Mortgages. Where a prospective regulated agreement is to be secured on land, the prospective mortgagor must receive a copy of the unexecuted agreement which contains a prescribed notice indicating his right to withdraw from the prospective agreement: C.C.A., s. 58. This agreement must be sent by post to the mortgagor for signature not less than seven days after the copy was given. During the "consideration period", the mortgagee must not communicate in any way with the mortgagor except at the mortgagor's specific request. The "consideration period" runs from the date when the copy of the unexecuted agreement is first given and expires seven days after the day the unexecuted agreement is sent for signature; or its return, with signature, by the mortgagor, whichever comes first: s. 61. A land mortgage securing a regulated agreement is enforceable on an order of the court only: s. 126. But remember that these provisions are not yet in force.

8. Legal and equitable interests. In English property law a distinction is drawn between legal interests in property (which are enforceable in any court and against any person), and equitable interests (which are personal rights against a particular individual and are not enforceable against other persons, save in certain exceptional circumstances: *see* below). Both legal and equitable interests in property can be used as security for loans, but the limited enforceability of equitable interests makes them less acceptable securities.

Differences between legal and equitable interests.

(*a*) *Creation.* A legal interest is one created in the correct form for the particular type of property, e.g. a deed of conveyance to create a legal interest or estate in land. An equitable interest is either (*i*) the result of an informal creation, e.g. a conveyance of land not under seal, or (*ii*) the result of a transfer of an existing equitable interest, since these cannot be converted into legal interests (even by conveyance under seal).

(*b*) *Enforceability.* If a person has a legal interest in property his claims are enforceable against all comers, and are indefeasible. But the holder of an equitable interest in property can (*i*) enforce his interest only against the person through whom he derives it, i.e. the owner of the parallel legal interest in the property, and (*ii*) can have his interest in the property destroyed if the legal owner sells the property to a purchaser for value without notice of the equitable interest attaching to the property.

(*c*) *Parallel interests.* In any one piece of property there may be parallel legal and equitable interests, vested in different persons. Thus, in a trust, the legal owner of property is compelled to hold the property as trustee for the benefit of the beneficiary, that is the owner of the equitable interest. (And the beneficiary's claims are enforceable only against the trustee, and can be extinguished if the trustee sells the property to a purchaser who buys without knowing of the beneficiary's interest.)

9. Legal and equitable mortgages. Just as there can be parallel legal and equitable ownership of property, mortgages can also be either legal or equitable. And where there are several mortgages of a piece of land some may be legal and others equitable.

Where the mortgagee obtains a legal interest in the property charged his mortgage is a legal mortgage; if he obtains merely an equitable interest, his mortgage is equitable (and is a weaker security).

PLEDGES AND MORTGAGES OF PERSONALTY

10. Mortgages of personalty. The method of mortgaging personalty is to transfer legal ownership to the mortgagee, subject to a condition for re-transfer on repayment of the loan.

The method of mortgaging therefore depends on the method of transfer of legal title appropriate to the particular form of personalty.

(a) Chattels are transferable by delivery without the need for any accompanying document, but in order to provide the mortgagee with documentary evidence (while leaving possession in the hands of the mortgagor) a conditional bill of sale is normally used: *see* **12** below.

(b) Choses in action are transferable by assignment, either legal (under L.P.A., s. 136) or equitable: *see* VI, **7**.

In some cases particular statutes lay down special requirements for the assignment of particular choses in action, e.g. insurance policies, copyrights, etc., and these requirements would have to be observed in a mortgage of such a chose.

11. Pledge or mortgage. Where chattels are to be mortgaged, a conditional bill of sale must be used. But this procedure is not popular: *see* **12** below.

An easier method of using small chattels as security is to pledge them, i.e. to deliver possession to the lender subject to a condition that he shall return the chattels on replayment of the loan. But pledging is only appropriate in connection with smaller chattels, which can be easily moved or stored. Larger chattels, such as pianos, motor cars, collections of furniture or paintings, etc., must normally be mortgaged by bill of sale.

12. Conditional bills of sale. An absolute bill of sale is a documentary assignment of chattels, giving title with or without delivery of the chattels comprised. Since chattels can pass by delivery, without documentation, and since most sales take effect in actual or constructive delivery, absolute bills of sale are rarely used. Their only use today is where the purchaser requires for some reason documentary evidence of his purchase, e.g. where he is buying goods for export and may have to prove to the customs authorities that he is the owner of the goods.

A conditional bill of sale is one used as documentary evidence of a mortgage of chattels, i.e. it transfers ownership to the mortgagee (while leaving the mortgagor in possession as bailee for the lender), subject to a condition that the chattels shall be re-assigned to the borrower on repayment of the loan.

13. Form of conditional bills of sale. These must comply with the requirements of the Bills of Sale Acts 1878 and 1882, as follows.

(*a*) The bill must be by deed, attested by at least one witness; otherwise it is void.

(*b*) The bill must be registered at the Central Office of the Supreme Court within seven days of creation; otherwise it is void.

(*c*) Consideration for the bill must be truly stated therein.

(*d*) Interest payable and date for repayment must be stated in the bill, together with any other conditions.

(*e*) The chattels comprised in the bill must be inventoried, and the inventory must be attached to the bill on registration.

(*f*) The lender's remedy under a conditional bill of sale which has been properly registered and drawn is seizure of the chattels. The right to seizure arises (*i*) on failure to repay the loan as agreed, (*ii*) on bankruptcy of the borrower, or (*iii*) on any fraudulent dealing by the debtor with the chattels with the intention of removing them from the lender's power, e.g. an attempted sale to another person.

NOTE: A conditional bill of sale takes its priority from the date of registration. Therefore a bill created earlier than a rival may rank after the rival if registered later. Because of the technicalities and publicity involved, bills of sale are not popular forms of security. They are sometimes taken by professional moneylenders, but very rarely by non-professional moneylenders such as bankers. From a borrower's point of view a pledge offers an easier way of raising money on security of chattels; the difficulty here is that a pawnbroker will not usually take a pledge of large and cumbersome chattels, which may then only be useful as security if someone can be found who is willing to take a conditional bill of sale, e.g. pianos, cars, collections of paintings, etc.

14. Pledges. A pledge of chattels involves actual or constructive delivery of chattels to the lender. Constructuve delivery might be by giving the pledgee the key to a warehouse in which the goods are stored.

The pledgor remains the legal owner of the goods, and the pledgee becomes a bailee who must return the goods on repayment as agreed. The pledgor is entitled to demand a receipt for deposit of the goods.

The pledgee owes a duty of care for the goods while in his possession, and if they are lost or damaged through his negligence he must make good the loss. (But if the goods were taken from him by robbery with violence, he is generally excused liability.) The pledgee generally has no right to use the goods deposited unless otherwise agreed.

The pledgee has a possessory lien over the goods entitling him to retain them until repayment, even if there is no written agreement stating the purpose of deposit.

15. Pawnbrokers. These are professional pledgees, who are required to be licensed under the Pawnbrokers Acts 1872 and 1960, to carry on business by lending money on security of goods pawned to them.

The Pawnbrokers Acts (applying to loans of £50 or less) lay down the following rules.

(*a*) A pawn-ticket must be given for the pledge.

(*b*) Pawns are to be redeemed any time within six months, plus seven days of grace.

(*c*) Pawns not redeemed within this period: (*i*) if for less than £2, belong absolutely to the pawnbroker, and (*ii*) if for more than £2, must be sold by public auction. (Surplus moneys after the pawnbroker has deducted the amount of his loan belong to the pledgor.)

(*d*) If the loan exceeds £5 the pawnbroker may make a special contract varying the provisions of the Act, providing such contract (usually in the form of a pawn-ticket) is signed by both parties.

(*e*) The pawnbroker must deliver up the goods on presentation of the pawn-ticket, and repayment of the loan. (He is entitled to presume that the person presenting the ticket is lawfully justified in claiming the goods.)

(*f*) If the goods are destroyed by fire, the pawnbroker is responsible for making good the pawner's loss. (Valuation is measured as the amount of the loan, plus interest, plus 25 per cent of the loan.) He is not liable for war damage.

NOTE: New rules about pawns and pledges, to replace the Pawnbrokers Acts, are contained in the Consumer Credit Act 1974, ss. 114–122. These provisions are not yet in force.

LIENS

16. Definition. A lien is a right over the property of another arising by operation of law (independently of any agreement), and gives the lienor a right (*a*) to retain the property until the owner has settled some debt owed to the lienor (a Common Law or possessory lien), or (*b*) to sell the property in satisfaction of the debt (an equitable lien).

A lien must be distinguished from a deposit of chattels by way of pledge. A pledge is security derived from express agreement; a lien generally arises independently of agreement.

17. Common Law or possessory liens. These arise where the creditor has actual possession of some of the debtor's property, and obtains a right to retain such property until an outstanding debt is paid.

NOTE: (1) A Common Law lien cannot arise independently of possession, i.e. the creditor is not entitled to obtain possession solely for the purpose of claiming such a lien. (Cf. Equitable liens: *see* **19** below.) (2) A Common Law lien is exercisable only by detaining the goods until the debt is paid, i.e. there is no right of sale, save in some exceptional cases where a right of sale is given by statute. A statutory right of sale is given to innkeepers (Innkeepers Liability Act 1878), unpaid sellers of goods (Sale of Goods Act 1893), and repairers (Torts (Interference with Goods) Act 1977). (3) A Common Law lien is extinguished by (*i*) agreement, express or implied, (*ii*)payment of the debt, (*iii*) loss of possession, or (*iv*) taking security for the debt. (4) A Common Law lien may be general or particular, i.e. may be available against any goods of the debtor coming into possession of the creditor, or only against the particular goods in connection with which the debt was incurred. Thus a carrier has a particular lien for his freight charges, while stockbrokers and factors have general liens. A banker's lien is also a general lien: *see* **20** below.

18. Maritime liens. A maritime lien is one attaching to a ship, in favour of the shipmaster (for disbursements and wages), seamen (for their wages), salvors (for charges in connection with salvage), etc.

The lien is exercised against the ship itself, not against the owners, and it arises independently of possession. A notice of lien is affixed to the ship, and proceedings may be taken in the Admiralty court to arrest the ship. If the lien is not discharged, the ship will not be allowed to leave harbour, and a court order for sale may be given to the lienor.

If the owner of a ship subject to a lien sells the ship, the purchaser takes it subject to the lien, i.e. becomes responsible for discharging the lien.

19. Equitable liens. Unlike Common Law liens these are not founded on possession, and can be exercised by a court order for sale of the property subject to the lien. But like all equitable rights they can be extinguished by the owner selling the property to a bona fide purchaser for value without notice of the lien.

They arise mainly in connection with the sale of land, e.g. a vendor of land who has given possession to the purchaser has a lien over the land for unpaid purchase money, and a purchaser who hands over a deposit before obtaining possession has a lien for his deposit.

20. Banker's lien. This is a general possessory lien arising at Common Law, but unlike other Common Law liens it gives the banker a right of sale of securities subject to the lien.

NOTE: (1) The lien arises out of a general course of dealing, and covers "All securities deposited with them as bankers, by a customer, unless there be an express contract, or circumstances that show an implied contract, inconsistent with the lien": *Brandao* v. *Barnett* (1846). (The lien therefore usually arises by implication from the relationship, but it appears that it may also be granted expressly unlike other liens.) (2) Property subject to the lien includes all securities coming into the banker's possession in the ordinary course of dealing, e.g. promissory notes, bills of exchange, foreign bonds, etc. It does not cover securities depositied merely for safe custody, unless at some time the customer agrees to allow the banker to hold these as security for an advance (in which case they are subject to an equitable mortgage, rather than a lien). (3) The banker's lien has been called an "implied pledge" (*Brandao v. Barnett*) which appears to confer a power of sale, at least in so far as it affects negotiable securities. The Bills of Exchange Act, s. 27, provides that any person having a possessory lien over a bill is deemed to be a holder for value to the extent of his lien, and can therefore sell and transfer the bill.

CHAPTER XVII

Guarantees and Indemnities

NATURE OF GUARANTEE

1. Definition of guarantee. A guarantee, or surety contract, is an undertaking "to be answerable for the debt, default, or miscarriage of another," Statute of Frauds 1677, s. 4.

Guarantees may be either specific or continuing.

(*a*) A specific guarantee relates to one isolated debt only. (Where a bank accepts a specific guarantee of a single loan, a separate account should be opened for that loan, otherwise the guarantee may be cancelled out by operation of the *Rule in Clayton's Case, see* V, **6**.)

(*b*) A continuing guarantee is one covering a series of transactions, e.g. a guarantee of an overdraft on a current account at a bank. (A bank, in order to enforce such a guarantee of an overdraft, should stipulate expressly in the guarantee form that the guarantee shall cover the final balance. Otherwise it will be interpreted as covering only the overdraft as it existed at the date of the agreement, and payments in after that date would thus reduce the guarantor's liability.)

2. Characteristics of guarantees.

(*a*) *Three parties:* principal creditor, principal debtor and guarantor (or surety).

(*b*) *Primary liability to pay* must attach to the principal debtor. The surety only becomes liable to pay if the debtor defaults.

(*c*) *The guarantor has no interest in the contract* between the principal debtor and the principal creditor, except in so far as he agrees to accept liability if the debtor fails to pay.

3. Form of guarantees. The Statute of Frauds, s. 4, requires any contract of guarantee to be evidenced in writing, by some sufficient note or memorandum; *see* III, **4–6**. (This requirement does not apply where the guarantee is part of some larger transaction, e.g. a contract of agency.)

Guarantees require to be supported by consideration, but the consideration does not need to be stated in the written memorandum: Mercantile Law Amendment Act 1856. (Thus the consideration may be proved by independent oral evidence if necessary.) Guarantee bonds do not require consideration.

NOTE: (a) Representations made in order to assist someone to obtain credit must be in writing, personally signed by the party making the representation. Otherwise the representation is not actionable: Statute of Frauds Amendment Act 1828. (b) Guarantees must normally be stamped within fourteen days of being signed. (c) Guarantees can also be securities within the Consumer Credit Act 1974: see XVI, 6.

4. Guarantees not uberrimae fidei. Neither the principal creditor nor the principal debtor are under any legal duty to disclose to the guarantor facts which might influence him against entering into the contract. Thus if A offers to guarantee B's bank account, the bank is under no obligation to reveal matters which show that B is a bad risk: *Wythes* v. *Labouchere* (1859).

BUT NOTE: (a) Active misrepresentation by the creditor (or by the debtor with the creditor's knowledge) will be grounds for rescission. (b) Active concealment of material facts may amount to misrepresentation, e.g. keeping silent about some facts so as to put facts disclosed into a deceptive light. (c) Once the contract of guarantee is made, the creditor owes a duty of the utmost good faith to the guarantor, who is entitled to be discharged if this duty is not observed. Thus the creditor must disclose material facts coming to his knowledge and affecting the guarantor's risk, but need not disclose mere suspicions, e.g. A guaranteed B's bank account, and B overdrew on the guaranteed account to pay off debts to another creditor. The bank suspected that A was being defrauded, but did not disclose this. HELD: They were under no duty to do so: *National Provincial Bank* v. *Glanusk* (1913). (d) Guarantees in the nature of insurance are *uberrimae fidei*, e.g. "fidelity guarantees" (of the character and good faith of some third person). Thus A gave a fidelity guarantee in respect of L to L's employer, B. B omitted to disclose that L had misappropriated some of B's money and was only being retained in employment in reliance on A's guarantee bond. HELD: L's former dishonesty should have been disclosed, and A was not liable on his guarantee: *London General Omnibus Co.* v. *Holloway* (1912).

5. Indemnity contracts. An indemnity contract is one in which the indemnifier promises to preserve the other party from loss. Unlike a guarantee (*a*) it is a contract of primary liability, and (*b*) it does not require written evidence, and (*c*) there are only two parties, i.e. the indemnifier and the person he promises to indemnify.

In *Birkmyr* v. *Darnell* (1704) guarantees and indemnities were distinguished thus:

A and B enter a shop and B asks X for goods on credit. Then (*i*) if A says to X, "Give B the goods, and if he does not pay for them I will," this is a contract of guarantee (since A will only become liable if B defaults, i.e. A's liability is secondary to B's); (*ii*) if A says to X, "Give B the goods and I will see that you get paid," this is an indemnity since A accepts the principal or primary liability for the debt.

NOTE: An indemnity may be a security within the Consumer Credit Act 1974: *see* XVI, **6**.

6. Capacity to contract. Capacity to guarantee is generally co-extensive with normal contractual capacity, but note:

(*a*) A partner as guarantor has no power to bind his firm unless (*i*) so authorised by his co-partners, or (*ii*) giving guarantees is part of the firm's normal business. Even where he has authority, he cannot bind the firm in a guarantee under seal unless (*i*) he is so authorised by deed (power of attorney), or (*ii*) all the partners sign the guarantee deed.

(*b*) Guarantees by married women are enforceable only against their separate estates. (Thus a bank considering a guarantee from a married woman cannot take her husband's status into account in assessing the value of her guarantee.)

(*c*) Trading companies have implied power to borrow money, but there is probably no implied power to give guarantees. (Thus a bank before accepting a guarantee from a company must examine the Memorandum and Articles of the company to make sure there is power to give guarantees.)

7. Position of creditor. His rights against the guarantor are dependent on the terms of the contract. But a continuing guarantee by or to a partnership is revoked as to future transactions by any change in the constitution of the firm: Partnership Act 1890, s. 18.

8. Joint and several guarantees. Sometimes several persons join in giving a guarantee, and the liability of such co-guarantors may then (depending on the agreement) be joint, or several, or joint and several.

(a) *Joint guarantors:* Each guarantor is personally liable for the full amount, but the creditor has only one cause of action against them and should therefore sue all in one action. If he elects to sue just one of the guarantors, he cannot later sue the others since he has exhausted his one cause of action, and is taken as having waived his claims against the others: The rule in *Kendall* v. *Hamilton* (1879).

Also on the death or bankruptcy of a joint guarantor, his estate is discharged from all liability. (As between themselves joint guarantors have a right of contribution for any sums paid beyond their fair share of liability.)

(b) *Several guarantors.* Each is fully liable for the whole debt, and can be sued separately and successively, i.e. the creditor has several rights of action and the rule in *Kendall* v. *Hamilton* does not apply. Further, the death or bankruptcy of a several guarantor does not release his estate from liability for claims arising before the death or bankruptcy..

(c) *Joint and several guarantors.* Here the creditor can either sue them jointly or separately and successively, and death or bankruptcy has the same effect as in (b) above. (From the creditor's point of view therefore a several, or joint and several guarantee is preferable, e.g. bank guarantees are nearly always drafted on the basis of joint and several liability.)

POSITION OF THE GUARANTOR

9. Liability of the guarantor. This arises only when the principal debtor has defaulted, and not until then.

The surety's liability depends partly on the terms of the contract and partly on the following rules of law:

(a) If the transaction between the creditor and the principal debtor is void, the surety is not bound by his guarantee, e.g. guarantees of loans to minors, which are themselves void under Infants Relief Act 1874, s. 1: *Coutts & Co.* v. *Browne-Lecky* (1947). Similarly since loans by a company for the purchase of the company's own shares are illegal, any guarantee on such loan is also illegal and void: *Heald* v. *O'Connor* (1971).

(*b*) The creditor may be entitled to treat the guarantor as a principal debtor, unless he makes it clear that he is a surety only and only secondarily liable.

(*c*) The creditor is under a legal duty not to prejudice the guarantor in any way, e.g. by increasing his liability by allowing release of any co-guarantor. (In such a case the guarantor can demand release also: *see* **11–17** below.)

(*d*) If the surety goes bankrupt, the creditor can prove in the bankruptcy for the amount guaranteed. (Bank guarantees usually provide expressly for this contingency, and for the bankruptcy of the debtor.)

(*e*) When he has accepted liability to the creditor, the guarantor immediately acquires a right of action against the debtor for the value of the guarantee. But this right does not arise until he has accepted liability himself (even though he has not yet actually paid the creditor): *Ascherson* v. *Tredegar Dry Dock Co.* (1909). (Under the Bankruptcy Act 1914, s. 24, discharge in bankruptcy does not release the debtor from liability to his guarantors: for discharge in bankruptcy *see* XVIII, **15**.)

10. Rights of the guarantor.

(*a*) *Indemnification by debtor.* The surety can sue the debtor for all sums properly paid under the guarantee plus damages for any additional loss. But he cannot recover the whole value of the guarantee if he was only made to pay a smaller sum. (This right to compensation arises as soon as he actually accepts liability to the creditor; but he cannot sue the debtor until he has actually paid the creditor himself.) However, a person who without being asked to do so guarantees payment of another's debt is not entitled on paying the debt to be indemnified by the principal debtor: *Owen* v. *Tate* (1975).

(*b*) *Set-offs and counter-claims.* If sued by the creditor, the surety can avail himself of any set-offs or counter-claims which the debtor has against the creditor, e.g. where he is sued on a £1,000 guarantee and finds that the creditor owes the debtor £200 for goods or services, he is entitled to set-off the £200 against the guarantee and so reduce his own liability to £800.

(*c*) *Delivery of securities held by the creditor.* On paying his guarantee to the creditor, the surety is entitled to possession of any securities the debtor may have earlier deposited with the creditor in respect of the same debt, even if the surety did not know of them when he made his guarantee.

(*d*) *Hotchpot.* A co-guarantor who has received securities from the principal debtor (or creditor) must share the benefit of them with other co-guarantors, even though they may have been unaware of their existence when they became guarantors.

(*e*) *Contribution from co-guarantors.* If one surety pays the whole debt, he is entitled to compensation from co-sureties (in a joint, or joint and several guarantee), even if (*i*) their guarantees are contained in different instruments, or (*ii*) he did not know of the existence of the co-sureties when he signed his own guarantee.

This right is implied by equity, and is independent of contract. (It may however be modified by contract.)

DISCHARGE OF GUARANTOR

Unless otherwise agreed, a guarantee is automatically discharged in the following circumstances.

11. Unauthorised variation of terms. The guarantor is automatically released if the debtor and creditor vary the contract between them, without the guarantor's knowledge and approval (even though the variation is not prejudicial to the guarantor).

EXAMPLE: A guaranteed D's overdraft. Without A's knowledge the bank allowed D to open a second account into which he paid substantial sums, while leaving his existing overdraft undiminished. HELD: This amounted to an unauthorised variation of the guarantee and A was discharged: *Nat. Bank of Nigeria Ltd.* v. *Awolesi* (1964).

12. Creditor relinquishes securities. If the creditor relinquishes securities of the debtor held by him in respect of the debt guaranteed, this automatically releases the guarantor (unless otherwise agreed).

13. Creditor omitting to do something to protect the surety. If the creditor omits to do something he reasonably should do for the protection of the guarantor, this operates as automatic release, e.g. where he fails to register an equitable mortgage granted to him by the debtor, since such a mortgage may be void if not registered (and the surety would be entitled to a transfer of such mortgage on payment of the guarantee).

14. Unauthorised extension of time to the debtor. If the creditor makes a binding agreement to grant the debtor an extension of time for payment of the debt, this automatically releases the surety.

EXCEPTIONS: (1) Where the extension was expressly or impliedly sanctioned by the original guarantee agreement (as in Bank guarantees in some cases). (2) Where judgment has already been obtained against the surety and the principal debtor together. (3) Where there are several distinct debts, extensions of time in respect of one debt will only discharge the surety in respect of that debt alone.

15. Release of co-surety, i.e. where the creditor discharges any co-surety, thus depriving the remainder of their rights of contribution against the surety discharged: *Smith* v. *Wood* (1929).

16. Revocation. This is only possible where the consideration for the guarantee is divisible, i.e. in continuing guarantees, which can always be revoked as to future liabilities (unless otherwise agreed).

Specific guarantees cannot generally be revoked, and revocation of a continuing guarantee does not affect liability for debts already incurred.

Also if the consideration for any guarantee is a forbearance to sue (i.e. a promise by the creditor not to sue the debtor for the debt, in reliance on the guarantee), it appears that the guarantee is irrevocable.

17. Release of debtor. Release of the debtor automatically releases the surety, unless the creditor expressly or impliedly reserves his rights against the surety in the original contract (as is usually done in Bank guarantees). However, a creditor's acceptance of a debtor's wrongful repudiation of a contract does not discharge a guarantor from liability under his guarantee, though the action against him is not to repay the debt but to pay damages for breach of contract: *Moschi* v. *Lep Air Services* (1972).

NOTE that if the debtor goes bankrupt and later obtains his discharge in bankruptcy this operates to release him from liability to the creditor in most cases, but it does not affect the liability of the guarantor.

18. Payment of debt by the debtor.

19. Death of guarantor. It depends on the terms of the contract whether his death will discharge his estate from liability under his guarantee. Thus bank guarantee forms usually stipulate that the guarantee shall remain operative until the bank receives notice of the guarantor's death.

Death of joint guarantor discharges his estate from liability, but surviving joint guarantors remain liable.

20. Bankruptcy of guarantor. The creditor can prove for the debt in the guarantor's bankruptcy, even if the debtor has not yet defaulted in payment himself, and even if he has received (but not yet realised) securities from the debtor: Bankruptcy Act 1914, s. 30(3).

If the surety obtains his discharge in bankruptcy, this operates to release him from his guarantee in most cases: B.A. 1914, s. 28 (2).

The bankruptcy of a joint guarantor does not relieve his co-sureties from liability.

21. Change in constitution of firm. A continuing guarantee given to a firm, or to a third party regarding transactions by a firm, is automatically revoked as to future liabilities by any change in the constitution of the firm, e.g. on the death or retirement of any partner: Partnership Act 1890, s. 18.

22. Limitation Act 1980. The creditor's rights against the guarantor are statute-barred after six years (twelve years if the guarantee was under seal), but time begins to run only when the debt becomes due from the principal debtor.

Thus bank guarantee forms usually stipulate that the guarantor shall not become liable until the bank formally notifies him that it proposes to call in his guarantee. Time then begins to run only after the bank makes this formal demand, even though the debtor may have become liable considerably earlier: *Bradford Old Bank* v. *Sutcliffe* (1918).

The Act also bars the guarantor's claim for indemnification against the debtor, and for contribution from co-sureties, after the limitation period has elapsed.

PROGRESS TEST 5

SECURITIES

1. What is a security, and what forms may it take? (XVI, **4, 5**)
2. Distinguish between legal and equitable interest in property,

and explain how ownership of the various forms of property can be transferred at law. (XVI, 3, 6)

3. How can personalty be (a) mortgaged, and (b) pledged? What sort of chattels are suitable for pledging? (XVI, 8–12)

4. Explain briefly the main provisions of (a) The Bills of Sale Acts, and (b) The Pawnbrokers' Acts. (XVI, 11, 13)

5. What is a lien? Distinguish between possessory, equitable and maritime liens. (XVI, 14–17)

6. When, if ever, does a lien confer a power of sale? (XVI, 14–18)

7. Define a guarantee. How does it differ from an indemnity contract, and what form must it take? (XVII, 1, 3, 5)

8. Guarantees are not *uberrimae fidei* contracts, but once formed a guarantee imposes similar duties upon the creditor. Explain. (XVII, 4)

9. Distinguish between joint, and joint and several guarantees. (XVII, 8)

10. What are the rights and liabilities of a guarantor under a contract of guarantee? (XVII, 9, 10)

11. In what circumstances is a guarantor discharged from liability? (XVII, 11–12)

12. In what circumstances may a guarantor revoke his guarantee? (XVIII, 16)

13. G guaranteed D's overdraft to the amount of £1,000. Later the bank allowed D to increase his overdraft to £1,200. What effect, if any, has this on G's liability? (XVII, 11)

14. In what ways, if any, does capacity to act as a guarantor differ from normal contractual capacity? (XVII, 6)

SPECIMEN QUESTIONS

1. "Guarantees are subject to the ordinary rule of English Law that all contracts, except those under seal, must be supported by consideration."

(a) Explain the meaning of the term "consideration" in this quotation.

(b) Is there any provision in English Law which requires that a contract of guarantee shall be in any particular form?

(c) In relation to a contract of guarantee, is there any provision in English Law which *either* requires that the consideration must be stated in the written agreement, *or*, on the other hand, provides that the consideration need not be stated there? *Inst. of Bankers, Part II, September* 1972.

2. E and F were partners in a furriers' business. G asked E whether the firm would guarantee G's overdraft with the H Bank up to £1,000. Without consulting F, E agreed and he gave the H Bank a written guarantee in the name of "E and F, furriers."

G has now failed to settle his overdraft and F consults you as to his legal position.

Advise him. *C.I.S., June* 1971.

3. What special rules govern a contract of suretyship?

X, who was employed in A's shop, stole some money from the till. When A discovered the theft he told X that he would overlook it but, nevertheless, thought it wise to obtain a guarantee of X's fidelity. This A asked B to do, and B signed a document to that effect. A did not tell B about the theft. Later X stole £50 from the till and absconded.

Advise A. *C.I.S., December* 1972.

4. (*a*) How far is it true to say that a creditor is not bound to disclose to a prospective guarantor facts about the debtor which might influence him against becoming guarantor?

(*b*) In what circumstances is a contract of guarantee automatically discharged? *A.C.A., December* 1971.

5. (*a*) Distinguish between a possessory lien, a maritime lien and an equitable lien.

(*b*) Eddy, a solicitor, acted for Roy and had possession of the title deeds to Roy's land. Roy mortgaged his land to Allan and the deeds remained with the solicitor who acted for both parties. Roy fails to pay Eddy the legal fees and Eddy claims a lien over the title deeds.

Advise Allan. *A.C.A., December* 1970.

6. State the essentials of a contract of guarantee.

A and Co. were stockbrokers who agreed with B that he should have half the commission earned as a result of his introductions and that he should pay half of any losses which might be sustained from them. Explain whether or not this is a contract of guarantee. *A.C.A., Intermediate, December* 1963.

7. (*a*) An executor finds that the deceased had, during his lifetime, given a continuing guarantee.

(*i*) In what circumstances would the guarantee be revoked by death?

(*ii*) If it is revoked, what action should the executor take?

(*b*) Jones gives Brown a continuing guarantee for the due ful-filment by a partnership firm, Robinson & Co., of its business transactions with Brown. A partner in the firm retires and another partner is taken in. What effect, if any, has the change in the partnership on Jones' guarantee? *I.C.A., Final, May* 1964.

8. When one of two sureties has paid the debt to the creditor what remedies are available to such surety against:

(*a*) the debtor,

(*b*) the creditor, and

(*c*) the co-surety? *I.C.A., Final, May* 1962.

9. G signed a guarantee in respect of the banking account of C. The latter is unable to repay his overdraft, and the bank has demanded payment from G under his guarantee. G wishes to deny liability on the ground that the bank failed to disclose to him: (*i*) that C's wife had served a prison sentence and (*ii*) that C's wife had authority to draw on C's account. Advise G whether or not he is liable to the bank. *Inst. of Bankers, Diploma Part II, April* 1962.

10. A customer has applied to his bank for an overdraft of £1,000, and he has offered as security a life policy on his own life for £5,000 with profits, the surrender value being £990.

Explain what is meant by "surrender value," and describe the steps which should be followed to enable the bank to obtain a legal mortgage of this policy. *Inst. of Bankers, Diploma Part II, April* 1964.

11. (*a*) Define a guarantee and explain how it differs from an indemnity contract.

(*b*) P orally hired A as his agent for the sale of some valuable paintings, and as part of the contract A guaranteed P against failure of any of A's clients to pay for the paintings they bought. State with reasons whether the guarantee is enforceable. *A.C.A., June* 1967.

PART SIX

BANKRUPTCY

CHAPTER XVIII

Bankruptcy

COMMENCEMENT OF PROCEEDINGS

1. Objects of bankruptcy. When a person is insolvent (i.e. unable to pay his debts as and when they fall due) either he or his creditors may petition for the court to take over the administration of his estate and its distribution among creditors. This procedure is called bankruptcy and is governed by the Bankruptcy Act 1914, as amended and the Insolvency Act 1976.

The objects of bankruptcy are:

(*a*) To secure fair and equal distribution of available property among the creditors.

(*b*) To free the debtor from his debts, so that he can make a fresh start as soon as he is discharged by the court.

(*c*) To enquire into the reasons for his insolvency, and so to deter people from rashly incurring debts they cannot pay.

2. Procedure in bankruptcies. For a debtor to be declared bankrupt he must first have committed one of the recognised acts of bankruptcy: *see* **5** below. The commission of such an act raises a presumption of insolvency and justifies presentation of a petition for the debtor's bankruptcy.

Procedure is then as follows:

(*a*) *Presentation of petition* by a creditor, or by the debtor himself. To present a petition a creditor must be owed £200 or more; *see* below. The petition should be presented (*i*) to the local County court in whose jurisdiction the debtor has carried on business for the greater part of the previous six months, or (*ii*) to the Chancery Division of the High Court, if the debtor does not reside in England, or his whereabouts are unknown.

(*b*) *A receiving order* is made out by the court if satisfied that the debtor appears to be insolvent. The receiving order makes the Official Receiver (an officer of the Department of

Trade) receiver of the debtor's property. The official receiver then (*i*) obtains a statement of affairs from the debtor, and (*ii*) conducts a public examination of the debtor as to the reason for his failure.

(*c*) *Creditors' first meeting*. The official receiver then summons the creditors to a meeting with the debtor to decide whether to accept any composition or scheme of arrangement he may wish to put forward, to save himself from bankruptcy. If he makes no offer, or the creditors reject what he does offer, the bankruptcy proceeds to the next stage. If they do accept, the bankruptcy normally ends there.

(*d*) *Adjudication order*. If no composition or scheme is accepted, the Court adjudicates the debtor bankrupt. His property then passes to his trustee in bankruptcy or, if none has been appointed, remains vested in the official receiver.

(*e*) *Discharge*. When all debts have been paid, or as much as can be, the debtor can apply for his discharge. He must first undergo a public examination to ensure that he has done all he can towards paying his debts, and if the court is satisfied it will order his discharge. This has the effect of freeing him from further liability on most of the debts still outstanding at his discharge.

3. Who may be bankrupted. Any debtor can be bankrupted (subject to the special rules in **4** below).

A debtor is any person, whether a British subject or not, who at the time he committed an act of bankruptcy was (*a*) personally present in England, (*b*) ordinarily resident, or possessing a residence, in England, (*c*) personally, or through an agent, carrying on business in England, or (*d*) was a member of a firm which was carrying on business in England: B.A. 1914, s. 1(2).

A non-resident can only be bankrupted in England if he was (*a*) domiciled in England, (*b*) resident in England within one year before presentation of the petition, or (*c*) trading in England either personally, or through an agent, or as a member of a firm: s. 4. (A debtor is still "trading in England" as long as any of his trade debts are outstanding: *Re Bird*, *Ex parte the Debtor*, v. *I.R.C.* (1962).)

4. Special classes of debtors.

(*a*) *Minors* can be bankrupted for debts enforceable against them, e.g. for necessaries, and for taxes. Voidable contracts ratified after majority are not sufficient to ground a petition. If a minor is a member of a firm, proceedings should be taken only against the adult members. (But all the firm's assets are available for the creditors, including the infant's share.)

(*b*) *Married women* are now fully bankruptable: L.R. (Married Women & Tortfeasors) Act 1935, s. 1. But a husband cannot prove in his wife's bankruptcy for debts owed to him until all the other creditors have been paid, i.e. he is a deferred creditor.

(*c*) *Persons of unsound mind* can only be bankrupted with the consent of the court (or, if the act of bankruptcy was committed before he was certified, without consent of court).

(*d*) *Companies and partnerships.* Companies are wound up, not bankrupted. Partnerships can be bankrupted and the separate estate of each partner may be bought into the firm's bankruptcy. If a person has been a director of at least two insolvent companies, he may be banned for up to five years from being a director or in any way concerned with the management of a company: Insolvency Act 1976, s. 9.

(*e*) *Deceased persons* cannot be bankrupted. But if the deceased's estate is unable to meet his debts it may be administered in bankruptcy, i.e. the administrators can be compelled to follow approximately the same procedure as in bankruptcy.

(*f*) *Aliens: see* 3 above.

5. Acts of bankruptcy: B.A., s. 1. Before bankruptcy proceedings can be commenced against him, the debtor must have committed one of the following acts of bankruptcy.

(*a*) Assignment or conveyance of his property to a trustee for the benefit of his creditors generally. If the conveyance is by deed, it comes within the Deeds of Arrangement Act 1914.

NOTE: (*i*) It must be a conveyance or assignment, i.e. an actual transfer. A mere contract to transfer is not enough. (*ii*) It must affect substantially all the debtor's property. (*iii*) It makes no difference whether assignment is honest or fraudulent. (*iv*) A creditor who has assented to it cannot rely on such assignment as an act of bankruptcy.

(*b*) Fraudulent conveyance, gift, or other transfer of any of his property.

NOTE: (1) Under this head any kind of transfer is sufficient; it need not be in favour of all the creditors, nor of all the debtor's property. But it must be fraudulent. (2) "Fraudulent" means seeking to prevent distribution in accordance with the bankruptcy laws. (This is a much narrower meaning than normally given to the word, which is usually intended to connote some intention to deceive.) (3) Such conveyance etc. is void, and the transferee must restore the property to the trustee in bankruptcy: s. 42. (4) By s. 172, Law of Property Act 1925, a conveyance is also void if it is intended to defraud the transferor's creditors.

(c) Fraudulent preference, i.e. a transfer of any of the debtor's property with the intention of paying the recipient creditor in full in preference to other creditors. Such transfer is void: s. 44.

(d) Departing or remaining out of England with intent to defeat or delay his creditors (or leaving his residence, or otherwise hiding from his creditors, even though he remains in England).

"Intent to defeat," etc., must be proved by the creditors, but can be presumed from circumstances, if they warrant it.

(e) Seizure of goods by a sheriff, under process of execution under a court order.

The goods must either (i) have been sold, or (ii) have been held by the sheriff for at least twenty-one days and the petition must be presented within three months thereafter.

(f) Declaration by the debtor of his inability to pay his debts.

The debtor may (i) file such declaration with the court, or (ii) present his own petition in bankruptcy, and either will constitute an act of bankruptcy.

(g) Failure to comply with a bankruptcy notice. A bankruptcy notice is one served by a creditor who has obtained judgment for his debt, and demands payment and warns the debtor that a petition will be presented for his bankruptcy unless he pays within ten days. But the debtor may resist the notice by (i) raising any set-off or counter-claim which was not available to him in the action in which the creditor obtained judgment, or (ii) paying the debt, or (iii) giving adequate security. Bankruptcy notices are construed strictly and the requirements of the Act must be fully complied with: *Re Cartwright* (1975).

(h) Notice by a debtor of suspension of payment of debts. The debtor may give the notice orally or in writing, and it will be grounds for a petition even if suspension is only temporary, or the notice is issued "without prejudice." The notice may not state expressly that suspension of payment is intended; it is sufficient if it gives a creditor reasonable grounds for believing that this is the intention: *Crook* v. *Morley* (1891).

NOTE: Where a County Court orders attachment of earnings against a judgment debtor, and in view of his other debts it appears that his over-all liabilities should be examined, the Court may order him to furnish a list of his creditors: Attachment of Earnings Act 1971, s. 4. This order operates as an act of bankruptcy, and may be grounds for a petition in bankruptcy.

Under the provisions of the Insolvency Act 1976 an application to the County court for an order for the administration of a debtor's estate is no longer an act of bankruptcy: s. 13. Where the court makes a judgment in money, and the debtor appears to have other debts, it must consider whether an administration order should be made. If the indebtedness does not exceed £1,000, an order can be made. But such an order is not an act of bankruptcy. (*See also Attachment of Earnings Act* above).

6. The petition. A petition can be presented by the debtor himself (because of inability to pay debts), or by a creditor.

A creditor's petition (verified by affidavit) can be presented if (s. 4):

(*a*) *his debt is* £200 *or more.* Several creditors can present a joint petition if their debts together aggregate £200;

(*b*) *the debt is a liquidated sum* (i.e. an ascertained amount, not for instance a claim for unliquidated damages for breach of contract), payable immediately or in the future;

(*c*) *the act of bankruptcy relied on occurred within three months:* before presentation of the petition;

(*d*) *the debtor is liable to English bankruptcy law: see* **3** *above;*

(*e*) *the act of bankruptcy is not one to which the creditor was privy,* e.g. not a deed of arrangement to which the creditor was a party.

NOTE: (1) A secured creditor can only petition if he relinquishes his security for the benefit of all the creditors, or if the security does not cover his debt fully. (2) Several petitions presented simultaneously can be consolidated and dealt with at one hearing: B.A., s. 110. (3) A petition can be dismissed if (*a*) the petitioner's motive is improper, e.g. malicious: *Re Shaw* (1901); *Re a Debtor No. 16* 1966 (1967) or (*b*) the debtor's sole property is a life interest terminable on his bankruptcy: *Re Otway* (1895), or (*c*) there are no assets and no reasonable likelihood of there being any: *Re Betts* (1897).

It is now no longer the case that no act of bankruptcy occurs where application is made to the County Court for the administration of an estate. But where the judge orders attachment of earnings under the A.E.A. 1971 and requires the debtor to provide a list of creditors, such an order constitutes an available act of bankruptcy. An order for the administration of a debtor's estate (available where the indebtedness does not exceed £1,000) does not constitute an available act of bankruptcy.

(4) A petition once presented can only be withdrawn with consent of the court: B.A., s. 5(7). (5) Before hearing the petition (usually eight days after presentation) the court may stay all actions or executions against the debtor's estate, and protect the available assets by making the Official Receiver their custodian: B.A., ss. 8, 9. (6) Where the petition is presented by a creditor, an affidavit must be filed unless it is dispensed with verifying the facts contained in the petition, a copy of the petition must be served on the debtor, and then the petition will be heard after not less than eight days from the date of service: Insolvency Act 1976, s. 5.

7. The receiving order.

(a) *When made.* (i) The order can be issued immediately after presentation of a petition by the debtor himself, but (ii) if the petition is presented by a creditor, a formal court hearing is a necessary prerequisite.

(b) *Advertisement of receiving order.* The making of the receiving order must be advertised in the *London Gazette* and a local newspaper: B.A., s. 11. (Also, if the debtor owns any land, the receiving order should be registered as a land charge to prevent dealings with the land: Land Charges Act 1925, s. 6.)

(c) *Effect of receiving order.* (i) The official receiver (an official of the Department of Trade attached to the court for bankruptcy purposes) becomes receiver of all the debtor's property, and may appoint a special manager of his business, if any. (ii) No actions can be commenced or continued against the debtor without leave of the court: B.A., s. 7.

NOTE: The receiving order does not make the debtor bankrupt. He only becomes bankrupt when the adjudication order is made: *see* **12** *below.*

(d) *Rescission of the receiving order* is allowed in the following circumstances:

(*i*) Where the court sanctions a composition or scheme of arrangement: B.A., s. 16.

(*ii*) Where it appears that the property should be distributed according to the laws of Scotland or Ireland, e.g. where a majority of the creditors in number and value, or the bulk of the debtor's property, is in Scotland or Ireland: s. 12.

(*iii*) Where the court exercises its wide discretion to rescind under B.A., s. 108, e.g. where the debts are paid in full, or the court is satisfied that the receiving order should never have been made. The fact that the creditors may ask for rescission is not binding on the court: *Re a Debtor* (D.C.) (1971).

8. Arrest of a debtor: s. 23. The court may order the arrest of the debtor and the seizure of books, papers, goods, etc., if the debtor:

(*a*) seems likely to abscond;

(*b*) seems likely to remove or conceal goods; or

(*c*) fails to attend any examination ordered by the court.

PROCEEDINGS AFTER RECEIVING ORDER

9. Proceedings after receiving order.

(*a*) The debtor must submit a statement of affairs to the official receiver and this must be verified by affidavit.

(*b*) After submitting the statement of affairs, the debtor must attend the first meeting of creditors, at which he may offer any composition or scheme of arrangement he has in mind.

(*c*) After a private examination by the official receiver, the debtor must attend a public examination. This may continue by successive adjournments, until his bankruptcy ends. The court, on application from the official receiver, may make an order dispensing with the public examination: Insolvency Act 1976, s. 6.

(*d*) If the creditors refuse to accept any composition or scheme offered by the debtor, the court will issue the adjudication order (which makes the debtor bankrupt, though commencement of the bankruptcy is back-dated to the date of the first available act of bankruptcy, i.e. up to as early as three months before the presentation of the petition).

10. Debtor's statement of affairs: s. 14. This (supported by an affidavit as to its truth and accuracy) must set out the debtor's debts and liabilities and the names of his creditors together with a list of his assets and such other matters as the official receiver may require.

The debtor has seven days to prepare his statement (or three where the petition was presented by himself).

The statement may be inspected by any person claiming in writing to be a creditor entitled to payment in the bankruptcy (if any person falsely so states he is guilty of contempt of court).

If for some reason the debtor himself cannot prepare the statement, the official receiver may do so at the expense of the estate: B.A., s.7 4. If the debtor refuses to prepare a statement of affairs he can immediately be adjudicated bankrupt.

11. First meeting of creditors: compositions.

(a) *When summoned.* Within fourteen days after the making of the receiving order the official receiver will summon and chair a meeting of the creditors, who will then decide whether or not they wish to have the debtor adjudicated bankrupt. The meeting is summoned by written notice to the creditors named in the statement of affairs, and by giving six days' notice, in the *London Gazette* and a local newspaper. The debtor must attend this meeting and answer any relevant questions as to his affairs.

(b) *Debtor's proposals.* At the meeting the debtor may put forward proposals, if any, for the payment of his debts, i.e. a composition or a scheme of arrangement. Such proposals must be submitted to the official receiver within four days after submission of the statement of affairs: s. 16.

If accepted by a majority in number, and three-quarters in value, of the creditors the proposals must then be submitted to the court for its approval.

(c) *Approval by court.* The court can approve or reject the proposals, but cannot vary them.

It must reject if of the opinion (*i*) that the proposals are unreasonable, (*ii*) that they will not benefit the general body of creditors, or (*iii*) that they do not obey the order of payments laid down by the Bankruptcy Act. The court also has a discretion to reject in other cases, if it appears just and equitable to do so.

(d) *Creditors bound.* Once approved by the court, a scheme or composition is binding on all the creditors. Its effect (so long as it is carried out) is to free the debtor from all debts provable in bankruptcy, and to release him from jurisdiction in bankruptcy.

(e) *Approval annulled.* An approved scheme or composition

may be annulled by the court because of (*i*) default in payment, (*ii*) injustice or impracticality, (*iii*) fraud of the debtor.

12. Adjudication order. If the receiving order is not rescinded and no scheme or composition is approved by the court, the court will issue the adjudication order declaring the debtor legally bankrupt.

(*a*) *When made.* The order must be issued if (*i*) the creditors so resolved at the first meeting, or (*ii*) at that meeting the creditors reached no decision, or (*iii*) there was no meeting for some reason, or (*iv*) no scheme has been approved within fourteen days after conclusion of the public examination, or (*v*) the debtor fails to give a reasonable account of his affairs: B.A., s. 14.

(*b*) *Effect.* The debtor becomes bankrupt and all his property vests in his trustee in bankruptcy, and becomes divisible among his creditors. In proceedings after a crown court bankruptcy order, the Official Receiver remains in charge. No trustee is appointed: Powers of Criminal Courts Act 1973, s. 39 and Sched. 2.

(*c*) *Annulment.* The order may be annulled if (*i*) a scheme or composition is accepted after adjudication (s. 21), (*ii*) the adjudication for some reason should not have been made (s. 29), (*iii*) the debts of the bankrupt have been paid in full (s. 29). On annulment the property of the bankrupt revests in him. (Notice of annulment must be published in the *London Gazette* and a local newspaper.)

13. Meeting of creditors.

(*a*) *First meeting* (*see* **11** above). If the creditors reject any scheme or composition put forward, they will usually at this meeting appoint the trustee in bankruptcy (upon whom falls the duty of paying the debts and managing the bankruptcy generally).

(*b*) *Voting at meetings.* No creditor can vote until he has proved his debt. A creditor entitled to vote can give a proxy (authority for someone else to attend on his behalf), which may be either (*i*) a eneral proxy to any adult employee to vote at any meeting (but not in order to secure any exceptional advantage for the appointor), or (*ii*) a specia¹ proxy to any adult to vote on the acceptance of any composition or scheme, the appointment of a trustee or committee of inspection, or any other specified matter. A proxy may not be used at any meeting unless deposited with the official receiver or the trustee before the meeting.

(*c*) *Resolutions.* (*i*) An ordinary resolution means a majority in value of creditors voting personally or by proxy at any meeting. (*ii*) A special resolution is a majority of three-quarters in value and more than half in number of creditors present personally or by proxy.

(*d*) *Chairman* is the official receiver at the first meeting, and the trustee thereafter. The chairman decides whether to admit proofs of any debt for the purpose of allowing a creditor to vote, etc.

14. Committee of inspection: s. 20. The creditors usually (but not invariably) appoint a committee consisting of not more than five and not less than three of their number to supervise the trustee in his management of the bankruptcy. No member may act on the committee until he has proved his debt and had proof admitted: *see* **26.**

The committee must meet at least once a month, and the trustee or any member may call a meeting at any time. It may act by majority of members present at any meeting, and a majority of the members forms a quorum, i.e. the quorum will usually be three.

Appointment of members is terminated by (*a*) resignation, in writing, (*b*) bankruptcy, (*c*) absence from five consecutive meetings, (*d*) removal by ordinary resolution of a general meeting of creditors (of which seven days' advance notice has been given).

If no committee is appointed, acts of the trustee usually requiring the consent of such committee require the consent of the Department of Trade (D.T.).

The committee supervises the trustee in the execution of his duties, and he must submit his accounts to the committee for examination, i.e. (*i*) trading accounts (if any) every month, (*ii*) cash book every three months, or more often. (The committee must sign the books if satisfied with them.)

15. Discharge of bankrupt: s. 26. The bankrupt may apply in open court for his discharge at any time after adjudication. The creditors must be given fourteen days' notice of the application, and they, the trustee or the official receiver can oppose it. Where the court declares that the debtor's examination has been concluded, or dispenses with his examination it may order an absolute discharge: Insolvency Act 1976, s. 7.

(*a*) *Court's discretion.* The court has a wide discretion to decide how far, if at all, discharge shall be granted. The court cannot grant any unconditional discharge where the bankrupt:

(*i*) has been convicted of any offence in connection with the bankruptcy;

(*ii*) has assets amounting to less than 50p in the pound on his unsecured liabilities (unless this is due to circumstances beyond his control);

(*iii*) has failed to keep proper books and accounts in business within three years immediately preceding the bankruptcy;

(*iv*) has continued to trade knowing himself to be insolvent;

(*v*) has contracted provable debts without reasonable expectation of being able to pay them;

(*vi*) has failed adequately to account for any loss or deficiency of assets;

(*vii*) has contributed to his own bankruptcy by gambling, extravagance or culpable neglect of his business;

(*viii*) has brought a frivolous action which has resulted in judgment being given against him, or has put up a frivolous defence to an action against him by a creditor;

(*ix*) gave undue preference to any creditor within three months before the receiving order;

(*x*) has been adjudicated bankrupt, or has made any composition with creditors on any previous occasion;

(*xi*) has been guilty of fraud or fraudulent breach of trust.

(*b*) *Kinds of discharge.* The discharge may be (*i*) unconditional, freeing the bankrupt from all further liability on his provable debts, (*ii*) conditional, having the same effect as (*i*) but subject to a condition that subsequently acquired property shall be disposed of in a certain way, (*iii*) suspensive, i.e. not becoming unconditional until after a certain period of time, or until the payment of certain debts, or (*iv*) conditional and suspensive. A conditional discharge can be revoked by the debtor not fulfilling the condition: *re Summers* (1970).

16. Effect of discharge order: s. 28. The order discharges liability on all debts except (*a*) Crown debts (unless the Treasury consents in writing), (*b*) liabilities incurred by fraud, and (*c*) judgment debts in affiliation proceedings or in a matrimonial cause.

Non-provable debts are not affected by discharge and can be sued upon in the normal way, unless statute-barred or waived.

An order of discharge does not necessarily relieve from liability any co-debtor, or any surety for the bankrupt.

The order may be revoked by the court at any time on cause shown, provided that such revocation does not affect the rights of third parties acquired since the discharge, unless they were fraudulent. Thus if after discharge the debtor sold certain property to X, and the discharge was revoked some days later, the property could not be recovered from X unless it could be shown that he was a party to some fraudulent scheme with the debtor.

NOTE: Where a debtor is fined for a criminal offence and the Crown fails to prove for the fines in his bankruptcy (even though he declared the fines as debts), this does not relieve the bankrupt from liability to pay the fines: *Re Savundra* (1973).

THE TRUSTEE IN BANKRUPTCY

17. How appointed: B.A., s. 19:

(*a*) By ordinary resolution of the creditors (usually at their first meeting).

(*b*) By the committee of inspection, if the power has been delegated to the committee.

(*c*) By the Department of Trade, if four weeks after adjudication no appointment has been made by (*a*) or (*b*).

NOTE: The official receiver cannot be appointed as trustee in bankruptcy except (*i*) where the value of the estate is not likely to exceed £4,000, or (*ii*) to fill a temporary vacancy in the office of trustee, or (*iii*) where the estate is that of a deceased debtor, or (*iv*) where directed by the D.T. in exceptional circumstances. (The appointment of a trustee must be approved by the D.T., which may refuse to approve because of (*i*) some irregularity in the appointment, or (*ii*) because the person appointed is not suitable, e.g. has been convicted of dishonesty, or is too closely and intimately connected with the debtor or any creditor to be truly impartial.)

18. Duties of trustee.

(*a*) To get possession of all the debtor's property, and to make the most of the available assets.

(*b*) To obey the instructions of the creditors in general meeting, and those of the committee of inspection

(*c*) To exhibit the utmost good faith.

(*d*) To summon meetings of creditors when required by one-sixth in value of them, or as directed by the creditors generally.

(*e*) To convert the bankrupt's assets into money as soon as possible.

(*f*) To keep proper accounts which can be inspected by any creditor (but not by the debtor). Such accounts must be submitted every three months to the committee of inspection (if any), and to the D.T. every six months. In addition a full statement of his dealings must be submitted to the D.T every twelve months, or more frequently if directed.

The accounts kept must include (*i*) a record book (minutes and proceedings of creditors' meetings, etc.), (*ii*) a cash book (receipts and payments from day to day, etc.), (*iii*) trading accounts, if he carries on the bankrupt's business: s. 85.

NOTE: All moneys realised by the sale or otherwise of the debtor's property must normally be paid into the Insolvency Services Account at the Bank of England: Insolvency Act 1976, s. 3.

19. Powers of the trustee: ss. 55–58.

(*a*) On his own authority he may:

(*i*) sell all or any part of the bankrupt's property;

(*ii*) give receipts for money;

(*iii*) in any other bankruptcy, draw and prove for a dividend owing to his bankrupt;

(*iv*) exercise any powers necessarily incidental to his duties and execute any necessary instrument;

(*v*) bar any entailed interest to which the bankrupt is beneficially entitled (so bringing it into the bankruptcy for the benefit of the creditors).

(*b*) With permission of the creditors, the committee of inspection or the D.T., he may:

(*i*) carry on the bankrupt's business (but only so far as is necessary for beneficially winding it up, e.g. so as to sell it as a going concern);

(*ii*) bring or defend any action affecting the bankrupt's property.

(*iii*) employ a solicitor or other agent where necessary;

(*iv*) mortgage or pledge any of the bankrupt's property;

(*v*) accept money payable at a future date on sale of any of the bankrupt's property;

(*vi*) agree a compromise of any claim by or against the bankrupt;

(*vii*) refer disputes to arbitration;

(*viii*) appoint the bankrupt to manage his own property;

(*ix*) make an allowance to the bankrupt for the support of

himself and his family, or any payment to him in consideration of his services in the winding up of his estate (subject to the court's power to reduce such payments).

20. Remuneration and expenses.

(a) *Remuneration.* The trustee is not automatically entitled to any remuneration, though payment is usually made. Remuneration is fixed by the creditors (or the committee of inspection if so agreed) as a percentage of the amount raised for distribution: s. 82.

Remuneration may however be fixed by the D.T. if one-quarter in number or value of the creditors so request, or at the bankrupt's request (if the amount fixed by the creditors is too large).

(b) *Expenses.* A trustee is automatically entitled to his expenses. But if he litigates unsuccessfully he is generally personally liable for the costs of the action, unless the creditors have agreed to reimburse him.

21. Vacation of office.

(a) *Release by the D.T.* discharges the trustee from all liability: B.A., s. 93. A trustee may apply to the D.T. at any time for his release and if it is refused he may then apply to the court.

(b) *Removal:* s. 95. A trustee appointed by the creditors may be removed by an ordinary resolution of a general meeting called for the purpose.

A trustee may also be removed by the D.T. for various reasons, e.g. misconduct, incapacity, lunacy, undue delay, etc. If the creditors disapprove of such removal they may apply to the court to set it aside.

(c) *Bankruptcy:* s. 94. If the trustee himself becomes bankrupt he is automatically removed from office.

(d) *Resignation* must be notified to a general meeting of creditors, who may accept or reject it.

DISTRIBUTION OF PROPERTY

22. Property available: s. 30. The trustee is entitled to all the debtor's property except as stated in **23** below.

The title of the trustee to the property available extends back to the date of commencement of the bankruptcy.

Under the *Doctrine of Relation Back*, commencement of the bankruptcy is the date on which the first available act of bankruptcy was committed, within three months before the presentation of the petition: s. 37.

(a) Property belonging to the debtor at commencement of bankruptcy. This includes (i) payments made to any creditor since commencement of bankruptcy, i.e. after the first available act of bankruptcy (under the doctrine of relation back), (ii) benefits of the bankrupt's existing contracts, except where these depend on the personal skill of the bankrupt.

(NOTE: Relation back does not occur regarding (1) money obtained by a creditor by sale of the bankrupt's property under a writ of execution either before the receiving order or before he has notice of the petition: s. 40. (2) protected transactions, i.e. payments *by* the bankrupt to creditors in return for valuable consideration (provided these were made before the receiving order and without notice of an available act of bankruptcy), and bona fide payments to the bankrupt before the date of the receiving order and without notice of presentation of a petition: ss. 45, 46, (3) sales of land to a bona fide purchaser for value without notice, who bought before the date of the receiving order and before registration of the petition in the Land Charges Registry: Land Charges Act 1972, s. 5 (1).)

(b) Property acquired by or devolving on the bankrupt before his discharge and after the commencement of bankruptcy.

Property coming to the bankrupt (i) after commencement of bankruptcy and before adjudication, vests in the trustee automatically, (ii) after adjudication, must be expressly claimed by the trustee.

(c) Capacity to exercise all powers over property which the bankrupt might have exercised for his own benefit.

(d) Goods in the bankrupt's reputed ownership: s. 38. This means: goods which at the commencement of the bankruptcy are (i) in his possession, order or disposition, (ii) in his trade or business, (iii) by consent of the owner, (iv) under such circumstances that he is reputed owner thereof. From a day yet to be announced, a section 38A will be inserted into the 1914 Act by the Consumer Credit Act. This states that issue of a default notice in respect of a hire-purchase or conditional sale agreement, or of a regulated agreement in respect of which a bill of sale has been granted, takes the goods out of the category of divisible property.

NOTE: (1) Goods includes all chattels personal but not choses in action (except debts due or growing due to the bankrupt in his business). (2) Reputed ownership may be excluded by trade custom, e.g. hotel furniture is customarily hired and this custom could defeat the reputation of ownership: *Re Parker* (1885) (3) If the owner of hired goods does not know they are used in the bankrupt's business, the reputed ownership provisions do not apply. (4) Possession by the bankrupt's agent suffices for reputed ownership. (5) If goods are taken by the trustee under s. 38 the owner can prove in the bankruptcy as a creditor for their value: *Re Britton* (1907).

(*e*) Property transferred gratuitously by the bankrupt to another person: s. 42, i.e. "voluntary settlements" made:

(*i*) within two years before commencement of bankruptcy, or

(*ii*) within ten years, unless the bankrupt could pay all his debts in full at the time of transfer, without recourse to the property in question. Where in divorce or nullity proceedings the Court has ordered transfer of any of the debtor's property to the spouse (or children) of the debtor, such transfers can be avoided in the debtor's subsequent bankruptcy: Matrimonial Causes Act 1973, ss. 24 and 39.

The following settlements are not voluntary, and are therefore not affected by bankruptcy.

(*i*) Settlements before and in consideration of marriage.

(*ii*) Settlements in favour of a purchaser for value.

(*iii*) Settlements for the wife or children of the bankrupt of property coming to him after marriage and by right of his wife.

(A settlement means any gift or transfer of property made with the intention that it shall be retained by the grantee.)

(*f*) Property used by the bankrupt to give fraudulent preference to any creditor over other creditors, within six months before becoming bankrupt.

NOTE: (*i*) There must be actual intention to prefer one creditor over another. (The burden of proving this lies on the trustee in bankruptcy, and he cannot claim back the property unless he can prove it.) (*ii*) The transfer must be voluntary, i.e. not under pressure by the creditor, for instance under threat of legal proceedings. (*iii*) A payment is not fraudulent if made (*a*) to revive a statute-barred debt or (*b*) by a trader in order to keep his business going, even though he knows he is insolvent at the time: *Re Clay & Sons* (1895). (*iv*) The burden of proving intention to prefer a creditor lies on the trustee in bankruptcy. (*v*) If the fraudulently preferred creditor sells the property given him to an innocent third party, the purchaser gets a good title, though the creditor may be compelled to reimburse the estate.

23. Property not available. The following classes of property do not vest in the trustee for distribution among the creditors.

(*a*) Property held by the bankrupt as trustee for any other person.

(*b*) Tools of the bankrupt's trade, necessary apparel and bedding (for the bankrupt and his family) to the value of £250: B.A., s. 38.

(*c*) Personal earnings, provided they are not more than are necessary to maintain the bankrupt and his family.

(*d*) Rights of action to sue for damages for bodily harm, or for injury to credit or reputation. (Rights of action for injuries to property do vest in the trustee.)

(*e*) Interests in property which are determinable on bankruptcy.

(*f*) The benefit of contracts requiring personal skill.

(*g*) Old age pensions, and benefits under the Social Security Acts.

NOTE: Copyrights of authors assigned to the bankrupt in return for royalty payments do vest in the trustee, but he must not dispose of them in such a way as to deprive the author of his royalties.

24. Discovery of bankrupt's property. The court can order the bankrupt, his wife, or any other person suspected of possessing information about, or possessing any of the bankrupt's property, to appear and be examined on oath and to produce any relevant documents, and may order delivery up of such property: B.A., s. 25.

25. Disclaimer of onerous property: s. 54.

(*a*) *Onerous property.* The trustee can rid himself of property which could be more trouble than it is worth, e.g. land subjected to burdensome covenants, stocks and shares in companies which may make calls upon them, unprofitable contracts, etc.

He cannot however disclaim the obligations and retain the rights in any property.

(*b*) *Form of disclaimer*. It must be in writing, signed by the trustee, and must be made (*i*) within twelve months after his appointment, or (*ii*) within twelve months after he becomes aware of the property (providing he did not become aware of it within one month of his appointment), or (*iii*) within such extended time as the court may allow.

(*c*) *Notice of disclaimer*. Any person interested in property which is likely to be disclaimed can compel the trustee to decide whether to disclaim or not, by serving notice on him requiring him to disclaim within twenty-eight days or not at all.

(*d*) *Leases* may not as a rule be disclaimed without leave of the court, except (*i*) where the bankrupt has not sub-let or mortgaged the premises and the value is less than £20 per year and the trustee has served notice on the lessor giving him seven days to appeal to the court against the disclaimer, or (*ii*) where the bankrupt has sub-let or mortgaged the property, but the trustee has served fourteen days' notice on such sub-tenants or mortgagees giving them fourteen days in which to appeal to the court against disclaimer.

(Failure to disclaim a lease which could properly have been disclaimed renders the trustee personally liable thereon.)

(*e*) *Effect of disclaimer* is to relieve the bankrupt's estate from all liabilities in connection with the property thenceforward. (It does not affect the rights and liabilities of other persons except insofar as is necessary to protect the bankrupt's estate, and the trustee. Disclaimer merely divests the trustee of the property, it does not vest it in any other person, and any person interested in the disclaimed property can apply to the court for an order vesting the property in him.)

Any person harmed by disclaimer can prove in the bankruptcy for the amount of his loss.

PAYMENT OF DEBTS

26. Proof of debts. Before he can be paid a creditor must prove his debt, as quickly as possible after the receiving order.

Proof is by a statement of the debt + affidavit asserting the creditor's claim and stating any surrounding circumstances. When proof is submitted, the trustee must within twenty-eight days (*a*) admit liability, (*b*) reject it, or (*c*) require further evidence. (The creditor can appeal to the court against rejection.)

A secured creditor (such as a mortgagee) must disclose his

security in his proof (if any) or he must surrender it for the benefit of the creditors generally. There is no need however why he should prove for his debt at all. He has in fact four choices: (*i*) to rely on his security and not prove, (*ii*) to realise his security and prove for the deficiency (if any), (*iii*) to surrender his security and prove for the whole debt, or (*iv*) to value his security and prove for any deficiency.

27. Provable debts. These are all debts and liabilities, present or future, certain or contingent, to which the debtor is subject at the date of the receiving order, or to which he may become subject before his discharge by reason of any obligation incurred before the date of the receiving order: s. 30(3).

(The obligation to pay must have arisen before the receiving order even though the debt may not be payable till after that date.)

If the debt is contingent (i.e. dependent on the happening of some future event), the trustee must assess its value and make allowance for it. If the creditor disagrees with the assessment he can appeal to the court.

Ordinary debts rank *pari passu* among themselves and are paid rateably, i.e. as fully as possible from the funds available.

28. Debts not provable.

(*a*) Unliquidated damages, not arising out of breach of contract or breach of trust: L.R. (Miscellaneous Provisions) Act 1934.

(*b*) Debts due to any person who knew of an available act of bankruptcy committed by the debtor, at the time the debt was incurred.

(*c*) Debts which in the opinion of the court are incapable of being fairly assessed.

(*d*) Debts contracted after the date of the Receiving Order.

29. Mutual dealings. Where in the course of dealings between the bankrupt and a creditor each has incurred liabilities to the other, the trustee must strike a balance and (*a*) if the balance shows a deficiency owing to the creditor, the debt must be paid, and (*b*) if the balance shows a credit in favour of the bankrupt, the creditor must pay this sum to the trustee: B.A., s. 31.

A creditor cannot claim any set-off against the bankrupt if, at the time of giving credit to the bankrupt, he had notice of an available act of bankruptcy: *Halesowen Presswork & Assemblies* v. *National Westminster Bank Ltd.* (1971).

The debts must be due between the same parties in the same right; thus a debt owed jointly by a partnership cannot be set off against a separate debt owed to one of the parties on his own: *Re Pennington & Owen* (1925).

Where a salesman employed by a bankrupt principal holds money collected from customers, he can keep it, setting of this debt due to the bankrupt against his claim for commission against the bankrupt. The salesman can also retain goods entrusted to him for sale, bringing their value into account: *Rolls Razor* v. *Cox* (1967).

The statutory provisions as to mutual dealings cannot be excluded by agreement: *National Westminster Bank Ltd.* v. *Halesowen Presswork & Assemblies* (1972).

30. Priority of debts: s. 33. Debts must be paid by the trustee in the following order.

(*a*) Official receiver's expenses, and other costs occurring before the bankruptcy proceedings.

(*b*) Trustee's expenses.

(*c*) Allowances to the bankrupt by the trustee.

(*d*) Trustee's remuneration (if any).

(*e*) Preferred debts.

(*i*) Rates falling due within twelve months before the receiving order, and taxes assessed up to 5th April preceding the receiving order but not exceeding the amount due for one year.

(*ii*) *Accrued holiday remuneration* for employees on the termination of their employment before the receiving order.

(*iii*) *National Insurance contributions* payable by the bankrupt employer as during the twelve months prior to the receiving order.

(*iv*) *P.A.Y.E. deductions* due from the bankrupt employer to the Crown.

An employee who loses his job when his employer (including a company) becomes insolvent can claim through the Redundancy Payment Fund arrears of wages, holiday pay and certain other payments: Employment Protection Act 1975.

(*f*) Ordinary debts, *pari passu*.

(*g*) Deferred debts: *see* **31** *below*.

31. Deferred debts. The following debts are not payable until all the preferred and ordinary debts have been paid in full.

(*a*) Loans to a business at a rate of interest varying with profits: Partnership Act 1890, s. 3.

(*b*) Amounts due to the seller of the goodwill of a business as a portion of profits (by way of annuity or otherwise).

(*c*) Loans by a husband to his wife (or vice versa) for trade purposes.

(*d*) Interest exceeding 5 per cent p.a. due under contracts including a moneylending contract: Moneylenders Act 1927, s. 9, B.A. s. 66 and Consumer Credit Act 1974, Sched. 5.

(*e*) Claims by the trustees of any settlement avoided in the bankruptcy: B.A., s. 42.

32. Distraint by landlord. A landlord has no priority for his rent unless he has distrained for it (i.e. seized the bankrupt tenant's goods and chattels found on the premises).

But if he has distrained the position is as follows.

(*a*) If he distrained before commencement of the bankruptcy, he can keep whatever he has obtained.

(*b*) If he distrained within three months before the receiving order, he can be made to pay the preferential creditors out of the proceeds of distraint. (He then steps into their shoes and acquires their priority.)

(*c*) If he distrains after commencement of the bankruptcy, he can distrain only for six months' rent accruing before the adjudication order. (For any balance owing, he must prove as an ordinary creditor.)

33. Bankruptcy of partnerships. A receiving order may be made against a firm, and it then operates as a receiving order against each individual partner also: B.A., s. 119.

Procedure is as follows.

(*a*) *The partners submit* (*i*) Statement of Affairs for the firm, and (*ii*) each partner submits a Statement of Affairs for himself.

(*b*) *The first meeting of creditors* will be attended by the firm's creditors, and by the creditors of the separate partners.

(*c*) *Any composition offered* may be accepted by the joint creditors and rejected by the separate creditors, and vice versa.

(*d*) *One trustee is appointed* to manage the firm's bankruptcy and those of the partners. (But the joint creditors, and each group of separate creditors may appoint their own Committees of Inspection.)

(e) *The joint estate is applied* first in payment of the firm's debts; and the separate estates are applied first in payment of the separate debts.

(f) *The firm's creditors* are entitled to prove in the separate bankruptcies of the partners and receive dividends, but only after the separate creditors have been paid in full.

(g) *The separate creditors* are entitled to prove and draw in the firm's bankruptcy, but only after the firm's creditors have been paid in full.

(h) *If there is no joint estate* and no solvent partner, the firm's creditors can prove against the separate estates and rank equally with the separate creditors.

(i) *If the bankruptcy was started by a firm's creditor* petitioning against one of the partners separately (as he may do), he is entitled to rank in that partner's bankruptcy with the separate creditors.

(j) *Where one partner is carrying on a separate business*, and there are debts outstanding between his business and the firm, his estate can prove against the firm and the firm can prove against him (providing the debts were incurred bona fide in the ordinary course of trading).

DEEDS OF ARRANGEMENT

34. Arrangements outside bankruptcy Where a debtor is insolvent and wishes to avoid bankruptcy, he and his creditors may reach an agreement for the arrangement of his affairs for the benefit of the creditors (without pushing the debtor into bankruptcy).

The Deeds of Arrangement Act 1914, applies to such agreements (whether under seal or not) made (a) for the benefit of creditors generally, or (b) by an insolvent trader for the benefit of three or more creditors. (The administration of the arrangement is entrusted to a trustee.)

Alternatively such agreement may take the form of a composition with creditors, i.e. a contract by which the creditors agree to accept (in complete discharge of their debts) a proportion of their claims, e.g. 75p in each pound owed. (This composition, despite the rule in *Foakes* v. *Beer* (*see* **III, 19**) is binding on all creditors who assent to it: the consideration for it lies in the mutual interchange of promises by the creditors not to sue for the whole debt, i.e. mutual forbearances.)

35. The Deeds of Arrangement Act 1914. If an arrangement or composition is embodied in a document (whether under seal or not) it is void unless:

(*a*) It is registered with the Registrar of Bills of Sale within seven days of execution, and is properly stamped: Deeds of Arrangement Act 1914, s. 2.

(*b*) It is assented to by a majority in number and value of the creditors (if made for the benefit of creditors generally) within twenty-one days of registration.

If the deed affects land it must also be registered at the Land Charges Registry, otherwise it will be void against a purchaser for value of the land: L.C.A., 1972, s. 4.

(The time limits for registration may be extended by the court.)

36. The trustee under a deed. He must within twenty-eight days of registration file a statutory declaration that the necessary majority of creditors have assented to the arrangement: D.A.A., 1914, ss. 2 and 3. (Once registered the deed can be examined by any person on payment of a fee.)

Unless all creditors have assented to it, the trustee must not act under the deed for three months after its execution. The reason for this is that if the debtor subsequently becomes bankrupt (and the trustee in bankruptcy's title relates back to a date three months before the presentation of the petition), the trustee under the deed may be personally liable in the bankruptcy for any property he has disposed of under the deed of arrangement. (Though usually the trustee in bankruptcy, if satisfied as to the good faith of the trustee under the deed of arrangement, will remunerate the latter for his services and treat his actions as those of his own agent.)

NOTE: (*i*) If the deed of arrangement is void merely because it failed to receive the assent of the majority of creditors required, and if the trustee was unaware of this, he is entitled to be exonerated from liability in any subsequent bankruptcy. (*ii*) If the trustee acts when he knows the deed is void, he is liable to penalties at the rate of £5 per day.

37. Duties and accounts of trustee.

(*a*) *Duties.* He must carry out the trusts stated in the deed, e.g. as to the distribution of the property assigned to him. He must pay creditors equally, except (*i*) those who can distrain for their claims i.e. landlords, and (*ii*) preferential creditors.

(The bankruptcy rules which go to swell the assets (e.g. the reputed ownership rule, the avoidance of voluntary settlements, the rules as to fraudulent preferences) do not apply in favour of the trustee under a deed, and his authority extends only to the actual property assigned to him.)

(*b*) *Accounts.* He must account annually to the D.T., and every six months to the assenting creditors. If a business is being carried on, a separate trading account must be rendered. His accounts are open to inspection by an interested person.

An audit may be ordered at any time on application of a majority in number and value of the assenting creditors, up to twelve months after the rendering of the final accounts of the D.T.

38. Deed of arrangement as act of bankruptcy. A creditor who has not assented to a deed or composition is not bound by it, and can sometimes use it as grounds for filing a petition in bankruptcy against the debtor: *see* **5** above.

In order to be cited as an act of bankruptcy, the deed must be for the benefit of creditors generally. Any creditor not assenting to the deed may ground a petition upon it any time within three months of its execution. (The trustee can reduce this time to one month by serving notice of the deed on non-assenting creditors.)

PROGRESS TEST SIX

BANKRUPTCY

1. What are the objects of bankruptcy, and who may be made bankrupt? (XVIII, **1, 3**)
Explain briefly the course of proceedings in bankruptcy. (XVIII, **1–4**)

2. Explain briefly the recognised acts of bankruptcy. What is their importance? (XVIII, **5**)

3. When and by whom may a petition in bankruptcy be lodged? (XVIII, **6**)

4. What is a Receiving Order? When is it made and what is its effect? (XVIII, **7**)

5. What are the duties of the Official Receiver after a Receiving Order has been made? (XVIII, **9–11**)

6. What meetings of creditors are held during a bankruptcy? How do creditors vote at such meetings, personally or by proxy? (XVIII, **11, 13**)

7. Explain the significance of (*a*) Adjudication Order, and (*b*) Committee of Inspection. (XVIII, **12, 14**)

8. When may a bankrupt apply for his discharge, and what power has the court on hearing the application? Explain also the effect of discharge. (XVIII, **15, 16**)

9. How is a trustee in bankruptcy (*a*) appointed, (*b*) removed, and (*c*) remunerated? (XVIII, **17, 20, 21**)

10. What are the duties and powers of a trustee in bankruptcy? When can he act on his own discretion, and when does he need the sanction of the court or of the creditors? (XVIII, **18, 19**)

11. What property of a debtor is available for distribution among his creditors in bankruptcy? Explain in particular what is meant by "reputed ownership." What property is not available in bankruptcy? (XVIII, **22, 23**)

12. When does bankruptcy commence? Explain what is meant by the Doctrine of Relation Back. (XVIII, **22**)

13. In what circumstances can a trustee divest himself of onerous property in a bankruptcy? (XVIII, **25**)

14. What debts are provable in bankruptcy, and how is proof effected? Explain also what debts are non-provable. (XVIII, **26–28**)

15. Explain what is meant by (*a*) mutual dealings, (*b*) preferred debts, (*c*) secured creditors. (XVIII, **26, 29, 30**)

16. What debts are not payable until all preferred and ordinary debts have been paid in full? Explain the position of a landlord who has distrained for rent owed by a bankrupt tenant. (XVIII, **31, 32**)

17. Where a member of a firm becomes bankrupt, how may this affect the other members of the partnership? Explain what happens when a partnership becomes bankrupt. (XVIII, **33**)

18. X is insolvent but wishes to avoid bankruptcy. Advise him how he may reach an agreement with his creditors. If any creditor is dissatisfied with an agreement so made, what can he do? (XVIII, **34–36**)

19. Explain the position of a trustee under a deed of arrangement, noting particularly his duty as to the rendering of accounts. (XVIII, **35–37**)

SPECIMEN QUESTIONS

1. What kinds of debts are provable in bankruptcy? Explain the meaning of, and describe the kinds of, "preferential" and "deferred" debts. *C.I.S., June* 1972.

2. Set out the main acts of bankruptcy. *C.I.S., June* 1970.

3. Explain the position of a trustee in bankruptcy in connection with the following matters:

(*a*) a lease held by the bankrupt;

(*b*) a claim by a bankrupt for damages arising out of a collision between a Post Office van and the bankrupt's motor car driven by the bankrupt;

(*c*) securities held by the bankrupt as trustee under a settlement created by his uncle;

(*d*) goods in the reputed ownership of the bankrupt. *C.I.S. Final, June* 1962.

4. (*a*) Explain the protected transactions which are governed by sections 45 and 46 of the Bankruptcy Act 1914.

(*b*) Is the following transaction protected, namely: the payment by a bank of a cheque drawn by a customer in favour of a third party if the payment takes place after the bank receives notice that the customer has committed an act of bankruptcy? *Inst. of Bankers,* 1964.

5. When a receiving order has been made against a debtor, it is necessary to call a first meeting of his creditors.

(*a*) By whom and in what way is such a meeting summoned?

(*b*) What are the purposes for which the meeting is held?

(*c*) What information are the creditors entitled to receive in advance of the meeting? *I.C.A., May* 1966.

Appendix

EXAMINATION TECHNIQUE

QUESTIONS in Mercantile Law are of two types: (*a*) text-book questions—asking the student to expound or discuss a topic, e.g. "What is specific performance and in what conditions will it not be granted?" (*b*) problems—in which the facts of a case are given and the student is asked to apply the various appropriate rules of law and discuss the situation (or advise one of the parties), e.g. "P's agent, A, exceeds his authority in contracting with C, and does not tell C that he is acting merely as an agent. Discuss." (Or "Advise C.")

These two types of question require slightly different approaches, but the following general points should always be borne in mind:

(*a*) First read the question carefully, to make sure you understand precisely what is involved. (If in doubt, underline *key-words*, or note the points you think are involved on a separate piece of paper.)

(*b*) Read the question a second time, noting down any points which may be involved but are not actually mentioned in the question. For instance in the problem on agency stated above: "breach of warranty," "ratification," "agency by estoppel," etc.

(*c*) Shuffle the points you have noted into a logical sequence. Thus in the agency problem above: (1) Agency, (2) Exceeding authority, (3) Breach of warranty of authority—damages; (4) Estoppel and Ostensible authority; (5) Undisclosed principal.

(Time spent on these preliminary stages is not wasted. It helps you to put your answer into logical order, saves you time in writing, and—most important—shows the examiner that you have taken the trouble to plan your answer instead of leaping into the question without preparation. It will also make your answer easier to mark, and go some way towards endearing you to the examiner.)

NOTE: Citation of cases, etc. In studying law you should first learn the facts and names of leading cases; secondly, the facts of other cases; thirdly, the names of all. If in an examination you cannot remember the name of a case but can remember the facts, cite the facts on their own. If you cannot remember either name or facts it is permissible to invent facts of your own to illustrate an argument, providing you make it clear that they are your own invention (and do not pretend they come from some fictitious case). As to the method of incorporating cases in an answer, note the method used in the model answers below. (Remember always to underline case-names and references to statutes; this is a legal tradition, and it also helps attract the examiner's attention.)

Textbook questions. These test: (*a*) your memory of your text-book and notes; (*b*) your ability to organise your information. Therefore before answering you should assemble your information carefully, and then write it down in a logical sequence. Use short sentences; long sentences tend to confuse you if you are in a hurry (and are also harder for an examiner to read).

In Mercantile Law, text-book questions do not usually require a very detailed knowledge, but they do require that the information sought should be known precisely.

Example: "Summarise (or 'state briefly' or 'state' or 'describe,' etc.) the conditions and warranties implied in contracts for the sale of goods, and explain how these terms may be excluded."

Model answer: Under the Sale of Goods Act 1893 (as amended by the Supply of Goods (Implied Terms) Act 1973), the following conditions and warranties are implied in every contract covered by the Act (unless excluded by express agreement):

1. A condition that the seller has or will have the legal right to sell the goods at the time the property is to pass: s. 12(1).

2. A condition, in sales by sample, that bulk shall correspond with sample and that the buyer shall have reasonable opportunity to examine and compare, and that the goods shall be free of any defect not likely to be apparent on reasonable examination: s. 15 (2).

3. A condition in sales by description (where the buyer merely describes what he wants and leaves it to the seller to select the goods) that the goods shall correspond with the description: s. 13.

4. A condition or warranty as to quality or fitness is only implied in the following cases.

(a) Where the seller is a dealer in the goods sold, and the purchaser makes clear that he relies on the seller's skill and judgment, a condition is implied that the goods shall be reasonably fit for the purpose intended: s. 14(3).

(b) Where the seller is a dealer in the goods sold, there is an implied condition that they shall be of merchantable quality, i.e. of a quality generally acceptable: s. 14(2).

5. A warranty that the buyer shall enjoy quiet possession: s. 12 (1).

Any condition (main term) or warranty (subordinate term) implied by the Act can be excluded by express agreement: s. 55(1). But exclusionary clauses are construed strictly against the party inserting them and certain clauses are in any case void against consumers: s. 55(3) and (4). The seller cannot avail himself of an exclusionary clause if he broke the contract in some other way: *Karsales Ltd.* v. *Wallis* (1956). Thus where printed conditions of sale excluded liability for misdescriptions, it was held that the express and written exclusion was cancelled by an express oral representation: *Couchman* v. *Hill* (1947).

Problems: This type of question tests: (a) your understanding of the application of basic rules of law to unfamiliar situations; (b) your ability to present a rational argument.

Consequently you should (i) state the points of law involved in the problem (ii) decide whether they are in fact applicable to the particular circumstances, and (iii) state your decision as to who is liable (if asked), etc. The most important parts of this answer are (i) and (ii). You can still get a good mark on a problem question, even if you fail to reach a decision on point (iii) or reach a wrong decision.

Example: "A is P's agent for the purchase of certain goods, and is authorised to pay up to £100. In fact he buys the goods from X at a price of £120. Can X enforce the contract against A and/or P? Would it make any difference to your answer if A had concealed the fact that he was merely acting as agent for P?"

Model Answer: This question appears to involve two main points, namely (i) excess of authority by an agent, and (ii) the doctrine of the undisclosed principal.

Where an agent exceeds his authority, his principal incurs no liability to the third party, but the agent is liable for damages for breach of his implied warranty of authority: *Collen* v. *Wright* (1857).

The principal may however incur liability where:

(*a*) He ratifies the agent's transaction, in which case the agent ceases to be liable. Ratification is only possible where:

(*i*) the principal had capacity to make the particular contract at the time the agent contracted, and at the time of ratification;

(*ii*) the agent contracted expressly as agent for the principal, naming him;

(*iii*) the principal was in possession of all material information or agreed to dispense with it;

(*b*) he is estopped from denying the agent's authority to make the contract in question, e.g.

(*i*) where the principal has held out the agent as having authority to make the contact in question (for instance where the agent has in the past made such contracts with the principal's concurrence); or

(*ii*) where the agent's ostensible authority covers the transaction in question, even though he has exceeded his actual authority (for instance where the agent occupies a position which normally carries with it authority to make such contracts, and the principal has imposed restrictions on that authority which are unknown to X).

Thus a factor has implied authority to sell goods in his possession, and can give a good title to a purchaser even though he was instructed not to sell the particular goods: Factors Act 1889, s. 2.

The doctrine of the undisclosed principal would be applicable to the problem stated if A had concealed the fact of his agency. The doctrine is that in such a case the third party (here X) can enforce the contract against the agent, and on discovering the identity and existence of the principal has an alternative right of action against the principal.

In the problem therefore it is submitted that:

(*a*) X has a right of action against A for breach of his warranty of authority, and is entitled to damages whether the breach was innocent or fraudulent;

(*b*) X has no right of action against P, unless P ratifies the transaction or is estopped from denying A's authority.

Index

Details of other Macdonald & Evans
publications on related subjects can be found in
the FREE Macdonald & Evans Legal Studies
catalogue, available from: Department BP1,
Macdonald & Evans Ltd., Estover Road,
Plymouth PL6 7PZ